Ecology and
Consciousness

Ecology and Consciousness

Traditional Wisdom on the Environment

edited by

Richard Grossinger

North Atlantic Books
Berkeley, California

Ecology and Consciousness: Traditional Wisdom on the Environment

Published by
North Atlantic Books
2800 Woolsey Street
Berkeley, California 94705

This is issue number 45 in the *Io* series.

Cover photograph: The Richat Hole in Mauritania, NASA photo
Cover design by Paula Morrison
Printed in the United States of America

Ecology and Consciousness: Traditional Wisdom on the Environment is sponsored by the Society for the Study of Native Arts and Sciences, a nonprofit educational corporation whose goals are to develop an educational and cross-cultural perspective linking various scientific, social, and artistic fields; to nurture a holistic view of arts, sciences, humanities, and healing; and to publish and distribute literature on the relationship of mind, body, and nature.

Table of Contents

Section I
Life and Spirit

Section II
Animal and Mind

Section III
Planet and Politics

Section IV

Evolution and Cosmos

Credits

Gregory Bateson: "Form, Substance and Difference" from General Semantics: The Journal of the Institute of General Semantics, 1971; simultaneously published in *Io*/14, *Earth Geography Booklet No. 3, Imago Mundi*, 1972. By permission of the author.

Harvey Bialy: "The I Ching and the Genetic Code" from *Io*/20, *Biopoesis*, 1974.

Gino Clays: "Omnia Mea Mecum Porto" from *A Pamphlet*, Idaho State College, Pocatello, Idaho, 1961; republished in *Io*/15, *Earth Geography Booklet No. 4, Anima Mundi*, 1973.

Maryse Conde: From *Segu*. Copyright © 1984 by Maryse Conde. English translation Copyright © 1987 by Viking Penguin Inc. Used by permission of Viking Penguin, a division of Penguin Books USA Inc.

Diane di Prima: "Revolutionary Letter No. 63" collected in *Selected Poems, 1956-1976*, North Atlantic Books, 1977.

Edward Dorn: "Dear Flabby: Vira Untwists the 'Murch'" from *Bean News*, San Francisco, 1973; republished in *Io*/20, *Biopoesis*, 1974.

"La Máquina a Houston" from *Recollections of the Gran Apachería*, Turtle Island Foundation, 1974. By permission of the publisher.

"This is the way I hear the Momentum" from *Io*/6, *Ethnoastronomy*, 1969.

Jule Eisenbud: "Evolution and Psi" from *The Journal of the American Society for Psychical Research*, Vol. 70, January 1978. By permission of the author and publisher.

"Interview" from *Io*/14, *Earth Geography Booklet No. 3, Imago Mundi*, 1972.

R. Buckminster Fuller: "Telegram to Senator Edmund S. Muskie of Maine" from *Io*/12, *Earth Geography Booklet No. 1, Economics, Technology, and Celestial Influence*, 1972.

Richard Grossinger: Section from *Embryogenesis*, North Atlantic Books, 1986.

Section from *The Night Sky*, Jeremy P. Tarcher, Inc., 1988. By permission of the author.

Robert Kelly: "First in an Alphabet of Sacred Animals" from *Io*/4, *Alchemy Issue*, 1967.

"On a Picture of a Black Bird" from *Finding the Measure*, Black Sparrow Press, 1968. By permission of the publisher.

"A Chapter of Questions" from *Io*/2, 1966.

Joanne Kyger: "A small field of tall golden headed grass . . ." from *Io*/16, *Earth Geography Booklet No. 4, Anima Mundi*, 1973.

Thomas Merton: "The Sacred City" from *Io*/7, *Oecology Issue*, 1970.

Michael McClure: Sections from *Wolf Net*, published in full in *Io*/20, *Biopoesis*, 1974.

Charles Olson: "Enyalion" from *Io*/14, *Earth Geography Booklet No. 3, Imago Mundi*, 1972.

Section I

LIFE AND SPIRIT

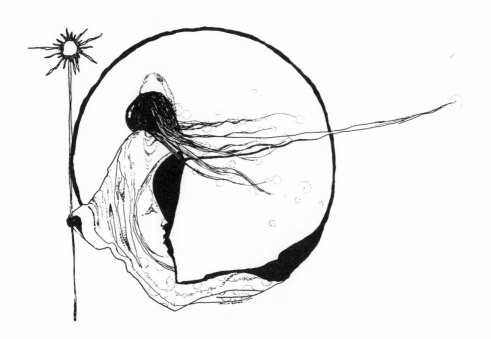

Joanne Kyger

A small field of tall golden headed grass, heavy with seed
     at the top
(Why did I travel so far from you who wishes to be
     snug in her home)
The grotesqueness of this california woman who wishes
     to take off her clothes but instead displays herself in
     provocative attitudes
Wrapping my shawl about my waist I went into sparkling water
     on shale reef.
     I am not empty
small sea anemones show their pink and blue insides.
Everything I walk on is alive.

There is something in me which is not open, it does not wish to live
it is dying
But then in the sun, looking out to sea
        center upon center unfold, lotus petals, the
     boundless waves of bliss

On the Meaning of Life
Talk, 25 July 1975, Plainfield, Vermont

Many of us are trying to understand the meaning of life and the spiritual quest. That seems to be inspiring, but at the same time it is problematic. When we talk about a spiritual reality—or the meaning of life—we automatically presume that there is one. We are told the world was created for us; it was God's will to create this world; everything is in the right place, karmically or whatever. You are born a child of God.

That is a very interesting psychology. Why should we think that we are a child of God, or why should we think that there is a meaning for life? Why should we? Is there any particular evidence which makes us think that there is meaning for life? Or is there particular proof that we are direct descendants of God? That is a very threatening and intrusive question, one we don't really want to ask. Even if we are able to ask such questions, we do so gently, rather than abruptly. Because abruptness is against spirituality and the entire question concerns seeking for peace. We therefore ask it peacefully, according to our notion of peace.

We could look at the question of the meaning of life in two different ways. Life as it is, and searching for the meaning of life, which are two separate categories. When we talk about the meaning of life we talk in terms of impressions, analogies, examples: how life *could* be seen. And when we talk about life as it is, we speak of naked life, raw life, rugged life, which does not require any introduction. Simple life, without any implication behind it, theoretical, philosophical, or metaphysical. Just life.

Life as it is, simple and straightforward, does not contain any extraordinary situations at all. We eat, we sleep, we shit, we bathe, we make love, we fight, we kill people, we do everything. We just live. Whatever we do, we just live. The living is life.

On the other hand, there is trying to find the meaning behind life—as though life itself is something bad, inefficient, not worth looking into, something that constantly presents problems, something that has to be disentangled, that is insufficient without some interpretation. We look for the meaning, for a way to view this complicated life from a different point of view. We become involved with all kinds of philosophical and spiritual thinking. We become involved with the myth of the past, which is what religion actually is. Anything connected with the practice of blind faith is purely myth. We try to get into that myth, and make it real. How to resurrect Robin Hood in the Twentieth Century; how to bring past dreams into this life situation. This whole process gets very confused, extremely confused.

We have basic reminders in our life, fundamentally speaking. Everybody has basic reminders, or we wouldn't be here discussing such subjects together at all. These reminders bring flashes of the confusion that we experienced in the process of our education and the confusion that we experience in our society, in our daily living with people; the confusion that comes from seeing people get into all kinds of trips, aggression, passion, materialism, spiritualism, all kinds of things. Those confusions, whether involved with a Madison Avenue business venture or with Rishikesh—spiritual adventure—seems to be the same. It is perhaps indiscreet to say that, but nevertheless it is so.

Last night and this morning I was reading a book called *The Sun King,* about Louis XIV. One of the quotations says that most men die of the remedy rather than the illness. I thought that was highly appropriate and took it as a message for my talk today. And I thought about it and what comes out of it seems to be a very wise thing. It seems that the problem really arises at the moment we try to cure ourselves. That in itself becomes the poison, a suicidal process. We want to cure ourselves from that problem, this problem. So we seek a solution. The solution itself contains poison.

In our work, we have developed a distinction between spirituality and religion. Religiosity is referred to as spiritual materialism. It is materialism in the sense that we are captivated by trying to *do* something, trying to block off certain areas that we don't want to acknowledge, and trying to bring out certain areas that we would like to enjoy. This still continues the warfare, the sense of trying to cure ourselves. It becomes truly violent in that we want madly to be cured. We eat our medicine—anti-death potion—spiritual message—madly. We get completely involved in it. We just gulp. We drink it, we swim in it, we eat it up. We get into it as much as we can, because this is what is supposed to save us.

It's true that openness can be beautiful, but there is a tendency to overdo it. Once we tend to do it more than necessary, we get a hangover from our medicine. It can become poisonous. If we cure ourselves completely, thoroughly, if we are cured from our illness we become completely white as opposed to black. Absolutely white. We become dazed in the white—there is no sense of discrimination at all. There is no spot of negativity. We have turned ourselves into zombies because we are so pure. We don't know how to react, how to relate to situations. There is no intelligence because we are so clean, so pure, absolutely cleansed by Ajax or Comet, superspiritual Comet. Clean—absolutely, peacefully. We washed out all the colors.

The rigidity of whiteness is like that of a corpse—there is no real smiling. We have been reduced into a tough, rigid, white, smiling—but deadly smiling—corpse. What seems to be a smile is actually the expression of death.

5

Spiritual materialism in that way has the quality of rigidity, unwillingness to accept the current situation of the world, our life situation, for what it is. We have good, we have bad, we have chaos. We never accept that. Rather we believe the whole thing should be whitewashed, turned into ultrawhite. There is no room at all for spontaneous responses.

That is dying of the remedy. We lose our individuality and inspiration by an overdose of the remedy. We become lifeless.

The alternative is to relate with our illness as illness, which is extraordinarily exciting. Each illness contains personal relationships. If we neglect our gall bladder we get an illness connected with that. If we abuse our muscles, then we get a direct reminder that we should pay attention to our muscles. We get aches in the muscles, we get aches in the bones, we get aches in our head. Whatever we neglect gives us a direct message, a reminder. It becomes very lively, a living situation.

Basically what we are discussing tonight is spirituality as a living practice, rather than a ideal one. According to the concepts of ideal spirituality, the cure would be based on living on the remedy. Actually, if we are living life as it is, we are not concerned with the cure as such. Life becomes just a simple living situation. We accept the actuality of the illness and live in the midst of it.

The psychological approach to this "ideal" spirituality is pushing ourselves as though we were a chicken laying an egg, or an excited mother in labor pain. Pushing and perching, rather than actually sitting, brings so much rigidity that our muscles begin to contract, our body and our psychological state begins to get tight, reduced into a lump of tense muscle. We become so tense that we begin to regard pushing or perching as meditation practices, spiritual acts. We begin to hear neurological buzzes in our ears. The tension becomes a reference point in our body. That tenseness of muscle begins to play what we would like to consider cosmic music. But it is the sound of tension, like what we would experience in a generator room, with the hum of electricity going on constantly. Electricity from this point of view is the embodiment of tension. Electrical energy goes on constantly, bringing out this buzz, this neurological buzz. Because we would like to give birth to wisdom or spirituality, we are rushing constantly. We perch on the egg, or grip the branches of the tree like a bird. It is what a constipated man would experience sitting on a toilet seat. He is still hearing the neurological buzz.

Any approach that involves trying to give birth is a problem in that we are not actually relating with things as they are, but with what they might be. We therefore have dreams of what might be and that might-be becomes so irritatingly seductive that we tend to reach beyond it, beyond our abilities. We end up perching and we take the tension buzz as a sign of our success.

William Irwin Thompson

Agriculturalization
from The Time Falling Bodies Take to Light

Human beings love to talk about the weather. When strangers are brought into an uncomfortable proximity with one another, as in an elevator or at a counter in a café, a brief reference to the weather will transform the uneasy atmosphere and create an occasion of human culture. Such little pleasantries are unconscious rituals that express the important relationship between weather and culture.

Each of the critical transformations of human culture is associated with profound climatic changes. The hominization of the primates is associated with a period of dessication in the Pliocene, a withdrawal of the forests and an opening up of the savannah in which the early hominids are pushed out into a new ecological niche. For almost a million and a half years thereafter that ecological niche is stable, and Homo erectus undergoes few evolutionary changes in his movement through time. But about 300,000 years ago, during the European Second Interglacial period, "the first evidence of sapientisation occurred,"[1] and the fossil remains begin to express the stages toward the emergence of modern humanity. At about this time the first engraved rocks and tools also make their appearance, and with them we can infer that the human is now miniaturizing her universe into symbolic forms. It is at this point that we can truly begin to speak of such a thing as "culture."

With the appearance of culture the rate of change seems to accelerate. Hominization occurred over millions of years, but Symbolization occurs within a time frame of hundreds of thousands. Once the climatic change opens up a new ecological niche, however, there does seem to appear a period of stability. Steady-state and transformation seem to alternate with one another. The culture of Ice Age humanity expresses a steady growth in the complexity of the tool kit, and a steady growth in complexity of artistic development. As Leroi-Gourhan has pointed out, the continuity of artistic traditions over millennia is remarkable. But, in the wisdom of the ancient Taoist sages, "Reversal is the movement of Tao," and every steady-state is followed by a period of transformation. For humanity this means that once again the weather changes and humanity is forced into yet another ecological niche.

During the Ice Ages the European tundra were covered with great herds of reindeer, horse, and bison, but when the winds shifted, the rains that once fell upon North Africa fell upon Europe. The land responded with an offering of trees. This time, however, humanity had so changed from its Pliocene origins that the return of its ancient forest home was no welcome event. The culturally elaborated adaptations of the Ice Age hunters melted away with the glaciers; now through the thick forest the hunter pursued a single animal with the new tool of the bow and arrow.

The climatic changes that stimulate these transformations of culture are not yet understood by science, but what is slowly emerging in the literature is a much more profound appreciation of how everything is very subtly involved with everything else. Explosions of volcanoes change the atmosphere; shifts in the earth's angle of rotation affect the movement of winds; and there is now dawning an almost mythopoeic sense that "our inconstant sun"[2] may be following cosmic seasons in its movement through the galaxy. Because so much of archaeology is guesswork, scientists have a tendency to fall into the old logical error of *post hoc, propter hoc:* things changed, therefore things changed because of the change. At one time, warming will be invoked as the cause of the change; at another period, the increasing cold will be seen as the cultural stimulant.

In the post-Pleistocene period the glaciers retreated, the seashore rose 300 feet, the tundra turned to forest, and the great herds disappeared from Western Europe. And gone with the animals was the great "high culture" of Ice Age humanity. It is not hyperbole to speak of the high culture of these hunters and gatherers, for cave paintings like Lascaux are complex works that speak rather eloquently for the abundant leisure and rich cosmology of their creators. Hobbes may have thought that life in a primitive condition of hunting and gathering was "nasty, brutish, and short," but we now know that these so-called primitives were what the anthropologist Marshall Sahlins has called "the original affluent society."[3] With a labor of a mere fifteen hours a week, hunters and gatherers can provide for all their needs. They have far more leisure time than an agrarian community, caught up as it is in what Marx called "the idiocy of rural life," and they certainly have more leisure time than the harassed factory and office workers of the industrial era. With their populations adjusted to the carrying capacity of the environment,[4] hunters and gatherers rarely starve, for they are not dependent on the fortunes of a single crop. With their need so easily provided for, primitive humanity devoted most of its spare time to matters of ritual and art. Small wonder that, as a contemplative people with time on their hands, they gave much thought to the relationship of menstruation and the moon, observed nature, constructed a calendar, told stories, and painted hundreds of thousands of images on the walls of the caves. As the Sistine Chapel expresses the flowering of the culture of the Renaissance, so Lascaux expresses the flowering of the culture of the Magdalenians. In more ways than one, the two great murals have much in common, for they are not mere decoration; they are mythological visions of the nature of time.

For the few thousand years that Magdalenian culture lasted, the relationships among religion, art, and technology seem to have achieved a condition of harmony and balance. But for humanity all steady-states are temporary, and just when we think we can take nature for granted, whether we live in a hunting or an industrial society, the weather changes, and we are forced to change.

8

Great ages of transition, with their attendant changes of climate—as we ourselves seem about to discover—are difficult times of decreasing culture. Adjusting to a new ecological niche calls for a new adaptation and takes the entire psychic energy of a culture. The Mesolithic was just such an age of transition; with none of the art of the Paleolithic Lascaux and none of the fine crafts of Neolithic Çatal Hüyük, it was—like the fifth century A.D.—a Dark Age.

*   *   *

The Magdalenian Culture of 12,000 B.C. was a temporary steady-state, a balance of the sexes in a harmonious division of labor celebrated in the juxtaposed male and female signs on the walls of the caves. The Mesolithic culture from 10,000 to 8000 B.C. was a Platonic *Magnus Annus* of loss and cultural disorientation, a Dark Age. The Neolithic culture from 8000 to 6000 B.C., however, was a brilliant period of the revival of crafts, the transformation of gathering into gardening, the growth of a cross-cultural obsidian trade, and the rise of towns. Astrologers, when they observe this pattern, insist that it corresponds to the zodiacal progression.[4] I am not an astrologer and I hold no brief for it, but I do believe the origins of astrology are not with the Chaldeans of Mesopotamia but with the hunters and gatherers of the Stone Age. Whether or not we believe in astrology is irrelevant; the question is, did the Magdalenians? If so, then in a self-fulfilling prophecy they may have been organizing their lives according to a religious belief system, and not simply an economic or ecological one. In the zodiacal procession of the poles, the 25,920-year cycle, Lascaux is the time of Virgo, and Virgo is associated with artistic excellence and discrimination. The Mesolithic transition is in the sign of Leo, a sign associated with masculine qualities of forcefulness and practicality. The Neolithic of 8000 to 6000 B.C. is in the sign of Cancer, a feminine sign associated with domesticity, retentiveness, and sentiment. Since the period from 8000 to 6000 B.C. saw the rise of domestic architecture and permanent villages and towns, the shift from the seasonal round to permanent settlement may have been inspired by religious as well as economic or environmental reasons.

The Mesolithic period is, I believe, one in which the traditional division of labor between the sexes is undergoing a change: the men are moving into the domestication of animals, and the women are ranging out to include a much broader spectrum of plant foods in their gathering. Physiological paternity has been discovered, but it is still subsumed under the mythological system of the religion of the Great Mother. Knowledge of a "fact" and its institutionalization in a society are quite distinct: murder, for example, was probably "discovered" in the Pliocene, but the institutionalization of murder in warfare does not seem to have occurred until the late Neolithic or the protoliterate period. The discovery of paternity does not mean, therefore, that the religion of the Great Mother is going to be replaced by one of the Great Father. That transformation is to come, but it will not be until humanity has shifted from the custom-bound life of the intimate matrilineal village to the law-ruled life of the complex, patrilineal state. If one wishes to gain an understanding of how humanity could shift from the one to the other, one needs to have an understanding of the enantiodromia (a movement that turns into its opposite) of the development of gathering into agriculture.

The archaeologists tell us that although the post-Pleistocene climate changed markedly in Western Europe, there was no pronounced change in Southwest Asia. The extinction of the Pleistocene megafauna had ended there long before it had in Europe, and so a "broad spectrum" of food collecting had been going on for some time. The decision to include wild cereals in the collection may have been initially a random act of gathering, but once that decision had been made it triggered a runaway system of positive feedback in which the entire culture was transformed.[5] There is, of course, the usual scholarly disagreement, with Braidwood disagreeing with the environmental-determinist theories of Childe, and Binford disagreeing with Braidwood's invocation of culture and human nature, but most seem to accept Flannery's cybernetic model.[6] The experts agree that in the foothills of the mountains of Southwest Asia certain forms of wild cereals grew and that women and children could collect enough grain in three weeks to feed a family for an entire year. The men would return from the hunting or fishing camp to find the home base filled and overflowing with grain. Once again, the miraculous nature of woman had asserted itself, and, armed with a crescent sickle shaped like the moon, she had gone out and gathered more life than any hunter could kill.

Woman had gone out and unconsciously taken nature into culture, for in gathering the wild wheat she struck the stalk with her sickle and thus helped to scatter the wild-blown seeds; in carrying the grasses home she increased the proportion of grains with large heads that stuck to the stalk. In her spilling of seeds around her home base, certain types of grain were being selected for; grains that could not easily reproduce themselves in the wild now had a helper, and the process through which crosses and hybrids become established was set into motion. As the seeds she spilled sprang up closer to home, it would seem as if the magical woman, the Great Mother and Mistress of Animals, was now becoming the Mistress of Plants. Ceres, the goddess of wheat, was about to make her appearance in prehistory. If we now say that "woman's place is in the home," it is not because men put her there, but because the home became the capitol of women's mysteries. It is the feminine vessel and container, the cornucopia brimming over with food. To deal with that problem of abundance, woman took another step and invented pottery to store the fruits of nature. Small wonder that pots were shaped like great-breasted matrons or were made round, not on the potter's wheel, but on the woman's breast.[7]

In the runaway system of positive feedback of collecting cereals, no conscious decision was made to change the culture; there was no Lenin at the Finland Station masterminding what V. Gordon Childe liked to call "the Neolithic Revolution";[8] yet a new culture began to develop at an increasingly rapid rate. Its growth could not help but push the old ways of hunting into the background. Of course men would still hunt, but it was more from the force of the three-million-year-old tradition, for the satisfactions of male bonding in their own

10

subculture, and as an escape from the furious activity of the women in gathering, grinding, cooking, and pottery. They could offer their obsidian to the women for use in the lunar crescent-shaped sickles, but even that contribution was ambiguous, for all the later myths would speak of castration with sickles; the standing grain cut down by the women would not create happy associations for the men. If we wonder now how easily men are threatened by women, and how the slightest expression of feminine power can generate castration anxieties in even a big man, then perhaps we would do well to think back on the origins of agriculture. As a gatherer, woman was a botanist; as a cook and a potter, she was a chemist; as a mother, she was a priestess of the Great Mother. Woman was a formidable creature in every way, and the origin of agriculture, rather than eliminating the religion of the Great Goddess of the Upper Paleolithic, ended by adding another miracle to the list of feminine wonders.

Whether or not Neolithic man longed to get away from women to go fishing or return to the hunting camp, the stored-up treasure in the granary would require his protective presence, and that was the beginning of the enantiodromia of agriculture for women. Hunters and gatherers have little property, and what they have they can carry, but sedentary collectors begin to have stores of grain, grinding stones, and clay bins that they cannot easily leave. They begin to have wealth, and the hunter with his spear and bow and arrow discovers a new use for his tool and his trade. If his manhood is insignificant in producing food in the chase, it can become significant in protecting women and wealth. It must have been frustrating for the Neolithic hunter to come home and lay his deer before all to admire, to realize his catch would last a few days, woman's a whole year. No doubt the hunter would demean the porridge of cereals and seeds as "woman's food" and make loud noises about a thick steak of venison, but the furious activity around him continued in spite of all his celebrations of the noble chase. And that too, triggered a positive feedback system of accelerating change. The more insignificant male activities were, and the more women's activities produced wealth, the more some men were attracted to steal and other men attracted to defend the new acquisitions. The men discovered a new way to get together and warfare was born. It was not ecological pressure or shortages of protein, as anthropologist Marvin Harris has claimed;[9] institutionalized violence, as opposed to the stylized agons of hunters over grievances, was the shadow side of the Neolithic Revolution. It is naive to look always to negative things for the cause of negative behavior; in the enantiodromias of history, we need to understand that even a positive change casts a shadow, we need to understand that the unique excellence of a thing is at the same time its tragic flaw. The collection of cereals produces wealth and increases the cultural distance between men and women, and both phenomena were to prove very dangerous.

End Notes

[1]Gail Kennedy, "The Emergency of Modern Man," *Nature*, Vol. 284, March 6, 1980, p. 11.

[2]David Clark, "Our Inconstant Sun," *New Scientist*, January 18, 1979, pp. 168-170.

[3]Marshall Sahlins, *Stone Age Economics* (Chicago, Aldine, 1972).

[4]Kent V. Flannery, "Origins and Effects of Early Domestication in the Near East and Iran" in *Prehistoric Agriculture*, ed. Stuart Struever (New York, Doubleday, 1971), p. 53.

[5]Grahame Clark, *Stone Age Hunters* (New York, McGraw-Hill, 1967), p. 94.

[6]See Erich Neumann, *The Great Mother* (Princeton, N.J., Princeton University Press, 1963), p. 114.

[7]Erich Isaac, "On the Domestication of Cattle" in *Prehistoric Agriculture*, ed. Stuart Struever (New York, Doubleday, 1971), p. 459.

[8]*Ibid.*, p. 462.

[9]Laurette Sejourné, *Burning Water: Thought and Religion in Ancient Mexico* (New York, Vanguard, 1956).

Knud Rasmussen

from

Intellectual Culture of the Iglulik Eskimos
(1929)

1   Takornaq

Another thing I remember about the white men is that they were very eager to get hold of women. A man with a handsome wife could get anything he wanted out of them; they never troubled much about what a thing cost as long as they could borrow the wife now and again. And they gave the women valuable gifts. I was only a little girl myself at that time, and had but little knowledge of what took place between man and woman when they were together, but I remember there were some of our men who would have no dealings with the white man, because they did not wish to share their wives with them. But most of the men did not mind; for it is quite a common thing among us to change wives. A man does not love his wife any the less because she lies with someone else now and again. And it is the same with the woman. They like to know about it, that is all; there must be no secrets in such matters. And when a man lends his wife to another, he himself always lies with the other man's wife. But with the white men it was different; none of them had their wives with them to lend in exchange. So they gave presents instead, and thus it was that many men of our tribe looked on it as only another kind of exchange, like changing wives. And there were so many things in our way of life that did not agree with the white men's ways, and they did not feel obliged themselves to keep our rules about what was taboo, so we could not be so particular in other matters. Only the white men had less modesty than our own when wishing to lie with a woman. Our men always desired to be alone with the woman, and if there was no other way, they would build a snow hut. But the white men on the big ship lived many together in one place, lying on shelves along the steep sides of the ship, like birds in the face of a cliff. And I remember a thing that caused great amusement to many, though the ones to whom it happened were not pleased. One evening when a number of women had gone to the white men's ship to spend the night there, we in our house had settled down early to rest. But suddenly we were awakened by the sound of someone weeping outside. And this was what had happened. A woman named Atanarjuat had suddenly fallen through the shelf where she was lying with one of the men on the ship, and rolled stark naked on the floor. She burst out crying for shame, put on her clothes in a great hurry and went home weeping, saying that she would never again lie with a white man.

2   Aua

I once went to Aua's hunting quarters on the ice outside Lyon Inlet to spend some time with the men. . . . For several evenings we had discussed rules of life and taboo customs without getting beyond a long and circumstantial statement of all that was permitted and all that was forbidden. Everyone knew precisely what had to be done in any given situation, but whenever I put in my query: "Why?", they could give no answer. They regarded it, and very rightly, as unreasonable that I should require not only an account, but also a justification of their religious principles. They had of course no idea that all my questions, now that I had obtained the information I wished for, were only intended to make them react in such a manner that they should, excited by my inquisitiveness, be able to give an inspired explanation. Aua had as usual been the spokesman, and as he was still unable to answer my questions, he rose to his feet, and as if seized by a sudden impulse, invited me to go outside with him.

It had been an unusually rough day, and as we had plenty of meat after the successful hunting of the past few days, I had asked my host to stay at home so that we could get some work done together. The brief daylight had given place to the half-light of the afternoon, but as the moon was up, one could still see some distance. Ragged white clouds raced across the sky, and when a gust of wind came tearing over the ground, our eyes and mouths were filled with snow. Aua looked me full in the face, and pointing out over the ice, where the snow was being lashed about in waves by the wind, he said:

"In order to hunt well and live happily, man must have calm weather. Why this constant succession of blizzards and all this needless hardship for men seeking food for themselves and those they care for? Why? Why?"

We had come out just at the time when the men were returning from their watching at the blowholes on the ice; they came in little groups, bowed forward, toiling along against the wind, which actually forced them now and again to stop, so fierce were the gusts. Not one of them had a seal in tow; their whole day of painful effort and endurance had been in vain.

I could give no answer to Aua's "Why?", but shook my head in silence. He then led me into Kublo's house, which was close beside our own. The small blubber lamp burned with but the faintest flame, giving out no heat whatever; a couple of children crouched, shivering, under a skin rug on the bench.

Aua looked at me again, and said: "Why should it be cold and comfortless in here? Kublo has been out hunting all day, and if he got a seal, as he deserved, his wife would now be sitting laughing beside her lamp, letting it burn full, without fear of having no blubber left for tomorrow. The place would be warm and bright and cheerful, the children would come out from under their rugs and enjoy life. Why should it not be so? Why?"

I made no answer, and he led me out of the house, in to a little snow hut where his sister Natseq lived all by herself because she was ill. She looked thin and worn, and was not even interested in our coming. For several days she had suffered from a malignant cough that seemed to come from far down in the lungs, and it looked as if she had not long to live.

A third time Aua looked at me and said: "Why must people be ill and suffer pain? We are all afraid of illness. Here is this old sister of mine; as far as anyone can see, she has done no evil; she has lived through a long life and given birth to healthy children, and now she must suffer before her days end. Why? Why?"

This ended the demonstration, and we returned to our house, to resume, with the others, the interrupted discussion.

"You see," said Aua, "you are equally unable to give any reason when we ask you why life is as it is. And so it must be. All our customs come from life and turn towards life; we explain nothing, we believe nothing, but in what I have just shown you lies our answer to all you ask.

"We fear the weather spirit of earth, that we must fight against to wrest our food from land and sea. We fear Sila.

"We fear dearth and hunger in the cold snow huts.

"We fear Takanakapsaluk, the great woman down at the bottom of the sea, that rules over all the beasts of the sea.

"We fear the sickness that we meet with daily all around us; not death, but the suffering. We fear the evil spirits of life, those of the air, of the sea and the earth, that can help wicked shamans to harm their fellow men.

"We fear the souls of dead human beings and of the animals we have killed.

"Therefore it is that our fathers have inherited from their fathers all the old rules of life which are based on the experience and wisdom of generations. We do not know how, we canot say why, but we keep those rules in order that we may live untroubled. And so ignorant are we in spite of all our shamans, that we fear everything unfamiliar. We fear what we see about us, and we fear all the invisible things that are likewise about us, all that we have heard of in our forefathers' stories and myths. Therefore we have our customs, which are not the same as those of the white men, the white men who live in another land and have need of other ways."

That was Aua's explanation; he was, as always, clear in his line of thought, and with a remarkable power of expressing what he meant. He was silent then, and as I did not at once resume the conversation, his younger brother Ivaluardjuk took up the theme and said:

"The greatest peril of life lies in the fact that human food consists entirely of souls.

"All the creatures that we have to kill and eat, all those that we have to strike down and destroy to make clothes for ourselves, have souls, like we have, souls that do not perish with the body, and which must therefore be propitiated lest they should revenge themselves on us for taking away their bodies."

3   Orulo

Orulo was, of all the Iglulingmiut I met, the most faithful storyteller and the most patient in answering all my questions. This was partly due to the fact that she was one of those who knew most about the old traditions. I was therefore surprised to find that the myth of the Sea Spirit, as she related it, differed from the versions I had heard elsewhere. Orulo makes the girl who married a dog and the girl who had a stormy petrel for a husband, one and the same woman. In most other places, these two myths are distinct, and regarded as two separate explanations of how the spirit of the sea originated. In both cases, the woman goes down to the bottom of the sea, and the story is content to assert, as its decisive feature, that the woman who was afterwards to obtain such extraordinary and determinative influence on human life, had once been married to an animal in human form, and was changed into a spirit after a violent death.

When I pointed out to Orulo the discrepancy between her description and those I had heard from others, she firmly maintained that hers was the correct one. Another thing I pointed out to her in this connection made not the slightest impression; and as her standpoint here is so characteristic of the Eskimo attitude generally towards myths which are actually of fundamental importance in their religious ideas, I will give our conversation as it took place.

I said to Orulo, that according to her account, all sea beasts originated from Takanakapsaluk. They were made from her fingers, and it was because she was their mother that human beings had to observe all the numerous and difficult rules of taboo, the purpose of which was to ensure that the thoughts and hands of unclean human beings should never come into contact with the "sacred" food. In a Greenland variant of the story, as I now told Orulo, the Mother of the Sea Beasts could only be the same as the girl who was married to a dog. In the story I knew, the girl let her offspring lick the blood from her father's kayak, with the result that the dog-children at last fell upon the girl's father and tore him to pieces. Their mother had asked them to do so. For she could not forget that it was her father who had degraded her by marriage with a dog, and therefore she wished that the very children of that marriage should themselves be the cause of her father's death. Thus she would be avenged, and her children bit her father to death. The body was thrown into the sea, but afterwards, the girl regretted that she had killed her own father. So great was her feeling of shame at what she had done that she could not bear to live any longer; so she sent her children out into the world, and flung herself into the sea where her father had been cast. She sank down to the bottom, and became a sea spirit, afterwards ruling over all the beasts of the sea.

"But where did the seals come from?" asked Orulo; "if the same girl was not married to a stormy petrel and thrown overboard when her husband was pursuing her, then that could never have taken place which led to

16

the cutting off of her fingers while she clung to the side of the boat. And if that had not happened, the beasts of the sea would never have been made at all."

To this I observed that in that case I also could not understand where the seals came from that lived in the sea long before the Mother of the Sea Beasts ever existed. For in the story Orulo herself had told me, the stormy petrel lived solely on young fjord seals.

At this Orulo laughed, and said:

"Too much thought only leads to trouble. All this that we are talking about now happened in a time so far back that there was no time at all. We Eskimos do not concern ourselves with solving all riddles. We repeat the old stories in the way they were told to us and with the words we ourselves remember. And if there should then seem to be a lack of reason in the story as a whole, there is yet enough remaining in the way of incomprehensible happenings, which our thought cannot grasp. If it were but everyday ordinary things, there would be nothing to believe in. How came all the living creatures on earth from the beginning? Can anyone explain that?"

And then, after having thought for a moment, she added the following, which shows in a striking fashion how little the actual logical sequence counts with the Eskimos in their mythology:

"You talk about the stormy petrel catching seals before there were any seals. But even if we managed to settle this point so that all worked out as it should, there would still be more than enough remaining which we cannot explain. Can you tell me where the mother of the caribou got her breeches from; breeches made of caribou skin before she had made any caribou? You always want these supernatural things to make sense, but we do not bother about that. We are content not to understand."

4 Aua

"Mysterious as the manner in which death came into life, even so mysterious is death itself," says Aua.

"We know nothing about it for certain, save that those we live with suddenly pass away from us, some in a natural and understandable way because they have grown old and weary, others, however, in mysterious ways, because we who lived with them could see no reason why they in particular should die, and because we knew that they would gladly live. But that is just what makes death the great power it is. Death alone determines how long we may remain in this life on earth, which we cling to, and it alone carries us into another life which we know only from the accounts of shamans long since dead. We know that men perish through age, or illness, or accident, or because another has taken their life. All this we understand. Something is broken. What we do not understand is the change which takes place in a body when death lays hold of it. It is the same body that went about among us and was living and warm and spoke as we do ourselves, but it has suddenly been robbed of a power, for lack of which it becomes cold and stiff and putrefies. Therefore we say that a man is ill when he has lost a part of his soul, or one of his souls; for there are some who believe that man has several souls. If then that part of a man's vital force be not restored to the body, he must die. Therefore we say that a man dies when the soul leaves him."

from

Segu

The *urubu* of death, invisible to the eyes of ordinary mortals, alighted on a tree in the compound and flapped its wings. It was exhausted. It had flown over miles and miles of sea, fighting against spray and air currents, then over dense forests swarming with a thousand different forms of fierce and violent life. Finally it had seen a tawny stretch of sand below and realized that its journey was nearly over. Then the walls of Segu appeared.

The *urubu* had a mission to perform. Naba had died far from home. His body lay in foreign soil and had not received the proper funeral rites. So his people had to be told he was in danger of having to wander forever in the desolate waste of the damned, unable to find reincarnation in the body of a male baby or to become a protecting ancestor, later a god. The *urubu* preened its feathers, got its breath back, and looked around.

It was morning. The sun had not yet answered the call of the earliest pestles and mortars, and still slumbered on the other side of the sky. The huts huddled together and shivered. But already the chickens were cackling, the sheep bleating, and from beneath the awnings of the open-air kitchens the smoke arose in white puffs. The women slaves were starting to prepare the morning porridge, while the men went to the bath huts, whetted their *dabas* on stones, and got ready to go out into the fields. The *urubu* looked with interest at all this activity, so different from that in the *fazendas*, where long before daylight the ox carts, preceded by the earsplitting sound of their axles, went up to the sugar mill laden with men in rags. There, working on the land was degradation. Here men only asked the earth for what was necessary to live. The landscape was different, too. There it was sumptuous and baroque, like the cathedrals the Portuguese built to worship their gods. Here it was bare, with the grass often as short as the pelt of an animal; but it was beautiful, too. The *urubu* hopped onto a low branch, facing the hut belonging to Koumare, fetish priest to Dousika's family. It was a wise move, for Koumare came out to divine what sort of day it was going to be, and didn't fail to notice the creature perched among the leaves.

Koumare had known for some time that the will of the ancestors concerning one of Dousika's sons was approaching fulfillment. One day when he was throwing his cowrie shells on his divining board they had told him so. But they wouldn't reveal anything more, however much he asked them. The coming of the bird was the sign it was all over. He went back into his hut, chewed some of the roots that allowed him to hear the speech of spirits, then took three stalks of dried millet out of a bowl. Then he went out under the tree, stuck the stalks into the earth, put his ear to them, and waited for instructions. They were not long in coming. Above his head the *urubu* had shut its eyes. It was going to sleep all day. Koumare went back to his hut, waved away his first wife's offer of gruel, put on a European blanket against the cold, and went out of the compound.

Segu was changing. Why? Was it because of the influx of merchants offering goods once rare and expensive, now quite common? Muslim robes, caftans, boots, European fabrics, furniture from Morocco, hangings and tapestries from Mecca.... It was Islam that was eating away at Segu like some incurable disease. The Fulani had no need to come any nearer—their breath had already fouled everything! Their jihad wasn't necessary any more! Everywhere there were mosques, their muezzins shamelessly bawling down their sacrilegious summons. Everywhere there were shaven heads. In every market people fought over talismans, powders, a whole lot of rubbish wrapped up with Arabic labels and therefore considered superior. And the Mansa wasn't doing anything about this new religion!

Koumare went into what used to be Dousika's compound, now in charge of Diemogo. He had to get a white cock and a white sheep from Diemogo, and then find out which tree Naba's umbilical cord was buried under. Diemogo was talking to the leader of a group of slaves just going off to clear a piece of hitherto uncultivated land belonging to the clan. He glanced at the fetish priest anxiously. What new calamity brought him here?

The family was already sorely tried. Tiekoro had not left his hut since Nadie's death, and he was as weak and sickly as old man. Princess Sounou Saro, his promised bride, feeling humiliated, had sent the dowry back by the royal griots, together with such presents as she had already received. Tiekoro's mission as ambassador to the sultanate of Sokoto was given to someone else. Nya, affected both by the recent tragedy and by her son's misfortunes, was not well either. She was getting thin and haggard and seemed to take no interest in anything. Without her supervision, everything went to rack and ruin. It was no use looking to the other wives: they had always been under the thumb of Dousika's *bara muso*. Diemogo went over to Koumare, who took him aside and told him what had happened.

"The ancestors have sent a messenger to me," he said. "One of Dousika's sons needs my help."

Diemogo trembled.

"Tiekoro?" he asked.

"Don't seek to know secrets too heavy for you," answered the other severely. "I need a white cock, a sheep without markings, and ten kola nuts. Have them all sent to my compound before nightfall."

Then he went to find the tree he needed for his ritual. As he was going through the compound he passed a hut where slaves were going busily in and out. It was Nya's hut. She had been taken ill with a violent pain near her heart and had collapsed unconscious. Koumare thought with wonder of the strength

20

of mother love and the intuition that went with it. It was just as powerful as the knowledge that came from intercourse with spirits.

Nya lay on her mat, her eyes closed, surrounded by women, co-wives, slaves. Two healers applied dressings of leaves to her forehead, rubbed her limbs with lotions, or tried to make her drink. In a corner a couple of fetish priests were consulting their cowries and kola nuts. When they saw Koumare, their uncontested chief, they rose respectfully.

"Help us, Komotigui,"* said one of them.

"Her life is not in danger," Koumare replied soothingly.

Then he crouched down by the patient.

He knew what she had been through since she'd been widowed. The family council, doling out Dousika's wives, had given her to Diemogo, for whom she had never had any respect and whom she considered, rightly or wrongly, as opposed to the interests of her own sons, especially those of Tiekoro. But from then on she owed him total submission and obedience. She couldn't refuse him her body. And now, on top of all these troubles, she had been mysteriously warned of Naba's death! Koumare decided to intercede for her with the ancestors, to try to lessen her sufferings. Meanwhile he took some powder from a goat horn and inserted it into her nostrils: at least she would now have a dreamless sleep.

Then he went out again. At the far end of the compound, near the paddock where the horses were kept, stood a group of trees, the tallest of which was a baobab, its branches covered with birds. Koumare walked around it three times, muttering prayers. No, the umbilical cord wasn't there. A white egret appeared, skimmed along the ground for a while, then swooped up like an arrow and alighted on a tamarind tree growing against the wall of the compound a few yards further on. Koumare saluted this messenger of the gods and the ancestors.

Nya slept all day, a deep sleep like that of childhood. When she opened her eyes, night had fallen. She found her pain was the same, but silent, like a presence that would never go away.

Her son Naba was dead. She could feel it, even though she didn't know where or how he had died. She saw him as he was when a baby, a little boy, always trailing behind his elder brother. Then she saw him as a hunter—her heart used to quake when Tiefolo took him into the bush. They often stayed there for weeks at a time. Then one day the sound of whistling would announce their return. The animals they had killed would be cut up while they were still warm: antelope, gazelles and warthogs. The heads and feet would be sent to Koumare, who had made the arrows that killed them; she herself received the animals' backs as her symbolic share. But those days were gone, gone forever. What sorrow, for a mother, not to know what earth covered her son's dead body! She turned onto her side, and the women watching over her bestirred themselves.

*Master of Komo, *i.e.,* high priest.

21

"Would you like some chicken broth?"

"Let me massage you, *ba!*"

"*Ba,* do you feel better?"

She indicated that she did. At that moment Diemogo entered the room and everyone else withdrew. Diemogo and Nya had never liked one another: he thought she had too much influence over Dousika. The reason why the family council had made them husband and wife was to try to resolve these tensions, to force them to forget personalities and think only of the family and the clan. But until now they had as little as possible to do with one another. Diemogo only spent the night with her so as not to cause her too much humiliation.

Now he felt a pity for her that resembled love. She was still beautiful. Beautiful with the characteristic arrogance of the Kulibaly, whose totem was the *mpolio* fish. He laid his hand on her brow.

"How do you feel?" he said.

She gave a fleeting smile. "My hour is not yet come, *koke,*" she answered. "I shall still be making your gruel tomorrow . . ."

He wasn't used to such mildness from her; she usually treated him like an enemy. Perhaps for the first time, he looked at her body with lust: her still-firm breasts, her wide hips, her long thighs visible through her *pagne*. All this had belonged to his elder brother, but now was his. For he was the master now—of lands, property, cattle, slaves. His heart, usually free of pride, swelled within him, and he was filled with an intoxication that merged into desire.

It was very dark now. All the noises of the compound had ceased apart from the crying of a child, trying to delay the sleep that marked the end of playtime. A drum could be heard in the distance. Diemogo, surprised at the vigor of his member, went nearer to Nya. It was as if another person had gotten inside his skin, taking over his heart and his sex. He lay down beside her.

"Let me sleep with you," he whispered. "A man's warmth is still the best cure."

She turned toward him, offering herself with a naturalness he had never seen in her before, and when he rather shyly touched her breasts he found them hot and ready. He entered her.

And so, that night, thanks to Koumare, Naba's wandering soul found its way back into his mother's womb.

Stanley Keleman

Professional Colloquium
29 October 1977

What do we mean by the life of the body? Does anybody know?
The shape of my life emerges, it is not something I plan.

$$* \quad * \quad *$$

With Freud nature is suddenly no longer outside man; it is now inside him, as his unconscious, with civilization around it. The governing and organizing part of the mind is to take more and more control over that inner nature (impulses, desires). Freud made explicit, and even established as a desired goal, the split from our biology that characterizes our contemporary awareness: where id is, so should ego be.

My conception of the human being is different. The human being is a process, a series of biological events that have learned and transmitted very circumscribed things, to translate into action, translations which then reflect the quality and quantity of the process by which we create a life, a bodily life, a life style, and perpetuate it, or not.

$$* \quad * \quad *$$

How does the individual, and the organism generally, translate his biology into social action? How are we connected socially?, and to what?

"I" for most people is a muscular sense, action-oriented. But we have been taught to idealize an image, so there is a feeling of disconnection between our "inner" process and our muscular organs. This is reflected in the general state of confusion about our values.

We are disengaged from a perception of our living process.

One hardly knows anymore what it means to experience and formulate from one's own bodily events.

We know this much: the embryo in utero pulsates with the uterus. The pulses are *linked* together. This linking is pleasurable or stressful, wanted or resisted, either way giving an emotional tone to the expression of connection.

We have been taught to be mostly cognitively aware, so much that we are out of the bodily experience. The languaging brain assumes it is the self but it blocks out a larger muscle-brain sense of our being.

In truth, we speak to ourselves in terms of sensations and feeings. They, not our words, form a life chain and sustain an awareness of continuity.

Our process is a living structure, containing, feeling, imaging, experiencing, and thrusting toward satisfaction. Individual event connecting to individual event, becomes a life.

We have given too much weight to how we feel about our actions or intended actions as a measure of self-value. This makes us disloyal to our own process.

Most of us live our life according to our image of the social milieu, copying values and patterns of action. But it is our own living process that brings social orders into being, and persons with a sense of inhabiting them.

We are not flesh with a spirit or genetic code dwelling in us. We are an event that sustains a particular life style. We are not a machine with a mind or with a spirit. We are a complex biological process that has many realms of living and experiencing. The body is a layered, ecological environment of ancient and modern lives, just like our planet's strata of life. The Human Being has many bodies: a water body, blood, lymph; an action body, bones, muscles, ligaments; a reflective body of brain and nerve; a child's body; an adult's body. The forming of a life style necessitates a continual series of events rather than living singular images, or experiencing a dogma.

What becomes evident is not how man should live his life, but how man evolves his life; not how man should be part of nature, but how man is part and parcel of the changing shapes of nature, and in what ways we change our shape and the shape of our biosphere. The human condition is situational or relativistic. The human being is capable of perceiving many levels of reality, many levels of his internal environment, his body, depending upon where he's located in his life.

Life is old, very old, and we are old in it. The continuum of existence we experience has no discrete beginning.

A living process is an eternal process.

A living event is committed by a continuum to billions of years of existence, an infinite chain of living events.

*   *   *

The act of living is a reward itself.

Does that sound strange? It is just a natural by-product. Ask people why they like being alive. They just like it.

If not, people die like prisoners of war die; they just lay down and die. Young and strong, yet you couldn't wake them up.

It is an important thing I am saying—most people who enter your office do not recognize *that the fact of their existence is satisfying; there is nothing to look for, even though they may be in an existential pain situation.*

*   *   *

Working with biological process is working with creation. In order to help us grasp the nature of the life of the body we need a way to sharpen our experience of these ancient events, and to live them in their present form, again to sharpen the connection of our social egos to the life of our body.

24

I'll use a method here to show how we continually shape ourselves, and I'll call it "somatic phenomenology."

*   *   *

The deprivation of actual physical contact is so enormous in our culture that anything that touches us has such an enormous impact, and anyone practicing touch becomes a guru.

One doesn't need ritualized methods to practice contact. We need to understand the organism and how it lives, and not develop methods.

What I practice comes from my understanding; it is not a method.

I am seeking a language of the basic metabolism of being, a matter-of-fact language arising out of the process of our biological existence.

For example, in loving, we participate in a whole series of events at different levels; there are cellular and blood components; there are interpersonal actions and symbols. Loving is a series of events: it is arousal, it is memory, it is pulsation, it is attraction, boundary-ending, connection, image-making. How these are shared is what contact is.

*   *   *

We can't see the inside of the body. We don't really know what the inside of the body is. I remember being in school, we were taught that what we were seeing on the slide or the autopsy table is the real thing. It is dead, taken from the inside. You have to look inside the body when it is alive. Then you have a different set of circumstances. The implication is that the actual pulsatory form that organizes the organism is sustaining a particular environment which is a picture. If you walk down to the ocean, and you look on the rocks, you see the beach, you see little tidal pools, you see a life in there; in the sand you see a different life. One environment supports one kind of image, another supports another kind of image. If you change the environment that the tidal pool creates, you don't have that environment and you don't have that life anymore. *So the quality of the environment is the image that it generates.* You take a person who tells you that his inner life and feeling life is a desert, that he is cold, doesn't have much empathy, that for him life is simply a sterile piece of equipment; you lay him down on the bed and ask him to move in such a way that you are suggesting that the viscera have a little bit more room to bounce around in: "Don't make your belly so tight." It won't be long and he will be angry, sad, or scared. You have changed the environment. You have changed the feeling the viscera have, and up pops the possibility of something else.

Most of us are so geared to pay attention to the images in the form that we can recognize them, that we, in fact, never pay attention to how those images are connected to the whole person. Images are concrete, hard. Most of us don't feel the pulsatoriness or the warmth to support that image-making. We are unaware that the patterns of sensations that arise from the muscles, from the joints, and from the viscera, *are* our images.

Richard Grossinger

from
Embryogenesis

We cannot be carnivores without being killers too. From the point of view of plants, we are just another mutant that has lost the ability to feed directly from the Sun. What if this ability were regained and transmitted through the cells? This would be remarkable, considering the thousands of years of predation our metabolism embodies. Our *apologia* for the whole animal kingdom is based on the circumstantial evidence that there is no other path to knowledge. Yogis still promise we can someday materialize the right chords to draw our sustenance from vibrations of air, without killing even plant life, to drink from the Sun and the psychic field around us, but if that's where we're headed, we obviously have a long way to go.

No diagnosis of the problem or possible solution is any longer too extreme. We miss the point when we act only conscientiously, so even our humanitarian gestures are confounded. This media-conscious, high-technology civilization creates the mirage of progress against famine, tyranny, and disease. But, in self-protection, we are blind. Between the unnamed forces of voodoo and the quantum dance of atoms lie untold universes of suffering and redemption. We may pretend to heal the Earth, but what about whole civilizations destroyed on other planets, individuals in pain on worlds around other suns? If we were to accomplish a lasting peace on our world, would we then have to worry about other planets that perhaps do not even exist? But if they do, they are part of the universe, part of consciousness; and, ultimately our sympathy must be extended through eternity to those victims too, creatures we could never know. Not because it does any good but because it forces us to view the crisis in its actual bigness while at the same time reminding us that we do not know who and where we are and thus what powers we have. If we could bring peace to this planet, we could probably bring peace to the universe.

We do not know. But that is not the problem. The problem is that we pretend we know, or think we should pretend. We think we know what we are and what the world should be. But nothing about cell life, or DNA, or the self-assembly of tissue suggests we have any idea of whence we come into being. Our whole culture and technology might be an evasion of our natural condition, our true dormant power. We could be avoiding our own natures, missing the solutions to our crises; worlds without end more fulfilling than this one might be within our grasp. But these lie in the margins of an unconscious inner life we presently flee in all our ideologies and institutions. It would seem now to have to begin in silence again. We must drop all our expectations and see just how

26

quiet and observant we can be—keeping our eye perfectly on each thing as it arises. We have created so much noise; yet the thing we are is so soundless and perfect it might simply become.

Section II

ANIMAL AND MIND

Robert Kelly

ON A PICTURE OF A BLACK BIRD GIVEN TO ME
BY ARTHUR TRESS

Raven   in Chiapas
beak up open to
flat white mexican light
against which an arch is breaking-its back to join the broken sky

barbs of its feathers hang down, it cries out
for a world full of carrion
but its claws
hold firm & flat
the top of the ruined sill

wings tensed back
it has swallowed its tongue
in hunger to eat
                    hunger to cry out loud   into the sky   I am here

feed me unmerciful gods
who made us feed on shit
                    feed me because I cry louder

because these holy stones are dead
& the grey moss & green fungus are dead in their pores
because men mumble & make the best of it,
                        put up with what comes down soft & they eat

because I am alive & make noise
because I can crack the cheap bowl of your sky with my shriek

                                    because I care
                                    because I am hungry
& cry louder than any other.

Gregory Bateson

Form, Substance and Difference
19th Annual Alfred Korzybski Memorial Lecture
9 January 1970, Oceanic Institute, Hawaii

Let me say that it is an extraordinary honor to be here tonight, and a pleasure. I am a little frightened of you all, because I am sure there are people here who know every field of knowledge that I have touched much better than I know it. It is true that I have touched a number of fields, and I probably can face any one of you and say I have touched a field that you have not touched. But I am sure that for every field I have touched, there are people here who are much more expert than I. I am not a well-read philosopher, and philosophy is not my business. I am not a very well-read anthropologist, and anthropology is not exactly my business.

But I have tried to do something which Korzybski was very much concerned with doing, and with which the whole semantic movement has been concerned, namely, I have studied the area of impact between very abstract and formal philosophic thought on the one hand and the natural history of man and other creatures on the other. This overlap between formal premises and actual behavior is, I assert, of quite dreadful importance today. We face a world which is threatened not only with disorganization of many kinds, but also with the destruction of its environment, and we, today, are still unable to think clearly about the relations between an organism and its environment. What sort of a thing is this, which we call "organism *plus* environment?"

Let us go back to the original statement for which Korzybski is most famous—the statement that *the map is not the territory*. This statement came out of a very wide range of philosophic thinking, going back to Greece, and wriggling through the history of European thought over the last 2,000 years. In this history, there has been a sort of rough dichotomy and often deep controversy. There has been a violent enmity and bloodshed. It all starts, I suppose, with the Pythagoreans versus their predecessors, and the argument took the shape of, "Do you ask what it's made of—earth, fire, water, etc.?" Or do you ask, "What is its pattern?" Pythagoras stood for inquiry into pattern rather than inquiry into *substance.** That controversy has gone through the ages, and the Pythagorean half of it has, until

---

*R. G. Collingwood has given a clear account of the Pythagorean position in *The Idea of Nature* (Oxford, 1945).

Prepared under Career Development Award (K2-21, 931) of the National Institute of Mental Health. This paper is Contribution No. 65 of the Oceanic Institute, Hawaii.

recently, been on the whole the submerged half. The Gnostics followed the Pythagoreans, and the alchemists follow the Gnostics, and so on. The argument reached a sort of climax at the end of the eighteenth century when a Pythagorean evolutionary theory was built and then discarded—a theory which involved Mind.

The evolutionary theory of the late eighteenth century, the Lamarckian theory, which was the first organized transformist theory of evolution, was built out of a curious historical background which has been described by Lovejoy in *The Great Chain of Being*. Before Lamarck, the organic world, the living world, was believed to be hierarchic in structure, with Mind at the top. The chain, or ladder, went down through the angels, through men, through the apes, down to the infusoria or protozoa, and below that to the plants and stones.

What Lamarck did was to turn that chain upside down. He observed that animals changed under environmental pressure. He was incorrect, of course, in believing that those changes were inherited, but, in any case, these changes were for him the evidence of evolution. When he turned the ladder upside down, what had been the explanation, namely, the Mind at the top, now became that which had to be explained. His problem was to explain Mind. He was convinced about evolution, and there his interest in it stopped. So that if you read the *Philosophie Zoologique* (1809), you will find that the first third of it is devoted to solving the problem of evolution and the turning upside down of the taxonomy, and the rest of the book is really devoted to comparative psychology, a science which he founded. *Mind* was what he was really interested in. He had used habit as one of the axiomatic phenomena in his theory of evolution, and this of course also took him into the problem of comparative psychology.

Now the status of mind and pattern as the explanatory principles which, above all, required investigation was pushed out of biological thinking in the later evolutionary theories which were developed in the mid-nineteenth century by Darwin, Huxley, etc. There were still some naughty boys, like Samuel Butler, who said that mind could not be ignored in this way—but they were weak voices, and incidentally, they never looked at organisms. I don't think Butler ever looked at anything except his own cat, but he still knew more about evolution than some of the more conventional thinkers.

Now, at last, with the discovery of cybernetics, systems theory, information theory, and so on, we begin to have a formal base enabling us to think about mind and enabling us to think about all these problems in a way which was totally heterodox from about 1850 through World War II. What I have to talk about is how the great dichotomy of epistemology has shifted under the impact of cybernetics and information theory.

We can now say—or at any rate, can begin to say—what we think a mind is. In the next twenty years there will be other ways of saying it and, because the discoveries are new, I can only give you my personal version. The old versions are surely wrong, but which of the revised pictures will survive, we do not know.

Let us start from the evolutionary side. It is now empirically clear that Darwinian evolutionary theory contained a very great error in its identification of the unit of survival under natural selection. The unit which was believed to be crucial and around which the theory was set up was either the breeding individual or the family line or the subspecies or some similar homogeneous set of conspecifics. Now I suggest that the last hundred years have demonstrated empirically that if an organism or aggregate of organisms sets to work with a focus on its own survival and thinks that that is the way to select its adaptive moves, its "progress" ends up with a destroyed environment. If the organism ends up destroying its environment, it has in fact destroyed itself. And we may very easily see this process carried to its ultimate *reductio ad absurdum* in the next twenty years. The unit of survival is not the breeding organism, or the family line, or the society.

The old unit has already been partly corrected by the population geneticists. They have insisted that the evolutionary unit is, in fact, not homogeneous. A wild population of any species consists always of individuals whose genetic constitution varies widely. In other words, potentiality and readiness for change is already built into the survival unit. The heterogeneity of the wild population is already one half of that trial-and-error system which is necessary for dealing with the environment.

The artificially homogenized populations of man's domestic animals and plants are scarcely fit for survival.

And today a further correction of the unit is necessary. The flexible environment must also be included along with the flexible organism because, as I have already said, the organism which destroys its environment destroys itself.

The unit of survival is a flexible organism-in-its-environment.

Now, let me leave evolution for a moment to consider what is the unit of mind. Let us go back to the map and the territory and ask: what is it in the territory that gets onto the map? We know the territory does not get onto the map. That is the central point about which we here are all agreed. Now, if the territory were uniform, nothing would get onto the map except its boundaries, which are the points at which it ceases to be uniform against some larger matrix. What gets onto the map, in fact, is *difference*, be it a difference in altitude, a difference in vegetation, a difference in population structure, difference in surface, or whatever. Differences are the things that get onto a map.

But what is a difference? A difference is a very peculiar and obscure concept. It is certainly not a thing or an event. This piece of paper is different from the wood of this lectern. There are many differences between them—of color, texture, shape, etc. But if we start to ask about the localization of those differences, we get into trouble. Obviously the difference between the paper and the wood is not in the paper; it is obviously not in the wood; it is obviously not in the space between them, and it is obviously not in the time between them. (Difference which occurs across time is what we call "change.")

A difference, then, is an abstract matter.

In the hard sciences, effects are, in general, caused by rather concrete conditions or events—impacts, forces, and so forth. But when you enter the world of communication, organization, etc., you leave behind that whole world in which effects are brought about by forces and impacts and energy exchange. You enter a world in which "effects"—and I am not sure one should still use the same word—are brought about by *differences*. That is: they are brought about by the sort of "thing" that gets onto the map from the territory. This is difference.

Difference travels from the wood and paper into my retina. It then gets picked up and worked on by this fancy piece of computing machinery in my head.

The whole energy relation is different. In the world of mind, nothing—that which is *not*—can be a cause. In the hard sciences, we ask for causes and we expect them to exist and be "real." But remember that zero is different from one, and because is different from one, zero can be a cause in the psychological world, the world of communication. The letter which you do not write can get an angry reply; and the income tax form which you do not fill in can trigger the Internal Revenue boys into energetic action, because they, too, have their breakfast, lunch, tea and dinner and can react with energy which they derive from their metabolism. The letter which never existed is no source of energy.

It follows, of course, that we must change our whole way of thinking about mental and communicational process. The ordinary analogies of energy theory which people borrow from the hard sciences to provide a conceptual frame upon which they try to build theories about psychology and behavior—that entire Procrustean structure—is non-sense. It is in error.

I suggest to you, now, that the word "idea," in its most elementary sense, is synonymous with "difference." Kant, in the *Critique of Judgment*—if I understand him correctly—asserts that the most elementary aesthetic act is the selection of a fact. He argues that in a piece of chalk there are an infinite number of potential facts. The *Ding an sich,* the piece of chalk, can never enter into communication or mental process because of this infinitude. The sensory receptors cannot accept it; they filter it out. What they do is to select certain *facts* out of the piece of chalk, which then become, in modern terminology, information.

I suggest that Kant's statement can be modified to say that there is an infinite number of *differences* around and within the piece of chalk. There are differences between the chalk and the rest of the universe, between the chalk and the sun or the moon. And within the piece of chalk, there is for every molecule an infinite number of differences between its location and the locations in which it *might* have been. Of this infinitude, we select a very limited number—which become information. In fact, what we mean by information—the elementary unit of information—is a *difference which makes a difference,* and is able to make a difference because the neural pathways, along which it travels and is continually transformed, are themselves provided with energy. The pathways are ready to be triggered. We may even say that the question is already implicit in them.

There is, however, an important contrast between most of the pathways of information inside the body and most of the pathways outside it. The differences between the paper and the wood are first transformed into differences in the propagation of light or sound and travel in this form to my sensory end organs. The first part of their journey is energized in the ordinary hard-science way, from "behind." But when the differences enter my body by triggering an end organ, this type of travel is replaced by travel which is energized at every step by the metabolic energy latent in the protoplasm which *receives* the difference, recreates or transforms it, and passes it on.

When I strike the head of a nail with a hammer, an impulse is transmitted to its point. But it is a semantic error, a misleading metaphor, to say that what travels in an axon is an "impulse." It could correctly be called "news of a difference."

Be that as it may, this contrast between internal and external pathways is not absolute. Exceptions occur on both sides of the line. Some external chains of events are energized by relays, and some chains of events internal to the body are energized from "behind." Notably, the mechanical interaction of muscles can be used as a computational model.*

In spite of these exceptions, it is still broadly true that the coding and transmission of differences outside the body is very different from the coding and transmission inside, and this difference must be mentioned because it can lead us into error. We commonly think of the external "physical world" as somehow separate from an internal "mental world." I believe that this division is based on the contrast in coding and transmission inside and outside the body.

The mental world—the mind—the world of information processing—is not limited by the skin.

Let us now go back to the notion that the transform of a difference traveling in a circuit is an elementary idea. If this be correct, let us ask what a mind is. We say the map is different from the territory. But what is the territory? Operationally, somebody went out with a retina or a measuring stick and made representations which were then put upon paper. What is on the paper map is a representation of what was in the retinal representation

---

*It is interesting to note that digital computers depend upon transmission of energy "from behind" to send "news" along wire from one relay to the next. But each relay has its own energy source. Analogic computers, e.g., tide machines and the like, are commonly entirely driven by energy "from behind." Either type of energization can be used for computational purposes.

of the man who made the map: and as you push the question back, what you find is an infinite regress, an infinite series of maps. The territory never gets in at all. The territory is *Ding an sich* and you can't do anything with it. Always the process of representation will filter it out so that the mental world is only maps of maps of maps, ad infinitum.* All "phenomena" are literally "appearances."

Or we can follow the chain forward. I receive various sorts of mappings which I call data or information. Upon receipt of these I act. But my actions, my muscular contractions, are transforms of differences in the input material. And I receive again data which are transforms of my actions. We get thus a picture of the mental world which has somehow jumped loose from our conventional picture of the physical world.

This is not new, and for historic background we go again to the alchemists and Gnostics. Carl Jung once wrote a very curious little book, which I recommend to all of you. It is called *Septem Sermones ad Mortuos,* Seven Sermons to the Dead.† In his *Memories, Dreams, Reflections,* Jung tells us that his house was full of ghosts, and they were noisy. They bothered him, they bothered his wife, and they bothered the children. In the vulgar jargon of psychiatry we might say that everybody in the house was as psychotic as hooty owls, and for quite good reason. If you get your epistemology confused, you go psychotic, and Jung was going through an epistemological crisis. So he sat down at his desk and picked up a pen and started to write. When he started to write the ghosts all disappeared, and he wrote this little book. From this he dates all his later insight. He signed it "Basilides," who was a famous Gnostic in Alexandria in the second century.

He points out that there are two worlds. We might call them two worlds of explanation. He names them the *pleroma* and the *creatura,* these being Gnostic terms. The pleroma is the world in which events are caused by forces and impacts and in which there are no "distinctions." Or, as I would say, no "differences." In the creatura, effects are brought about precisely by difference. In fact, this is the same old dichotomy between mind and substance.

We can study and describe the pleroma, but, always, the distinctions which we draw are attributed *by us* to the pleroma. The pleroma knows nothing of difference and distinction; it contains no "ideas" in the sense in which I am using the word. When we study and describe the creatura, we must correctly identify those differences which are effective within it.

---

*Or we may spell the matter out and say that at every step, as a difference is transformed and propagated along its pathway, the embodiment of the difference before the step is a "territory" of which the embodiment after the step is a "map." The map-territory relation obtains at every step.

† Written in 1916, translated by H. G. Baynes and privately circulated in 1925. Republished by Stuart & Watkins, London, and by Random House, 1961. In later work, Jung seems to have lost the clarity of the Seven Sermons. In his "Answer to Job," the archetypes are said to be "pleromatic." It is surely true, however, the constellations of ideas may seem subjectively to resemble "forces" when their ideational character is unrecognized.

I suggest that "pleroma" and "creatura" are words which we could usefully adopt and it is therefore worthwhile to look at the bridges which exist between these two "worlds." It is an oversimplification to say that the "hard sciences" deal only with the pleroma and that the sciences of the mind deal only with creatura.

There is more to it than that.

First, consider the relation between energy and negative entropy. The classical Carnot heat engine consists of a cylinder of gas with a piston. This cylinder is alternately placed in contact with a container of hot gas and with a container of cold gas. The gas in the cylinder alternately expands and contracts as it is heated or cooled by the hot and cold sources. The piston is thus driven up and down.

But with each cycle of the engine, the *difference* between the temperature of the hot source and that of the cold source is reduced. When this difference becomes zero, the engine will stop.

The physicist, describing the pleroma, will write equations to translate the temperature difference into "available energy," which he will call "negative entropy," and will go on from there.

The analyst of the creatura will note that the whole system is a sense organ which is triggered by temperature difference. He will call this difference which makes a difference "information" or "negative entropy." For him, this is only a special case in which the effective difference happens to be a matter of energetics. He is equally interested in all differences which can activate some sense organ. For him, any such difference is "negative entropy."

Or consider the phenomenon which the neurophysiologists call "synaptic summation." What is observed is that in certain cases, when two neurons, A and B, have synaptic connection to a third neuron, C, the firing of neither neuron by itself is sufficient to fire C; but that when both A and B fire simultaneously (or nearly so), their combined "impulses" will cause C to fire.

In pleromatic language, this combining of events to surmount a threshold is called "summation."

But from the point of view of the student of creatura (and the neurophysiologist must surely have one foot in the pleroma and the other in creatura), this is not summation at all. What happens is that the system operates to create differences. There are two differentiated *classes* of firings by A: those firings which are accompanied by B and those which are unaccompanied. Similarly there are two classes of firings by B.

The so-called "summation," when both fire, is not an additive process from this point of view. It is the formation of a logical product—a process of fractionation rather than summation.

The creatura is thus the world seen as mind, wherever such a view is appropriate. And wherever this view is appropriate, there arises a species of complexity which is absent from pleromatic description: creatural description is always hierarchic.

38

I have said that what gets from territory to map is transforms of difference and that these (somehow selected) differences are elementary ideas.

But there are differences between differences.

Every effective difference denotes a demarcation, a line of classification, and all classification is hierarchic. In other words, differences are themselves to be differentiated and classified.

In this context I will only touch lightly on the matter of classes of difference, because to carry the matter further would land us in problems of Principia Mathematica.

Let me invite you to a psychological experience, if only to demonstrate the frailty of the human computer. First note differences in texture are *different* (*a*) from differences in color. Now note that differences in size are *different* (*b*) from differences in shape. Similarly ratios are different (*c*) from subtractive differences.

Now let me invite you, as disciples of Korzybski, to define the differences between "different (*a*)," "different (*b*)," and "different (*c*)" in the above paragraph.

The computer in the human head boggles at the task.

But not all classes of difference are as awkward to handle.

One such class you are all familiar with. Namely, the class of differences which are created by the process of transformation whereby the differences immanent in the territory become differences immanent in the map. In the corner of every serious map you will find these rules of transformation spelled out—usually in words. Within the human mind, it is absolutely essential to recognize the differences of this class, and, indeed, it is these that form the central subject matter of *Science and Sanity*.

An hallucination or a dream image is surely a transformation of something. But of what? And by what rules of transformation?

Lastly there is that hierarchy of differences which biologists call "levels." I mean such differences as that between a cell and a tissue, between tissue and organ, organ and organism, and organism and society.

These are the hierarchies of units or Gestalten, in which each sub-unit is a part of the unit of next larger scope. And, always in biology, this difference or relationship which I call "part of" is such that certain differences in the part have informational effect upon the larger unit, and vice versa.

Having stated this relationship between biological part and whole, I can now go on from the notion of creatura as Mind in general to the question of what is *a* mind.

What do I mean by "my" mind?

I suggest that the delimitation of an individual mind must always depend upon what phenomena we wish to understand or explain. Obviously there are lots of message pathways outside the skin, and these and the messages which they carry must be included as part of the mental system whenever they are relevant.

Consider a tree and a man and an axe. We observe that the axe flies through the air and makes certain sorts of gashes in a pre-existing cut in the side of the tree. If now we want to explain this set of phenomena, we shall be concerned with differences in the cut face of the tree, differences in the retina of the man, differences in his central nervous system, differences in his efferent neural messages, differences in the behavior of his muscles, differences in how the axe flies, to the differences which the axe then makes on the face of the tree. Our explanation (for certain purposes) will go round and round that circuit. In principle, if you want to explain or understand anything in human behavior, you are always dealing with total circuits, completed circuits. This is the elementary cybernetic thought.

The elementary cybernetic system with its messages in circuit is, in fact, the simplest unit of mind; and the transform of a difference travelling in a circuit is the elementary idea. More complicated systems are perhaps more worthy to be called mental systems, but essentially this is what we are talking about. The unit which shows the characteristic of trial and error will be legitimately called a mental system.

But what about "me"? Suppose I am a blind man, and I use a stick. I go tap, tap, tap. Where do *I* start? Is my mental system bounded at the handle of the stick? Is it bounded by my skin? Does it start halfway up the stick? Does it start at the tip of the stick? But these are nonsense questions. The stick is a pathway along which transforms of difference are being transmitted. The way to delineate the system is to draw the limiting line in such a way that you do not cut any of these pathways in ways which leave things inexplicable. If what you are trying to explain is a given piece of behavior, such as the locomotion of the blind man, then, for this purpose, you will need the street, the stick, the man; the street, the stick, and so on, round and round.

But when the blind man sits down to eat his lunch, his stick and its messages will no longer be relevant—if it is his eating that you want to understand.

And in addition to what I have said to define the individual mind, I think it necessary to include the relevant parts of memory and data "banks." After all, the simplest cybernetic circuit can be said to have a memory of a dynamic kind—not based upon static storage but upon the travel of information around the circuit. The behavior of the governor of a steam engine at Time 2 is partly determined by what it did at Time 1—where the interval between Time 1 and Time 2 is that time necessary for the information to complete the circuit.

We get a picture, then, of mind as synonymous with cybernetic system— the relevant total information-processing, trial-and-error completing unit. And we know that within Mind in the widest sense there will be hierarchy of sub-systems, any one of which we can call an individual mind.

But this picture is precisely the same as the picture which I arrived at in discussing *the unit of evolution.* I believe that this identity is the most important generalization which I have to offer you tonight.

In considering units of evolution, I argued that you have at each step to include the completed pathways outside the protoplasmic aggregate, be it DNA-in-the-cell, or cell-in-the-body, or body-in-the-environment. The hierarchic structure is not new. Formerly we talked about the breeding individual or the family line or the taxon, and so on. Now each step of the hierarchy is to be thought of as a *system,* instead of a chunk cut off and visualized as *against* the surrounding matrix.

This identity between the unit of mind and the unit of evolutionary survival is of very great importance, not only theoretical, but also ethical.

It means, you see, that I now localize something which I am calling "Mind" immanent in the large biological system—the ecosystem. Or, if I draw the system boundaries at a different level, then mind is immanent in the total evolutionary structure. If this identity between mental and evolutionary units is broadly right, then we face a number of shifts in our thinking.

First, let us consider ecology. Ecology has currently two faces to it: the face which is called bio-energetics—the economics of energy and materials within a coral reef, a redwood forest, or a city—and, second, an economics of information, of entropy, neg-entropy, etc. These two do not fit together very well precisely because the units are differently bounded in the two sorts of ecology. In bio-energetics it is natural and appropriate to think of units bounded at the cell membrane, or at the skin; or of units composed of sets of conspecific individuals. These boundaries are then the frontiers at which measurements can be made to determine the additive-subtractive budget of energy for the given unit. In contrast, informational or entropic ecology deals with the budgeting of pathways and of probability. The resulting budgets are fractionating (not subtractive.) The boundaries must enclose, not cut, the relevant pathways.

Moreover, the very meaning of "survival" becomes different when we stop talking about the survival of something bounded by the skin and start to think of the survival of the system of ideas in circuit. The contents of the skin are randomized at death and the pathways within the skin are randomized. But the ideas, under further transformation, may go on out in the world in books or works of art. Socrates as a bio-energetic individual is dead. But much of him still lives as a component in the contemporary ecology of ideas.*

It is also clear that theology becomes changed and perhaps renewed. The Mediterranean religions for 5,000 years have swung to and fro between immanence and transcendence. In Babylon the gods were transcendent on the tops of hills; in Egypt, there was god immanent in Pharaoh; and Christianity is a complex combination of these two beliefs.

---

*For the phrase "ecology of ideas," I am indebted to Sir Geoffrey Vickers' essay "The Ecology of Ideas" in *Value Systems and Social Process* (Basic Books, 1968). For a more formal discussion of the survival of ideas, see Gordon Pask's remarks in Wenner-Gren Conference on "The Effects of Conscious Purpose on Human Adaptation," 1968.

The cybernetic epistemology which I have offered you would suggest a new approach. The individual mind is immanent but not only in the body. It is immanent also in pathways and messages outside the body; and there is a larger Mind of which the individual mind is only a sub-system. This larger Mind is comparable to God and is perhaps what some people mean by "God," but it is still immanent in the total interconnected social system and planetary ecology.

Freudian psychology expanded the concept of mind inwards to include the whole communication system within the body—the autonomic, the habitual and the vast range of unconscious process. What I am saying expands mind outwards. And both of these changes reduce the scope of the conscious self. A certain humility becomes appropriate, tempered by the dignity or joy of being part of something much bigger. A part—if you will—of God.

If you put God aside and set him vis-à-vis his creation and if you have the idea that you are created in his image, you will logically and naturally see yourself as outside and against the things around you. And as you arrogate all mind to yourself, you will see the world around you as mindless and therefore not entitled to moral or ethical consideration. The environment will seem to be yours to exploit. Your survival unit will be you and your folks or conspecifics against the environment of other social units, other races and the brutes and vegetables.

If this is your estimate of your relation to nature *and you have an advanced technology,* your likelihood of survival will be that of a snowball in hell. You will die either of the toxic by-products of your own hate, or, simply, of over-population and over-grazing.

The raw materials of the world are finite.

If I am right, the whole of our thinking about what we are and what other people are has got to be restructured. This is not funny, and I do not know how long we have to do it in. If we continue to operate on the premises that were fashionable in the pre-cybernetic era, and which were especially underlined and strengthened during the Industrial Revolution, which seemed to validate the Darwinian unit of survival, we may have twenty or thirty years before the logical *reductio ad absurdum* of our old positions destroys us. Nobody knows how long we have, under the present system, before some disaster strikes us, more serious than the destruction of any group of nations. The most important task today is, perhaps, to learn to think in the new way. Let me say that *I* don't know how to think that way. Intellectually, I can stand here and I can give you a reasoned exposition of this matter; but if I am cutting down a tree, I still think "Gregory Bateson" is cutting down the tree. *I* am cutting down the tree. "Myself" is to me still an excessively concrete object, different from the rest of what I have been calling "mind."

The step to realizing—to making habitual—the other way of thinking—so that one naturally thinks that way when one reaches out for a glass of water or cuts down a tree—that step is not an easy one.

And, quite seriously, I suggest to you that we should trust no policy decisions which emanate from persons who do not yet have that habit.

There are experiences and disciplines which may help me to imagine what it would be like to have this habit of correct thought. Under LSD, I have experienced, as have many others, the disappearance of the division between self and the music to which I was listening. The perceiver and the thing perceived become strangely united into a single entity. And this state is surely more correct than the state in which it seems that "I hear the music." The sound, after all, is *Ding an sich,* but my perception of it is a part of mind.

It is told of Johann Sebastian Bach that when somebody asked him how he played so divinely, he answered, "I play the notes, in order, as they are written. It is God who makes the music." But not many of us can claim Bach's correctness of epistemology—or that of William Blake who knew that the Poetic Imagination was the only reality.

The poets have known these things all through the ages, but the rest of us have gone astray into all sorts of false reifications of the "self" and separations between the "self" and "experience."

For me another clue—another moment when the nature of mind was for a moment clear—was provided by the famous experiments of Adalbert Ames, Jr. These are optical illusions in depth perception. As Ames' guinea pig, you discover that those mental processes by which you create the world in three-dimensional perspective are within your mind but totally unconscious and utterly beyond voluntary control. Of course, we all know that this is so—that mind creates the images which "we" then see. But still it is a profound epistemological shock to have direct experience of this which we always knew.

Please do not misunderstand me. When I say that the poets have always known these things or that most of mental process is unconscious, I am not advocating a greater use of emotion or a lesser use of intellect. Of course, if what I am saying tonight is approximately true, then our ideas about the relation between thought and emotion need to be revised. If the boundaries of the "ego" are wrongly drawn or even totally fictitious, then it may be nonsense to regard emotions or dreams or our unconscious computations of perspective as "ego-alien."

We live in a strange epoch when many psychologists try to "humanize" their science by preaching an anti-intellectual gospel. They might, as sensibly, try to physicalize physics by discarding the tools of mathematics.

It is the attempt to *separate* intellect from emotion that is monstrous, and I suggest that it is equally monstrous—and dangerous—to attempt to separate the external mind from the internal. Or to separate mind from body.

Blake noted that "A tear is an intellectual thing," and Pascal asserted that "The heart has its *reasons* of which the reason knows nothing"; and we need not be put off by the fact that the reasonings of the heart (or of the hypothalamus) are accompanied by sensations of joy or grief. These computations are concerned with matters which are vital to mammals—namely, matters of *relationship,* by which I mean love, hate, respect, dependency, spectatorship, performance, dominance, and so on. These are central to the life of any mammal and I see no objection to calling these computations "thought," though certainly the units of relational computation are different from the units which we use to compute about isolable things.

But there are bridges between the one sort of thought and the other, and it seems to me that the artists and poets are specifically concerned with these bridges. It is not that art is the expression of the unconscious, but rather that it is concerned with the relation *between* the levels of mental process. From a work of art it may be possible to analyze out some unconscious thought of the artist, but I believe that, for example, Freud's analysis of Leonardo's "Virgin on the Knees of St. Anne" precisely misses the point of the whole exercise. Artistic skill is the combining of many levels of mind—unconscious, conscious and external—to make a statement of their combination. It is not a matter of expressing a single level.

Similarly, Isadora Duncan, when she said "If I could say it, I would not have to dance it," was talking nonsense, because her dance was about *combinations* of saying and moving.

Indeed, if what I have been saying is at all correct, the whole base of aesthetics will need to be re-examined. It seems that we link feelings not only to the computations of the heart but also to the computations in the external pathways of the mind. It is when we recognize the operations of creatura in the external world that we are aware of "beauty" or "ugliness." The "primrose by the river's brim" is beautiful because we are aware that the combination of differences which constitutes its appearance could only be achieved by information processing, i.e., by *thought.* We recognize another mind within our own external mind.

And last, there is death. It is understandable that, in a civilization which separates mind from body, we should either try to forget death or to make mythologies about the survival of transcendent mind. But if mind is immanent not only in those pathways of information which are located inside the body but also in external pathways, then death takes on a different aspect. The individual nexus of pathways which I call "me" is no longer so precious because that nexus is only part of a larger mind.

The ideas which seemed to be me can also become immanent in you. May they survive—if true.

Edward Dorn

Dear Flabby: Vira Untwists the "Murch"

Dear Flabby:

I am a Carbonaceous meteorite who fell in Australia never mind when. The point is as luck had had it (I believe thats the idiom but I hope you'll excuse any error as I was programed for English & Swedish at the same time, Simultaneous is the word for that. In fact, if you can believe a coincidence like this, Simultaneous is the word for THAT where I come from never mind where. Swedish so if there were a Noble Prize for Meteorites I should be able and ready to accept it in the tongue of the Great Creator of Firecrackers. Of course, I soon learned that the object is never awarded the prize, to my great dismay, since I come here as a perfectly innocent object. Thus those who scrutinize meteorites are given prizes but not meteorites. Those who write poems but not the poems etc. An odd practice, and had I known this Id of got into another system.

Anyway, as luck has had it, I landed in Australia, where, because so little lands, I was taken immediately (the word for This where I come from, for instance we say, Immediately or Simultaneously for This or That) to the site where something called the Ames Team noticed that my Amigo acid chains turned right as much as left when apparently your whole natural world turns left! Which I understand is rather embarrassing to Keynsian biology. Vell, it' something to think about. Be that as it might, we was quite chagrinning when I met some totally nasty types who came in concealed in the noses of the Ames Team and spread all over thir Kleenex. They could do Everything very simple minded I can do both ways and no kidding! Called by my Ames Team Virus. So what I want to know, Flabby, exactly who is these Virus?

> The Murchison Meteorite
> for all the 'clules on this
> trip,
>
> left & right—

Dear "The Murch:"

A Virus is the simplest known biological entity on Earth. It is made up of a single strand of DNA surrounded by a protective protein coat which keeps it warm during the long glacial winter, or when the courier sneezes. By itself, a virus is not really alive. When a group of them are hanging around the candy store dried up they form a crystal. They can wait like this for years! But when dissolved in liquid and allowed to penetrate a cell, they become alive, acting out their ancient need to gobble up the amino acids and nucleotides of the primordial soup. Once inside a cell they fuck with its genetic machinery and use its rich stash of amino acids and nucleotides to make copies of **Themselves.** They're the **heaviest** ego trip around!

> Good luck to all the objects
> down at the site,
> sighnd, Flabby

Dear Flabby:

This is in regards to a letter you published last week from the Murchison Meteorite and your cozy reply. Because The Murchison Meteorite doesnt speak for All the 'cules down at that site or any other. I just want your readers to know that "the Murch" wasnt that special a job and he ought to realize what he fell into before he complains about getting fucked over by the Ames Team (a bunch of real jokers anyway) and duplicated by us. The fact is there aint nothing down here but us virus and the reason we're not worried bout who gets the prize is the same reason we're not worried about who takes the cake and we dont worry about any subject-object relationship because we're completely into where those two lines **converge** —and by the way, if the Murch wants to know what Simultaneous really does he can try **that** the way we do it around here!

Furthermore, I can say without any sarcasm that **we're** perfectly satisfied to all look alike and do our one thing—and rather pleased, when we get to them, Everybody else begins to look like us. Such an arrangement takes care of all those **decisions** I've heard youre up against out there. You oughta try it. Of course, as a virus individual I admire myself (which is the same thing) a very Great Deal—and why not? That's what I'm here for. But it's a strictly private affair between reality and me (which is the same thing) and there isnt one of us who is even slightly concerned with the public ego of an acceptance speech. So by now you will begin to understand. Me can speak for all of us because we are all of us. You better believe I don't have to speak Swedish to tell you that.

> sighnd, Vira
> somewhere in case 10^{19}
> Culture 54321-21

PS   On the basis of whats predicted here of organisms of so-called complex extensions (a very gross aspect of evolution indeed) I can believe theyd get it off accepting almost anything. But I'd like to remind everyone how that prize got there in the first place. Down at the site we're the biggest thing on the set and none of us are interested in "soup" whoever that is, altho of course primordial is another matter, and the way things look out there is not necessarily duplicated in here. Sure, we get into crystal and I can recommend it as a way to really structure your rigidities if thats what you need to do but if any of you out there get serious about that trip youd do well to reconsider an aesthetic which makes a distinction like Alive or Not Alive before you bring it along. Because like there aint any magazines at all in this waiting room!

Robert Kelly

A CHAPTER OF QUESTIONS

Coming back through the names
will it all be the same?

Going outward where it is
will be there easy?

What is the form of it does the
voice count does the anxious
ness of the voice count does
the speaker of the voice
count?

What is the form of it?
Why do they not know how to question?
Why do I know how to question?
Who are they?
Are they good?
Are they enough?
Is good enough?
Is bad enough?
Is ever enough?
What's the good
word?
Who is the woman?
Does she have red hair?
Does she go bare?
Does she go back?
Was she ever there?
Is one enough?
Or more?
Is it possible?
Which way was he looking?
Is it positive?
Are you positive?
Are you negative?
Are you neutral?
Do you hear me?
Are you neural?
Do you feel me?

Do you ever?
Is this too late?
Too early?
What do you ask of reality?
How do you beg a question?
What is an empty chair?
Why is a door?
What did you do in the dark?
What did it do in you?
Do you know that there is violence in the air?
Do you care?
Is rhyme ever true?
Where does it lead?
Whom does it need?
What do you need?
Can you go fishing in the air?
If it was empty who ate what was there?
Do you care?
Can you go fishing in the air?
Does it count?
Are you there?
Do you count?
Will it be there?
Will it be all the same?
Who made me?
Why did he make me?
Who made you?
Will the air?
Care?
Does her beauty matter?
Is her beauty matter?
Is it a running matter?
Fire?
Will I find the question?
Where are they who came before us?
Do you care?
Do you dare not answer?
Coming in from the rain is it wet?
Going out into the rain is it wetter?
Will you ever get better?
Is it now?
Tomorrow is it forever?
Never?
When will it be?
Spicer spicer over the wall

which is the truest word of them all?
Do your eyes?
Does your name?
Will it ever?
Put it together?
Who killed Cock Robin?
Is he risen?
Is he not here?
Does he go before you into Galilee?
What's the good word?

from

The Wise Wound

It is at least arguable that our children are born in modern obstetrical practice by a series of aggressive acts. The child's first experience of life in the world is a panic breath, due to cutting the cord which is still supplying oxygenated blood, or glaring lights and noise of the hospital delivery room. The possibility that altering the conditions of birth might affect favorably the aggressive tendencies of the adults into which these babies grow, and by the same token the aggressive tendencies of those societies that practice such birth-methods, is a barely explored field. But it is at least worth a hypothesis that aggression may thus grow in people and societies by a "snowballing" or feedback effect.

Another unexplored field is the examination of how a different experience of her menstrual cycle might enhance the growth and powers of individual women, though there is much evidence, as we shall show, that such growth and powers are possible. It is up to every woman to determine for herself, so far as she is able, her wishes toward her own labor-experience, and also toward her menstrual experience. It is only in recent years that women have begun to be able to do the former, and the effects on society may soon be seen, as the children grow up. We believe that menstrual experience may soon take its place in the total picture.

There is the great anomalous myth of the Holy Grail within Christian history. The holy male knights sought through the desolation of their wasteland for that Grail which would bring back life, and make the Wasteland bloom. The legend tells that the perfect knight, Parsifal, at last found and entered the Grail Castle, and saw the procession of dancing youths and maidens carrying the spear dripping with blood and the great chalice of the Grail brimming with blood. King Amfortas, its guardian, whose wounds bled day and night, and all the assembled company in that castle waited for Parsifal to ask the simple and natural but magical question that would put an end to the desolation that surrounded them. But Parsifal was so full of astonishment and the inappropriate kind of awe, that he forgot to ask the small necessary question.

And that question was no more than, "This Cup that bleeds, what is it for?"

We think that the mythic question has such power in the legend precisely because it can be asked in fact. The question we can ask is: "What does my bloodshed every month mean?" Women through the ages have asked this question, and the Wasteland answer they have received from the male knights (who believe that because they do not bleed they do not have to ask the question), when they have been answered at all, has been: "It is a Curse."

51

Peggy Beck

The Fool and the Beginning of Wisdom

> ... he existed on the edges of a society which did not recog-
> nize him in any way, and, as he might himself have put it, he
> had not done so very badly at all.
>
> He lived as a bird lives, or a fish, or a wolf. Laws were for
> other people, but they were not for him; he crawled under or
> vaulted across those ethical barriers, and they troubled him no
> more than as he had to bend or climb a little to avoid them. . . .
> He stood outside of every social relation, and within an organ-
> ized humanity he might almost have been reckoned as a differ-
> ent species.*

A Fool is compelled to wander because he has been dispossessed by
society. The Fool is at once both a prisoner of definition, i.e. abnormal,
and free for this reason to come and go in the guise of folly. The Fool, like
freedom, is outside of definition. He comes and he goes. The Fool's irrev-
erence and guerrilla existence makes the Fool's time and place so precisely
an event of the present that he could properly be said to be a mere quality,
still and empty space. But as the Fool is that still point in the conception of
space, he is also the juggler, minstrel and clown at every turn of the
universe.

The notion at the root of my thinking is that *folly* or the way of the Fool
is the guiding principle of an epistemology that equates ecological balance
in the natural world with moral and ethical balance in the human community. An epistemology that will demonstrate that human consciousness is
compatible with ecological imperatives and will, by its own structure, com-
pel us to wisdom. This epistemology which embraces both ecological complexity and human folly, wisdom and madness, is, I believe, an analogue
for *grace*. The moment that consciousness dovetails with ecological imperatives we divine the world. The key to this epistemology is that human
play and human folly are the only conscious human acts that coincide with
the conscious or formative movements of the universe.

The archetypal figure of the Fool is the only metaphorical gate I know of
that might admit one within sight of consciousness itself. The Fool is, I
believe, the archetype of the impulse to make connections, to see patterns,
to reflect the world with the human mind, and to eventually dissolve this
impulse into *being*. The task of the Fool is to demonstrate the epistemological premise that it is the structure by which we perceive which opens us

---

*The Irish author James Stephens, *The Demi-Gods* (New York: Macmillan, 1919), p. 60.

to the forms we perceive. The way of the Fool is a manner of living which impels us out of our limited perspective on the world and forces us never again to name that which in fact has no name: ecological permutations which have no definition—only continuity, circularity, and grace.

> His mind is natural and true, unshadowed by reflection or ulterior designs. For wherever conscious purpose is to be seen, there the truth and innocence of nature have been lost.*

When human beings exploit the basic need we have to survive or the means with which survival can be accomplished; when human beings view themselves as more efficient, more knowledgeable than the ecosystems of which they are but a small part; or when human beings feel certain that science can replace dreaming, both the human species and the planet will be destroyed. Wisdom, derived from our Fool's epistemology, includes a knowledge of the "larger interactive system." It includes pieces of information obtained from barely visible sources, from indefinable though perceptible sources, from highly irregular or idiosyncratic sources—from minutiae which though absolutely necessary for the maintenance of health and balance in ecosystems, are usually ignored by our shortcuts to efficiency. These sources exist as part of a wise person's "second nature." Minutiae give the shaman's art an air of simplicity that belies the highly complex sources of his/her final designs or poetry. Minutiae make gestures in aboriginal dances weighty with "information" or meaning. Given the normal insistence on linear/logical thought and expression; unable to communicate the nature of one's existence in a langauge simple (and complex) enough to match it, the scope of communications between human beings about their ecosystems is reduced and contact with the wonder of minutiae limited. Those human beings who are wise, Fools and others, will be found attempting to catch our attention at odd moments, to impel us unexpectedly out of our frameworks of limited perspective in order to put us in touch with the wonder that lies at the origin of language, ethics, and consciousness.

> He had culture too, and if it was not wide it was profound; he knew wind and weather as few astronomers know it; he knew the habit of the trees and the earth; how the seasons moved, not as seasons, but as days and hours.†

In the universe there are no beginnings or endings, only interference patterns, synchronicities, momentary connections, and topological twists. In essence: relationships, dissonance, differences, and transformations. In

---

*From the hexagram *Wu Wang*, Innocence (The Unexpected). *I Ching.*

†James Stephens, *The Demi-Gods*, p. 58.

turn, the universe is composed of rather strict laws which govern its essential play. These laws impel matter to take shape, to permute and transform. Consequently, we are able to perceive a diversity of forms and a complex of events or relationships. These laws of form are patterns of transformation which turn chaos into a great Druid Circle, a play ground, a matrix sensitive to fluctuations, moods, and other intimations. We might call this matrix a *field* upon which any boundary surface or fluctuation designates a threshold in our consciousness. The Fool is the archetype for this threshold. The Fool is a point of change, a manifestation of "difference," a relationship—any negative space which introduces a hiatus in our consciousness.

In order to merge consciousness with ecology, to become synchronous with the field of the universe, a hiatus in convention is required. Incidences of slippage and accident transform chaos into designs, patterns, and images as well as into a matrix of forms again. When this happens to our perception, consciousness becomes equal to the formative matrix of all ecosystems. Existence, we find, is no more or less than play. When we command the folly and the passion of play in our acts we will then act with wisdom.

The Fool shows us that there is an "order" to the universe that can be manipulated but that there is no "meaning" to that order. Knowing this, information generated by our infinite imagination can never outrun ecological imperatives. Fools manipulate by stepping aside and pointing out. Fools ride with destiny because their intuitions are perfectly attuned to the daily potential for dramatic irony let loose by love, by the wind, by the changing seasons, and by the mortal mind. Folly is a form of detachment—a detachment grounded in passion and love. A detachment which watches the folly of humankind cascade in a saturnalian dance—fate and fortune swirling together like the foam on tidal breakers, like crows in a March wind.

The Fool is a mediator for the idea of consciousness and ecology. Between each level of cognition on the path of knowledge there is a threshold. Every threshold met and mediated produces moments of awareness that in turn are the carriers for the next threshold of knowledge. This process of "awakening" is its own metaphor. The structure of the journey and the wisdom we gain at the end of the journey are the same. The labor of journeying a spiral into infinity is only the labor of a dance.

"What do you like best in the world, Shepherd Girl?"
Caitlin's eyes were fixed on his.
"I don't know yet," she answered slowly.
"May the gods keep you safe from that knowledge," said Pan gravely.
"Why would you say that?" she replied. "One must find out all things, and when we find out a thing we know if it is good or bad."

"That is the beginning of knowledge," said Pan, "but it is not the beginning of wisdom."

"What is the beginning of wisdom?"

"It is carelessness," replied Pan.*

The Fool is stripped of a proper name, dispossessed of property and status except as that of the lowest and most pitiful. He has been thrown out of every world but that of the carnival, the turret basement or the asylum; and so he skillfully makes his way in the undergrounds and underworlds that exist in the shadow of every inhabited place. This peculiar perspective on the world puts the world a little out of shape. Consequently, the Fool mimics a grotesque version of the world but one that is absolutely true since it lies at the very base of real life, its backroads, its wild places, its subways. So his wisdom does not exactly fit; it is too basic and too unplanned to be "useful." The Fool knows that usefulness is not always the test of goodness since he knows too well that what is premeditated can easily turn into deceit. Not only this but premeditation also holds the world at bay and instills fear into the heart.

The Fool is without plans for himself except that he is *compelled* to live in a certain way. This is the plan of an epistemology that is arrived at by the very nature of human play reciprocating the play of the universe on human fortunes.

---

*Pan, the half-goat half-man flute player/wanderer/fool, speaking in James Stephens' *The Crock of Gold* (reprint: Collier Books), pp. 68–69.

Robin Grossinger

Concerning the Interests of Insects

March 21, 1990

To the E.S. Board,

This is a copy of a letter to the T.A. concerning the Entomology Lab 108L, accompanying and explaining the film I completed in place of the assigned specimen collection. I think the letter raises issues about education and the goals of Environmental Studies which need to be addressed, so I am submitting this as a sort of class evaluation. I hope you will find it relevant and take the time to consider it.

Sincerely,
Robin Grossinger

Comment

I want to make clear the context in which this project arose. I am turning in this collection of insects on film not because I was incapable of doing the assigned specimen collection but because it contradicted my values. I took Entomology because I am interested in the life of insects as members of a complex living world. I found searching for, discovering, and observing insects of all different form and behavior in myriad habitats to be a wonderful, educational experience. But taking the step of appropriating their lives and watching them slowly die seemed to go against my beliefs and goals as a biology (the study of life) major oriented towards environmental issues and questions of how humans relate to the world.

I agree that in some cases it is important to possess a specimen to permit identification and that there is valuable scientific knowledge to be gained by collecting and examining insects, but this does not translate into an automatic validation of killing insects; it means we are dealing with a complex and non-clear-cut issue which can only be decided on the basis of the relative value one places on certain types of knowledge and different modes of experience and interaction. So I am not saying that my values are right and others are wrong, but I do want to bring attention to the fact that it is important, and an important part of college, to define and act upon one's own values. In that way this class has been a stimulating experience for me. I originally thought that I would persevere and do the project despite my distaste, so that I would understand what it was that bothered me about the assignment. But the sadness I felt after catching an active, lively bumble bee and watching it slowly cease to move made up my mind that this was not the right thing to be doing, for myself or the bee. Unfortunately, though, I think you have belittled me, for what you see is not my seeming to handle this conflict responsibly, because to you it is a *fait accompli*; you are an entomologist and have come to terms with the struggle—the case is closed in your mind. You also have been unaware of the fact that for many people in the class the collection has been a powerful, thought-provoking experience, not nearly so light and inconsequential as the comment "Happy Hunting!!" on the assignment sheet implies. Both you and the professor have suggested that I am out of place, that I shouldn't have taken the lab, that "Maybe entomology isn't for you," but making it my problem is a simplistic solution to a complicated dilemma which, as it turned out, affected a substantial proportion of the class. And saying that you hoped I stayed away from these types of conflicts in the future seems to bespeak a very narrow and twisted sense of what education is—what is education if it is not wrestling with difficult and significant questions?

When I decided I could not do this project I focused my energy on creating an appropriate, alternative project which would serve much of the same purposes as the original collection and not contradict itself by encouraging admiration and appreciation and then objectification and destruction. I first proposed a collection of structured, organized observations of each insect found, using terminology learned in the class and filling out an equivalent sheet for each and including a photograph. The response was that a photograph, or preferably, a slide would be acceptable. I bought slide-compatible film and spent hours trying to find a method of getting meaningful pictures with my 35mm camera, but was unable to get a close-up lens and could get nothing but a useless dot, or at best, smudge, in the center of the field.

Thus my dad's old 8mm camera with excellent close-up lenses seemed a much more effective solution since it actually had the capacity of re-presenting the observed insect and even had the potential to capture a glimpse of the insect's life by its movements, behavior, and surroundings. The movie camera was a risk since I had never used it before and its light meter is nonfunctional because the required batteries are no longer made. Consequently, the film has its problems, but not for lack of effort or time. Despite a late start, many subjects that are difficult to see and not identifiable, and all the ones that escaped as I tried to film them, my point total still approaches fifty. I also transferred the film to videotape for your convenience. This project (1) did not necessitate a disjunction between my values and my actions and (2) is less antagonistic to an attitude of appreciating and respecting the insects for what they are in their environment. The original project (and collection) can obscure this way of relating to the natural world and easily degenerate into a focus on converting the insects into tangible, material possessions.

Clearly, by your uncomfortableness with it, though, this project is not what you want. It suffers in comparison to the original collection on several criteria, including gradability. It will be harder for you to judge exactly how many points I deserve because the film clips are not an absolute representation of what I saw and based my identification on, as bringing in the actual insects would be. You may have to rely on less numerically tangible data to get a sense of how much work I put into this collection. Secondly, the film does not permit keying out, only comparative identification. Your main contention, though, involves my not contributing to the school's collection. You feel that I have been hypocritical in studying and learning from our insect collection while not contributing to it through my own collecting. If we had such a limited collection that it was difficult to learn from them I would have been more sympathetic to that cause. But I certainly felt there was sufficient material in all but a few areas to allow an excellent educational experience. I question how necessary the majority of the approximately one thousand specimens (20 students x about 50 per student) annually are needed to maintain the collection and make it more useful for students. Which is really the goal here—a more educational collection or a larger, more prestigious one? And if the overriding justification for individual collecting is, as the point has been made, to contribute to the college's collection, then would the assignment be discarded or modified if we ever finally have enough insects stockpiled to cover those that are broken in use? The emotional attachment and lack of consciousness implied in the "Happy Hunting" comment (which was pointed out to me by another class member who found it disconcerting) as well as the little attention paid to the issues involved in taking life lead me to think not.

You have the sense that these issues were addressed by a few sentences early in the class, before anyone had used a killing jar, telling us not to get duplicates and if we did, to trade them. On the contrary, the discussions I've had with about a half-dozen classmates about their own struggle with the assignment show that this is an important part of the class and should not be limited to discussion outside of class. Instead the questions should be addressed at points throughout the quarter, when people are really thinking about them. What I find really striking is that many people were actively examining the issues raised, such as the value of different types of scientific knowledge and ethical questions of taking life for human purposes, but nobody knew that other classmates were contending with and contemplating similar questions. This is an extreme disservice to the educational process of the students, denying an experience of just as much, if not more (and not mutually exclusive of), importance than learning to identify the insects. Examining the basic assumptions of a collection may seem to be provoking havoc in an entomology lab, but mature, thoughtful college students ought to be given the respect to address a difficult issue instead of having it ignored. Everyone deals with it when they go out with their killing jar.

I know I would have responded differently had this class been endowed with a depth which allowed me to respond within its structure. Instead I wrestled with my seemingly "off-the-wall" intuitions (judging from the class' quietness— I was genuinely surprised to find other people were experiencing the same

58

questions) that collecting was a debatable activity for a number of weeks, hoping that my distaste for the project would fade and I would not have to "make waves."

I think the crux of the problem was touched upon when you explained to me that we collect insects "for science." Science is a much more problematic entity than that justification suggests. While they are extremely valuable and powerful human achievements, science and scientific knowledge have also played a powerful role in legitimating personal prejudices and systems of domination from sexism and racism to Nazism and environmental degradation. The distinction between "values" and "science" is part of our scientific tradition and is not only false and misleading, but, historically, catastrophic (*e.g.*, atomic energy). What appears to be a radical suggestion—to include this sort of discussion as an integral part of entomology lab—seems with further thought to be clearly appropriate. I think that, as an educational trend, bringing science into a position where it can be examined and discussed in an ethical, social, political, etc. context is of critical importance to developing an awareness and ongoing dialogue concerning our role and behavior in the world as the human species. This dialogue will be necessary to respond to the modern crises of an interconnected world in which issues of relation between countries (as in contemporary re-thinking of the usefulness of the traditional economic, political, and environmental disjunction accepted in the superpower alignments), or between species, can no longer be overlooked. If this type of analysis is not cultivated here, in an undergraduate class in Environmental Studies at UC, then where else?

In summary, that is why I am submitting this film. I hope you will see it not as challenge to the teacher student hierarchy, but as a personal response to an unaddressed but real conflict. Because I feel it is important and relevant, I am submitting a copy of this letter to the E.S. Board, in the spirit of a class evaluation.

Robert Kelly

First in an Alphabet of Sacred Animals

The ANT for all his history is a stranger
& his message is the gospel of an alien order
& his & his & his

works are furious in the crust of the earth
his house & his bread

(We must start with him because he is other,
he comes from a nowhere underneath us
& returns again & does not know us)

this is the easiest animal to kill.

Today I did not kill an ant
                            a great big black one
& it became necessary to think
of the price of an ant's death:
                            nothing we do
is without consequence
                            (nothing the ant does
can be without consequence)
                            & in the taking of an ant's life
is the taking of life

But the ant is not an albatross & dies easy
& soon his carcass is gone, who knows where they go
the bodies of insects we kill,
                            when we take life
                            what do we give?
–What is the price
of killing an ant
–What intricate microscopic karma do we fulfill
in crushing him
–What cosmic debt does he repay under my foot
–Will we notice the pain
with which we must one day surely atone for his death
–Or are there beings (& are there beings)
who step on us as lightly as we tread ants?

that is the hideous question someone is always asking
Egypt after Egypt

But all this touches us & what touches the ant?
the ant I can barely feel as it walks the innocent
topside of my foot?

By our social order we seek to understand the ant's
we speak of their *cities* & their *queens* & their *work*
& call their aphids *cows* & say ants *milk* them
We understand ants to be industrious, plenteous, sober & secure
in the merciless absolute of their numbers

There are many ants

That is there are more ants than men

or so it seems for who has seen them
billion after billion moving together
investing a planet & controlling an atmosphere?

It is without hope
we may not understand the ant
& if the ant teaches us any lesson
it is this lesson:

here is an alien being doing alien things
wordless timeless neither beautiful nor ugly
as readily on a planet of Toliman as here

while from our need to identify with the ant
& render its institutions such homage
as it may be to call them by our names

we may observe (here is the lesson) how lonely we are.

*   *   *

The GOD of ants is Saturn, initiator of timeless incomprehensible works.
The patron SAINT of ants is Saint Joseph (husband of Mary the Mother of
Jesus); he submitted himself to the operations of an alien intelligence &
was exalted without comprehension. The RELIGION most favorable to ants
is Islam : submission. The holy PLACE of ants is Riverside Drive & 114th
Street, the park between city & river, a river which also is ocean, where
between rows of paths we have made lie patches of what we have not made:

61

over each the ant travels with equal ease & profit. The DAY of ants is Saturday in Summer. Ants will separate & sort each kind of grain in Psyche's heap, all for their own purposes.

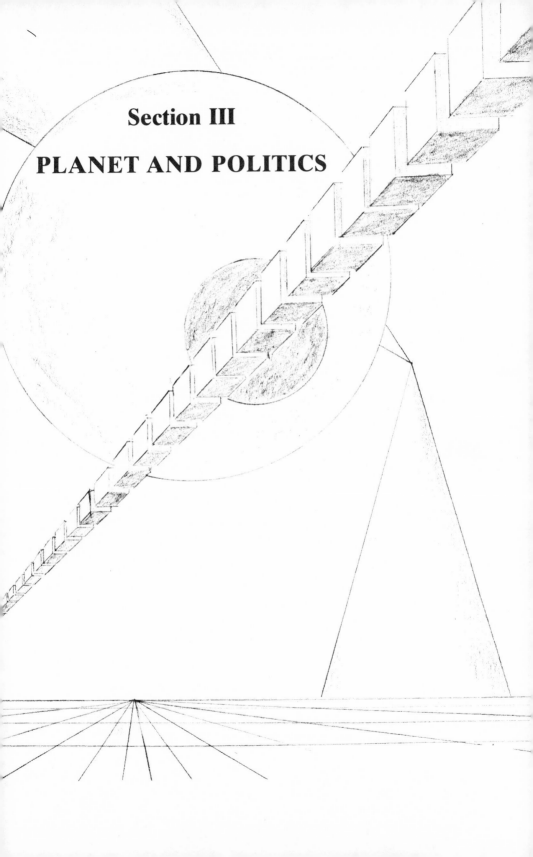

Section III

PLANET AND POLITICS

Edward Dorn

La Máquina a Houston

The train has come to rest and ceased its creaking
We hear the heavy breathing of the máquina
A relic in its own time
Like all the manifestations of technical art
And without real gender
And hidden from direct appeal
By the particulates of the English language
Itself the agent of frag mentation
And lonely accuser of the generic lines
The heavy breathing of the lonely máquina
Stopped in its tracks waiting for the photograph.

The Apache are prodded out into the light
Remember, there are still dark places then
Even in the solar monopoly of Arizona and Tejas

We are the man with the camera
They step off the train and wait among the weeds
They never take their eyes off of us, wise practice
We motioned the way with our shotguns
They are almost incredibly beautiful

We are struck and thrilled
With the completeness of their smell
To them we are weird while to us
They are not weird, to them we are undeniable
And they stop only before that, they are like us
Yet we are not like them
Since we dont recognize that. We say:
One cannot have a piece of what is indivisible
Is natural Apache policy
Where for us, that is a philosophical implication
We are alike, but we see things
From behind dis-similar costumes,
The first principle of warfare
Where *All of Us* is the Army, and they are the people
Precisely they step off the train
And this is an important terminal moment

In the Rush Hour begun in this hemisphere

This is the moment before the leg irons
They look Good. They look better than we do.
They will look better than we look forever
We will never really look very good
We are too far gone on thought, and its rejections
The two actions of a Noos

Natches sits alone in the center
Because he is the elegant one among them
Hereditary, proper as a dealer
He is inherent and most summary of themselves
Supple, graceful, flexible hands
Goodnatured, fond of women

As the train moves off at the first turn of the wheel
With its cargo of florida bound exiles
Most all of whom had been put bodily
Into the coaches, their 3000 dogs,
Who had followed them like a grand party
To the railhead at Holbrook
                                    began to cry
When they saw the smoking creature resonate
With their masters,
And as the máquina acquired speed they howled and moaned
A frightening noise from their great mass
And some of them followed the cars
For forty miles
Before they fell away in exhaustion

Gino Clays

Omnia Mea Mecum Porto

Nate sat in his room staring at the same walls that probably his father had stared at all through Europe and he thought perhaps there is a room somewhere in Austria or Hungary just like this one with the faded blue plaster crumbling and peeling and the stained water murals. One generation American who is now leaving the shell that was destroyed long ago before there was electricity and television. —I didn't last long as long as my ancestors remained in Europe but then they were still building buildings for shelter and working for food and what have I to do with a hammer but set off a chain reaction and they still had dreams of fortunes and Junker estates along the Donau and Strauss waltzes captured in Mosel Wine and I can hear them shout build that house plant those crops the Huns have left us long centuries ago and deposited their seeds in our soil and a new generation later one of my ancestors put rosin on his eyes to decrease the epicanthic fold and requested a visa to Oberammergau. And they were still building when Herr Schickelgrüber came marching over vineyards shouting Heute hört uns Deutschland und morgen die ganze Welt and loaded up boxcars of dreamers with Alle Räder müssen rollen für den Sieg written on the side and deposited their ashes over the pastures of Deutschland and the years following the wine-crop was excellent. So my father singing to himself omnia mea mecum porto traveled across ashes with a rifle in his rectum and spent tormenting nights in hotels such as this telling himself that America would be different. And when the boat left Lisbon he lived like a pig in the bottom deck crammed in with eight hundred other visioners and at eight knots a day across the Atlantic while German planes above were skywriting denn die todten reiten schnell. New York City is a blackout and the war became a reality he found all the ghettos completely filled and someone said foreigners are not allowed but then this is war and you should try Jersey and my father found a job and procured a wife in a cafe next door and then the apartment was filled with a screaming youth who thought his mothers teat was paradise. But the war did not end in 1945 and I was fighting with gravel in my elbows and wiping the blood from my nose and my father said that things will be better with a college education but I found out early that no one really respects education but only for the pragmatic diploma that lets you sell life death hospital car accident baby home crop failure insurance and what can be insured when no one is living and there are no crops and I saw mans exterior crumbling and the psychiatrists treating the interior when there was no interior to treat. There is no home to build father the ground is sterile, the people impotent and I instinctively headed West for I saw no purpose and I kept going as my greatest grand-father did as he chased dreams across the Gobi desert and what did he find but no purpose and so I kept chasing myself until I reached San Francisco and this room with some understanding of inseparability with the universe and with no purpose I was liberated and I checked on a boat to the Orient where Tin Sung was waiting for me inside Buddha's triple body with no ego and where there is an innate trust in good and evil and here is balance and not the land of used car salesmen and wax flowers over dead people that had always been dead because the Westward migration of man had been too soon based on greed and wealth and exterior pomp and so I am leaving America in the womb of a saline world of Pacific for I am going to be reborn inside the world and I knew that the circle would be completed and the last of mans migration for the next migration would be inside of the world and not across.

Thomas Merton

The Sacred City

The valley of Oaxaca is one of the poorest and least productive areas of Mexico today. It was once one of the richest and most fertile. It was also the center not only of a great culture, but of what was probably the first real city in America: Monte Alban. What was this city? What kind of culture flourished there? What kind of people lived there?

Archaeological studies* have now brought to light some very rich and detailed material concerning the "early urban" and "pre-classic" Zapotecan culture of the Oaxaca valley and its central city. We are finally in a position to fit Monte Alban into the general picture of Mesoamerican civilization of the "classic" age, before the rise of the Mixtecs, Toltecs and Aztecs, whose culture was essentially decadent.

Before we even begin to speak of Monte Alban and of the ancient Mayan cities which had much in common with it, we must put out of our minds the generalized idea of ancient cities which we have associated with Egypt and Mesopotamia, or with our sketchy knowledge of post-classic Mexican (Toltec and Aztec) culture in the five centuries preceding the Spanish conquest. In these ancient cultures, which are more familiar to us, the city stands out as the stronghold of a monarch or tyrant, a potential empire-builder, with an army and a culture based upon slavery. The City, in other words, comes into being with kingship or at least with militaristic autocracy, and urban culture is a culture not only of commerce but above all of war and conquest. True, the less well known archaic cultures of Cretans and Etruscans seem to have been less warlike, but they were also more isolated.

The popular estimate of Mexican and Mayan culture, based primarily on the reports of the Spanish conquerors and on their observations at the time of the conquest, gives us an idea of a very colorful but also bloodthirsty and necrophilic city life, in which war, slavery and human sacrifice play a dominant part. (This view of American Indian civilization is typically re-

---

*This essay is essentially an appreciation of a new collection of studies—reports on "Discoveries in Mexican Archeology and History" edited by John Paddock under the title *Ancient Oaxaca,* and published by Stanford University Press (1966). It contains two very important surveys: "Mesoamerica before the Toltecs" by Wigberto Jiménez Moreno and "Oaxaca in Ancient Mesoamerica" by John Paddock. Eight other shorter papers by archeologists like Alfonso Caso, Ignacio Bernal, and other scholars, are mainly concerned with the relations of Zapotec and Mixtec cultures after the "Classic" period. The two longer studies are essential for a contemporary evaluation of Zapotec culture in its relation to other civilizations of Middle America. We also refer to the new edition of the standard work of Sylvanus Morley, *The Ancient Maya,* revised by George W. Brainerd, 3rd edition, Stanford, 1956 (reprint 1963).

peated in the *Time-Life Book on Ancient America* by Jonathan Norton Leonard, "Great Ages of Man" [New York, 1967].) In a word, when we think of the first cities we instinctively think also of "war," "power," "wealth," "autocracy," "empire," and so on. Possible exceptions (such as Jerusalem, the "city of peace") are ambivalent enough to be no exceptions. But the first cities in America were not like Nineveh, Babylon, Ur or Thebes—or Rome. The Western "ideal" city has always been Athens the independent, the democratic, the sophisticated. Could Monte Alban or Tikal be compared with Athens? Not really, except in so far as they were highly esthetic cultures and seem to have been in a certain sense "democratic," though perhaps not in a way that fits our own familiar humanist, rationalistic and Western concept of democracy.

The most recent studies of Mesoamerican culture enable us to reconstruct a general picture of man and civilization on our continent, and in order to situate Monte Alban correctly, it might be well to look first at the general picture. This will help correct the foreshortening of perspectives in the popular view of Mexico.

We now know that hunters of mammoth were established in the Valley of Mexico as far back as 12,000 B.C.—when the continental ice sheet came as far south as the Ohio River and Mexico had a cool, rainy climate. With the extinction of the big game a new kind of culture developed. Agriculture seems to have been introduced after 7000 B.C. with the rudimentary cultivation of maize. It is, of course, on maize culture that the whole Mesoamerican Indian civilization is built.

Where was maize first grown? For a long time the highlands of Guatemala were thought to be the place where corn was originally cultivated. Recently, discoveries in a dry area of northern Oaxaca have given us a complete sequence of ancient remains of maize in its evolution from a wild to a domesticated plant. This domestication certainly goes back beyond 4000 B.C. At any rate, for a thousand years or more there flourished a neolithic, maize growing, semi-nomad, pre-ceramic culture in Mexico. Ceramics began to be made around 3000 B.C. and of course the ceramic art became one of the most highly developed and sophisticated of the Indian civilization. Metal tools were known about 1000 B.C. but never entirely supplanted stone implements, which continued in use down to the Spanish conquest. Thus we have some two millennia and more of neolithic village life before the appearance of a city in Mexico.

How does the Mesoamerican city develop? It is not primarily the result of a population explosion. The first city develops as a cult center, and about the year 1000 we find evidence of such centers among the Olmecs in the jungle lowlands of Vera Cruz. Many of the Mayan cities were merely centers for worship, sometimes uninhabited except by a small population of priests and scholars occupied with the important social task of determining the proper dates for clearing, planting, etc., as well as fortunate and unfortunate days for various activities. For the authentic urban center, what is required is a moderate concentration of population and of economic activity, a development of science that includes the knowledge of writing and of chronology—and of course astronomy and mathematics. And one also seeks evidence of planning, as well as of permanent monumental public buildings: evidence in other words of a relatively advanced culture, prosperous and creative, which at the same time stimulates and satisfies the higher esthetic and intellectual needs of the community. This appears for the first time in Monte Alban, several hundred years before the construction of the Maya cities of Guatemala.

The city of Monte Alban was built somewhere between 1000 and 500 B.C. by Zapotecan Indians who knew writing, had a calendar, were astronomers and were probably the first city dwellers in America. Pottery finds at Monte Alban have brought to light an archaic style, examples of which go back to about 800 B.C. But with the paving of the Great Plaza after 300 B.C. we definitely enter upon the great period of urban culture at Monte Alban. There is a certain amount of complexity in the terms used by scholars, due to the fact that the word "Classic" has become ambiguous. Morley used it to designate the Mayan culture of the fourth to tenth centuries A.D. It was until recently assumed that the Mexican and Mayan urban cultures were all roughly contemporaneous and "Classic" was used loosely of any urban culture. Attempts to find a more accurate classification have resulted in complex charts and correlations, with Pre-Classic and Post-Classic or Epiclassic, broken up into numerous subdivisions, and reaching out to include the widely different cultures of Guatemala, Yucatan, Vera Cruz, Mexico, Oaxaca, etc. These charts may be very illuminating to the experts, but to the general reader they are not much help.

To put it in the simplest terms, we can lump together everything from 1000 B.C. to 900 A.D. as "Classic" or "Early" (though it includes various degrees of Pre-Classic and late Classic). This is a convenient and clear division because about 900 A.D. Monte Alban was abandoned and so were the "Classic" Maya cities like Peten, Uaxactun and other centers in Guatemala. After this time, the Mayan culture spread out in Yucatan in a Post-Classical civilization under Toltec domination, and in the Oaxaca Valley the old Zapotec society yielded to Mixtec conquerors, who occupied fortified towns of the region like Mitla and Yagul. The six-hundred-year period between 900 A.D. and the Spanish conquest can be called "Post-Classical" or "Late." Note that by the time the Spaniards arrived, even the last, post-classic Mayan cities of Yucatan had been abandoned. Mayan urban civilization was at an end. But the Aztecs had a flourishing city of three hundred thousand at Tenochtitlan (on the site of Mexico City).

The great difference between the two cultures and the two periods is this: In the early or Classical cultures there is almost no evidence of militarism, of war, or of human sacrifice until very late. The late, post-Classical civilization results from the radical change from a peaceful to a warlike and militaristic way of life brought in by conquering and relatively barbarous tribes from the north. The Mixtecs conquered the Zapotecs who had abandoned Monte Alban (though still sporadically worshiping there). The Toltecs overcame the Mayas and produced a hybrid Toltec-Mayan culture in Yucatan, centered especially in Chichen Itza. It is with the "late" period that history really begins. The history of the Oaxaca Valley begins with the important Mixtec codices—such as the famous Bodley Codex 14-IV-V which tells the story of the Cacique called "Eight Deer Tiger Claw" who ends up being sacrificed. Alfonso Caso's study in Paddock (*op. cit.*) shows that the value of Mixtec codices is greatly enhanced by recent discoveries in tombs of the Oaxaca valley.

But in the Classic period there are no chronicles. Even though there are many dated *stelae* in classic Mayan architecture and at Monte Alban, the "dates" are at first non-historical. They refer to cosmic cycles, to the stars, and to events that may be called "divine" rather than historical. In other words, the Classic chronologists were more concerned with cosmic happenings than with the rise and fall of kings and empires, with gods rather than with kings. Not that this concern with the gods excluded care for human existence; for by liturgy and celebration, the lives of men, cultivators of maize, were integrated in the cosmic movements of the stars, the planets, the skies, the winds and weather, the comings and goings of the gods. That this society was not dominated by what Marx called religious alienation is evident from the fact that its art did not represent the gods until very late: the early art represents the people themselves, the celebrants officiating in liturgical rites and feasts, vested in the splendid and symbolic emblems of their totem.

We are only just beginning to realize the extraordinary sophistication of totemic thought (as interpreted by Claude Lévi-Strauss). Living records left by such North American Indians as Black Elk and Two Leggings suggest that the elaborate symbolic association of the human person with cosmic animals represents something more intimate than an "alienated" subjection to external forces. We know something of the profoundly interior relationship of the North American hunter with his "vision person," and we know that the Central American Indian remained in extremely close relationship with the divinity that ruled the day of his birth and gave him one of his names. What we have here is in fact not a matter of alienation but of *identity*. But it is obviously a conception of identity which is quite different from our subjective and psychological one, centered on the empirical ego regarded as distinct and separate from the rest of reality.

This "objective" identity seems to have been fully integrated into a cosmic system which was at once perfectly sacred and perfectly worldly. There is no question that the Indian in the "sacred city" felt himself completely at home in his world and perfectly understood his right place in it. And this is what we are to understand, apparently, by the splendor and symbolism of an art which signified that the gods were present not in idols or sanctuaries so much as in the worshipper, his community and his world.

The individual found himself, by his "objective" identity, at the intersection of culture and nature, crossroads established by the gods, points of communication not only between the visible and the invisible, the obvious and the unexplained, the higher and the lower, the strong and the helpless: but above all between *complementary opposites which balanced and fulfilled each other* (fire-water, heat-cold, rain-earth, light-dark, life-death). "Self-realization" in such a context implied not so much the ego-consciousness of the isolated subject in the face of a multitude of objects, but the awareness of a network of relationships in which one had a place in the mesh. One's identity was the intersection of chords where one "belonged." The intersection was to be sought in terms of a kind of musical or esthetic and scientific synchrony—one fell in step with the dance of the universe, the liturgy of the stars.

What kind of life was led in the "Classic" cities of Guatemala or Oaxaca? We can say that *for roughly two thousand years* the Zapotecan and Mayan Indians maintained an entirely peaceful, prosperous civilization that was essentially esthetic and religious. This civilization was focused in urban cult-centers, but it was not what we would call a truly urban culture.

Although it has been maintained that Tikal once had a population of a hundred thousand, the Maya cities were usually quite small—and indeed had few permanent residents apart from the priests and scholars who served the temples and observatories. Most of the population was more or less rural, living outside amid the cornfields (*milpas* or *col*) which were periodically cleared from the jungle and then allowed to run wild again. Since there was no war, at least on any scale larger than perhaps family or tribal feuding, there was no need to concentrate the population within fortified towns—until, of course, the Post-Classical period. It was perfectly safe for families, clans and other small groups to live in jungle villages as they had done from time immemorial. The city was where they came together for special celebration, for the worship which included the games and dances in which they took intense satisfaction and gained a heightened awareness of themselves as individuals and as a society. This worship was also completely integrated in their seasonal round of clearing the milpa, burning brush, planting, cultivating and harvesting of the maize. This work did not take up an exorbitant amount of time, and in the great periods of enthusiasm and prosperity the people gave their surplus time and energy to the common construction projects which some of the modern scholars still find hard to understand. The example of Egypt and Assyria would suggest slave labor, yet all the evidence seems to indicate that the Mayans and Zapotecans built their classic cities spontaneously, freely, as a communal expression of solidarity, self-awareness, and esthetic and religious creativity. There is no evidence of slavery until the Post-Classical period.

The success of these two thousand years of peaceful, creative existence demanded a well-developed sense of coordination, a division of tasks under the direction of specialists, a relatively high proportion of skilled labor, and above all a completely unanimous acceptance of a common vision and attitude toward life. One must of course avoid the temptation to idealize what was still in many respects a Stone Age culture, but one cannot evade the conviction that these must have been very happy people. The Mayan scholar Morley quotes an English statesman who said that "the measure of civilization is the extent of man's obedience to the unenforceable" and comments that by this standard the Mayans must have measured high. John Paddock, writing of the Zapotecs of Monte Alban, and remarking that there is no evidence of slavery there, says: "No whip-cracking slave driver was needed. The satisfaction of helping to create something simultaneously imposing, reassuring and beautiful is enough to mobilize endless amounts of human effort." He goes on to argue from the persistence of pilgrimage and generosity in the Mexican Indian of today:

"It is common for tens of thousands of men, women and children to walk 50 or more miles to a shrine. They are not slaves: they would revolt if denied the right to make their pilgrimage. . . . Mexico's shrines of today are in most cases far less beautiful and the worshipper's participation (with money) is far less satisfyingly direct; but they still come by the thousands voluntarily."

What Paddock is trying to explain here is not merely the fact that a religious center, a "sacred city" like Monte Alban existed, but that it was in fact built on a mountain ridge, without the use of wheels for transport and without draft animals—as also without slave labor. The fantastically difficult work was carried out with immense patience and love by people whose motives cannot even be guessed if we try to analyze them solely in economic or technological terms.

Here was a major religious capital, an urban complex which at the height of its prosperity "occupied not only the top of a large mountain but the tops and sides of a whole range of high hills adjoining, a total of some fifteen square miles of urban construction" (Paddock). The maintenance of the city "would necessarily require the services of thousands of specialists: priests, artists, architects, the apprentices of all these and many kinds of workmen, including servants for the dignitaries and their families." The peaceful and continuous *growth* of this city and its culture—with continued renewal of buildings and art work century after century—can only be explained by the fact that the people liked it that way. They wanted to build new temples and to dance in the Great Plaza dressed in their fantastically beautiful costumes. Nor were they particularly anxious to find quicker and more efficient methods of doing their work. They were in no hurry. An artist was content to grind for months on a jade pebble to carve out a glyph. And he was not even paid for it!

"In purely economic terms, in fact, the whole accomplishment seems fantastic. But if we attempt to comprehend it in economic terms alone we are neglecting the crucial factors. For over a century we have been living in a world where technology has been the great hope, solving one problem after another. Perhaps we may be forgiven if we have come to demand material-mechanical explanations for everything, overlooking the possibility that they may often be insufficient.... To ask these questions only in economic, technological or political terms will produce only some of the needed answers. Questions about religion and art must be included, and they may be in this case the most basic ones" (Paddock).

The chief economic factor in the success of the Zapotec civilization was that in the fertile, isolated Oaxaca valley, a relatively small population, which remained stable, had a highly effective system for exploiting the natural advantages of their region. They could produce the food they needed—plenty of corn, squash, tomatoes, peppers, avocados, red and black beans, cacao, along with tobacco and cotton. They engaged in some commerce with the so-called "Olmec" civilization in the jungle lowlands of what is now the state of Vera Cruz, and later with the people in the Valley of Mexico to the north. But their surplus time and energy went into art, architecture and worship. The result was a city and a culture of great majesty and refinement, integrated into a natural setting of extraordinary beauty, dominating the fertile valley surrounded by high mountains. The people who collaborated in the work and worship of the sacred city must have enjoyed a most unusual sense of communal identity and achievement. Wherever they looked, they found nothing to equal their creative success, which antedated that of the Clasic Mayan culture by more than five hundred years, and was not outshone by the latter when it finally dawned.

The archeology of the Oaxaca Valley is still only in its first stages and further discoveries will bring to light more that has been barely guessed at so far. But we know enough to accurately surmise what it was all about. Paddock says:

"Monte Alban was a place electric with the presence of the gods. These gods were the very forces of nature with which peasants are respectfully intimate . . .

"Every temple stood over half a dozen temples of centuries before. Buried in the great temples were ancient high priests of legendary powers, now semi-deified; centuries of accumulated wealth in offerings, centuries of mana in ceremonies, centuries of power and success, lay deep inside that masonry. But with their own humble hands, or those of their remembered ancestors, the common people had made the buildings.... They were participating in the life of the metropolis; they could see that they were making it possible. They could stand dazzled before those mighty temples, stroll half an hour to circle the immense open plaza, watch the stunning pageantry of the ceremonies, stare as fascinated as we at the valley spread out mile after mile below. They knew that no other such center existed for hundreds of miles—and even then their city had only rivals, not superiors."

Three things above all distinguish this "sacred city" from our own culture today: the indifference to technological progress; the lack of history;

and the almost total neglect of the arts of war. The three things go together, and are rooted in an entirely different conception of man and of life. That conception, of which we have already spoken as a network of living inter-relationships, can be called synthetic and synchronic, instead of analytic and diachronic.

In plain and colloquial terms it is a difference between a peaceful, time-less life lived in the stability of a continually renewed *present,* and a dynamic, aggressive life aimed at the future. We are more and more acutely conscious of *having arrived,* of being at the heart of things. Mircea Eliade speaks of the archaic meaning of the sanctuary or the sacred place as the *axis mundi,* the center or navel of the earth, for those whose lives revolve in the cycles of its liturgy.

Perhaps the inhabitants of these first American cities, who remained content in large measure with Stone Age technics, who had no sense of history (and certainly no foresight into what was to come after their time!) simply accepted themselves as having more or less unconsciously achieved the kind of successful balance that humanity had been striving for, slowly and organically, over ten thousand and more years. Their material needs were satisfied and their life could expand in creative self-expression. This was the final perfection of the long relatively peaceful agrarian society that had grown out of the neolithic age.

According to our way of thinking, the Zapotecs were crazy not to make use of the wheel when they knew of its existence. The curious thing is that they *had* wheels, but only for toys. And they *did* use rollers to move heavy blocks of stone. They were, in a word, perfectly capable of "inventing the wheel" but for some reason (which must remain to us profoundly mysteri-ous) they never bothered with it. They were not interested in going places.

The Indian cultures of Mesoamerica are typical archaic societies in which the creative energy of the people found expression in artistic and religious forms rather than in applied science. This is, to us, one of the most baffling of problems. Greco-Roman civilization—which was more pragmatic and practical than that of the Indians—also presents this problem. The science of the Alexandrian scholars in the Roman empire was sufficiently advanced to permit the development of steam engines. The industrial revolution *might have* taken place in 200 A.D. But it didn't. So might the discovery of America, for that matter, as the Alexandrian geographers were aware that the earth was round!

What is most perplexing to us is that, as a matter of fact, economic con-ditions called for this kind of development. To our way of thinking, the Zapotecs *needed* wheels and machinery, and the economy of the late Roman empire *demanded* a technological revolution. Just as the Meso-american Indians used wheels only for toys, so the Romans also used hydraulic power, but only for shifting heavy scenery in the Circus!

A few modern scholars have tried to grapple with this enigma, and Hanns Sachs, a psychoanalyst, contends that the urge for technological

Progress was suppressed in the ancient world because of the radically different disposition of narcissism and libido in ancient man. Tools and machines *replace* the body and absorb or alienate libido energy, which is frankly cathected by sensuous man.

Once again we come upon the curious question of archaic man's *sense of identity*. His sense of his own reality and actuality was much more frankly bound up with sensual experience and body narcissism, whereas we have been split up and tend to project our libido outward into works, possessions, implements, money, etc. In the lovely sculptured "danzantes" (dancers) of Monte Alban with their frank and sensuously flowering male nakedness we apprehend a bodily awareness that substantiates what Sachs says: "To these men of antiquity, the body, which they could cathect with a libido still undeviated, was their real being. . . . Animistic man vitalized the inanimate world with such narcissism as he could not find other use for."

The "reality" and "identity" of archaic man was then centered in sensuous self-awareness and identification with a close, ever-present and keenly sensed world of nature: for us, our "self" tends to be "realized" in a much more shadowy, abstract, mental world, or indeed in a very abstract and spiritualized world of "soul." We are disembodied minds seeking to bridge the gap between mind and body and return to ourselves through the mediation of things, commodities, products and implements. We reinforce our sense of reality by acting on the external world to get ever new results. More sensuous, primitive man does not understand this and recoils from it, striving to influence external reality by magic and sensuous self-identification.

The primitive, like the child, remains in direct sensuous contact with what is outside him, and is most happy when this contact is celebrated in an esthetic and ritual joy. He related to things and persons around him with narcissistic joy. Our narcissism has been increasingly invested, through intellectual operations, in the money, the machines, the weaponry, which are the extensions of ourselves and which we venerate in our rituals of work, war, production, domination and brute power.

Obviously the Zapotecs of Monte Alban knew what violence was. They knew what it meant to fight and kill: they were not a "pacifist society" (which would imply a conscious and programmatic refusal of war). They just had no use for war, as a community. It was pointless. They were not threatened, and it evidently did not enter their heads to threaten others—until the far end of the Classic period when a growing population had exhausted the reserves of land, when the deforested mountains were eroded and the hungry, restless community began to look for places to plant corn in the territory of others—or to fight others who came looking for more room in Oaxaca.

By this time, of course, the long centuries of high classic civilization were coming to an end everywhere in Mexico and Yucatan. Already in the seventh century A.D. the metropolis of the Valley of Mexico, Teotihuacan, had been sacked or burned. In the tenth century, Monte Alban was deserted. But it was never conquered, never even attacked. There were never any fortifications—and indeed there was never a need for any. There is no evidence of violent, revolutionary destruction—the city was not harmed. It just came to an end. The enterprise of sacred culture closed down. Its creativity was exhausted.

There is no satisfactory explanation as yet of why the classic sacred cities of the Mayans and Zapotecs were simply abandoned. Presumably the ancient civilization grew too rigid and died of sclerosis. Its creative and self-renewing power finally gave out. Sometimes it is assumed that the people became disillusioned with the ruling caste of priests and revolted against them. But we also hear of a migration of priests and scholars into the south, under pressure of invasion from the north. In any case, the cities were abandoned.

The Zapotecs were conquered by their neighbors the Mixtecs after Monte Alban was abandoned, but they continued to lived under their conquerors, maintaining, it is said, a "government in exile" somewhere else. Today, the Zapotecs persist. Their language is still spoken, and in their ancestral territory they have outlasted the Mixtecs, who remain a minority.

The Spanish conquered Mesoamerica in the sixteenth century. The bloodthirsty Aztec empire, built on military power, ruled Mexico. But it was hated and decadent. It was willingly betrayed by other Indians and collapsed before the guns of Christian Spain. Much of the ancient Indian culture was destroyed; above all, anything that had to do with religion. But we must remember that the finest Mesoamerican civilizations had already disappeared seven or eight hundred years before the arrival of the Europeans.

After the conquest, the Oaxaca valley, once rich and fertile, gradually became a near-desert as the ancient agricultural practices were forgotten and the soil of the deforested mountains washed out. Contact with the Europeans was in many ways a human disaster for the Mexicans. The Indian population of Mesoamerica was probably twenty million in 1519. In 1532 it was already under seventeen million, in 1550 it was down to six million and in 1600 there were *only a million Indians left!* The population dropped nineteen million in eighty years! This was not due to systematic genocide but to diseases which the Indians could not resist. The impact of Spain on Mexico was in effect genocidal. Fortunately, a slow recovery began in the mid-seventeenth century.

To summarize: the extraordinary thing about the Zapotec civilization of the Oaxaca Valley is that, like the Classic urban civilization of the Mayas and the so-called "Olmec" or Tenocelome culture, it maintained itself without war and without military power for many centuries. We can say that Monte Alban, in its pre-urban as well as in its urban development, represents a peaceful and prosperous culture extending over two millennia without a full-scale war and without any need of fortifications or of a defense establishment.

In the present state of our knowledge of Zapotec culture, we can say that for two thousand years Monte Alban *had no history but that of its arts and its creative achievement. Indeed, the only chronology we have is determined by different styles in ceramics and sculpture.* We may hope that further archeological finds and a better understanding of hieroglyphic writing may give us an idea of the development of scientific, philosophical and religious thought in Monte Alban. But we have here an almost unique example of a city-state whose history is entirely creative, totally centered in artistic work, in thought, in majestic ritual celebration. We may add that it is intensely and warmly *human* and often marked with a very special charm, humor, and taste. Even in its baroque stage, Zapotec Classic art is less bizarre than Mayan, and of course it never approaches the necrophilic bad taste of the Aztecs.

A more detailed knowledge of the religious thought and development of the people at Monte Alban may perhaps show us a gradual change, with an archaic, totemistic, ancestor-plus-fertility religion and a few "high gods," giving place eventually to a more and more hierarchical religious establishment, an increasingly complex theogony and a whole elaborate pantheon of deified nature forces and culture heroes to be bought off by sacrifice.

In other words, it may be that at Monte Alban and in the ancient Maya cities we may witness the gradual transition from neolithic village-agrarian culture to the warlike imperial metropolis, through the theocratic establishment of urban power in the hands of priest-kings. But it appears from the recent studies that life in the Classic era for Monte Alban was still "democratic," not in the sophisticated sense of the Greek polis but in the archaic sense of the neolithic village. It was a life of creative common participation in the general enterprise of running the sacred city as a permanent celebration.

This was made possible by special circumstances: a fertile and productive region, not too thickly populated, which allowed all the material needs of the people to be satisfied with a small amount of field work, and liberated the surplus energies for common urban projects in art and architecture, as well as for religious celebration. The energy and wealth that other cultures put into wars of conquest, the Zapotecs simply put into ennobling their common agrarian and city life. But of course they did this entirely without self-consciusness, and their art, unlike ours, was spontaneously and completely integrated in their everyday lives. They did not take courses in art appreciation or go dutifully to the opera, or seek out good paintings in a museum.

Since this kind of life was impossible except in a small and isolated population, it flourished under conditions which have become practically unthinkable in our present day world. We have to look for some other formula. Nevertheless, it will not hurt us to remember that this kind of thing was once possible, indeed normal, and not a mere matter of idealistic fantasy.

By way of summary and conclusion: the purpose of this study is not merely to draw an unfavorable contrast between the peaceful, stable, esthetic existence of the "sacred city," and the turbulent, unstable and vulgar affluence of the warfare state—the "secular city." To say that Monte Alban was nice and that New York is ghastly would be an irrelevant exercise, especially since the writer likes New York well enough and does not think of it as ghastly—only as a place where he is well content to be no longer a resident. It is all too easy for people who live, as we do, in crisis, to sigh with nostalgia for a society that was once so obviously tranquil and secure. Yet there is some advantage in remembering that after all peace, tranquillity and security were once not only possible but real. It is above all salutary for us to realize that they were possible only on terms quite other than those which we take for granted as normal.

In other words, it is important that we fit the two thousand warless years of Monte Alban into our world-view. It may help to tone down a little of our aggressive, self-complacent superiority, and puncture some of our more disastrous myths. The greatest of these is doubtless that we are the first civilization that has appeared on the face of the earth (Greece was all right in so far as it foreshadowed the U.S.A.). And the corollary to this: that all other civilizations, and particularly those of "colored" races, were always quaintly inferior, mere curious forms of barbarism. We are far too convinced of many other myths about peace and war, about time and history, about the inherent purpose of civilization, of science, of technology and of social life itself, and these illusions do us no good. They might be partly corrected by a sober view of the undoubted success achieved by the Zapotec Indians.

The "sacred cities" of Monte Alban and of Guatemala, as we see them, looked back rather than forward. They were the fulfillment of a long development of a certain type of culture which was agrarian and which flourished in small populations. With the growth of populous societies, the accumulation of wealth, and the development of complex political and religious establishments and above all with the expansion of invention and resources for war, human life on earth was revolutionized. That revolution began with what we call "history" and has reached its climax now in another and far greater revolution which may, in one way or another, bring us to the end of history. Will we reach that end in cataclysmic destruction, or—as others affably promise—in a "new tribalism," a submersion of history in the vast unified complex of mass-mediated relationships which will make the entire world one homogeneous city? Will this be the purely secular, technological city, in which all relationships have been absorbed in technics? Will this usher in the millennium? Or will it be nothing more than the laborious institution of a new kind of jungle, the electronic labyrinth in which tribes will hunt heads among the aerials and fire escapes until somehow an eschatological culture of peace emerges somewhere in the turbulent structure of artifice, abstraction and violence which has become man's second nature?

Inevitably, such a culture will have to recover at least something of the values and attitudes that were characteristic of Monte Alban.

R. Buckminster Fuller

Telegram Sent to Senator Edmund S. Muskie of Maine

There is dawning world-around comprehension
Of the existence of a significant plurality
Of alternative energy source options
Available for all Earthians' vital support
Which now intuitively fortifies
Maine's far-sighted citizens' and friends'
Spontaneous expression of abhorrence
For any petroleum refineries or storage
Anywhere along its complexedly meandering
Deep-tide coastline.
Because humanity is born
Helpless, ignorant and naked
Nature must anticipatorily provide,
Protect and nurture humanity's regeneration
By spontaneously assimilatible
Environmental resource availabilities
Under omni-favorable conditions.

But originally permitted ignorance
No longer may be, self-excusingly, pleaded
As justification for failure to employ
The now known to exist
Omni-self-supporting technical capabilities
To produce unprecedently advanced
Standards of living
And freedoms of thought and actions
For all humanity,
Without any individual
Being advantaged
At the expense of another,
All of which feasibilities
Are inanimately powerable
Well within our daily energy income
From extraterrestrial sources
And all accomplishable without pollution.

By tapping the billion years' long
Safe-depositing of fossil fuel energies, ---
As petroleum and coal, within the planetary crust
Humanity was self-startered
Into inauguration of World-around
Electromagnetic energy resources integration,
Accomplished exclusively
By industrialization's ever-evolving knowledge
Regarding ultimate feasibility
On non-biologically harvested
Metabolic support of all humanity.

Humanity had to be self-startered
Into bounteously underwritten
Trial and error gropings
From whence gradually emerged
Mind-discovered comprehension
Of some of the eternal principles
Governing the availability and feasible employment
Of cosmically-constant, astronomical quantities
Of inherently inexhaustible energies
Of self-regenerative Universe.

Because humanity now has learned
How to gear directly into the inexhaustible energy
Of the main engines of Universe
It is no longer justified in attempting
To accommodate its ever-expanding,
Knowledgeable functioning in Universe
By ignorantly keeping its foot on the self-starter
To obtain its evolutionary propulsion
Only from the swiftly exhaustible
Fossil-fuel storage battery energies
Or from its perishable, one-season crops.

Realistic accounting
Of the time and foot pounds
Of energy-work, invested by nature,
Into the land-born agriculture's---
And seaborn algae's
Impoundment of Sun energy,---
Exclusively by photosynthesis,---
And its progressive conservation
As dead organic residues progressively covered
By wind and waterborne dustings

Siftings and siltings buried and sunken
To critical, gravitationally actuated,
Pressure depths and temperatures
Within which unique conditions
The hydrocarbon residues are chemically converted
Into coal and petroleum,
Discloses an overall time and pressure
Energy accounting cost
Of one million dollars per gallon of petroleum
(Or its energy equivalents in coal)
As calculated at the present
Lowest commercial rates
At which kilowatt hours of energy
May be purchased from public utility systems.

Failure to reckon
The fundamental metabolic costs,
Is to be economically reckless.
Further reckless expenditures
Of our fossil fuel energy saving account
To which future generations
Needs must have emergency access
As a self-re-starting recourse,
Is equivalent to drilling a hole
From the sidewalk into a bank vault
Pumping out money
And calling it free-enterprise discovery
Of an energy wealth bonanza
Physical energy convergent as matter
Or divergent as radiation,
Compounded by weightless metaphysical know-how,
Have altogether provided the means
For Earthians' progressively greater participation
In Universe's inexorable evolutionary transformings,
The participation being accomplished exclusively
By Human-intellect directed ingenuities,
In progressive rearranging
Of the physical furnishings
Of our spherical, space-boat home,
In such a way as progressively to support
Ever-more lives in ever-more ways
With ever-increasing health.

Naught gets *spent* but human time
As cosmically inexhaustible energy
Is tapped exclusively
By intellect-discovered and employed
Cosmic principles
Which to qualify as principles
Must be eternal.

Real wealth
Is Universally self-regenerative energy
Harnessed by mind to regenerate
Human lives around our Planet,---
Increasing wealth means
More regeneratively self-supporting days ahead
For more lives
Ranging first within Earth's biosphere
And subsequently by ever-increasing exploration
With Earth's extra-terrestrial
Cosmic neighborhoods.

Such ever-evolving greater know-how wealth
Provides the means
With which specifically to augment
The ever-expanding anti-entropic
Intellectual responsibilities of humanity
As local Universe's local problem solver
Which problem solving is human intellect's exclusive,
Complementary and essential functioning,
In support of total, scenario-Universe's
Self-regenerative integrity.

Physics shows
That universal energy is undiminishable.
Experience teaches
That every time humanity initiates
Intelligibly logical experiments
Human intellect always learns more.
Intellect cannot learn less
Intellect is growthfully irreversible.
Both the physical and metaphysical advantage gains
Of intelligently harvested know-how,---
Reinvested as competent energy-transforming,---
Always produces
Inherently irreversible wealth growth.

This is contrary to yesterday's
Now scientifically and technically obsolete
Concept of a self-exhausting,
Ergo, progressively expendable---
And ultimately spent Universe,
With assumedly progressive failure phases
And their negative economic accountings
Whose bankruptcies are as yet employed
By all political economies,
Together with their depletion tax evasions
Covering only physical property depletions
With no capitalization, nor depreciation allowances
Of the metapysical competence of humanity's mind
Without which there would be
Neither human life self-awareness
Nor its wealth
Of capable conceptioning.

Modern physics renders it incontrovertible
That celestial energy is nonexhaustible
Only the fossil fuel savings account
And perishable human muscles
And the self-startering, but limited
Hydro-carbon impound energies
Are terrestrially exhaustible.
Humanity's economics are as yet ignorantly geared
Exclusively to the annual energy harvesting cycles
And bankruptcy accounting
Of ignorance permeated yesteryear's
Human brain reflexing
As conditioned, by floods, fires, droughts, and pestilence,---
And frequently ruined crops,
Whereby millions of humans perished.

Brilliant and potentially effective
Managerial capabilities and leadership potentials
Are as yet diminishingly extruded
Through minuscule accounting and customs apertures.
Which force those capabilities
To concentrate exclusively and myopically
Only upon *this* year's production
This year's election and
This year's profit
While blindly overlooking
The infinitely reliable cyclic frequencies

Governing the 99 per cent of reality
Lying outside human sense apprehending
And lying outside this year's considerability
Which vast, invisible reality
Is the great electromagnetic spectrum
And its astrophysical even recurrency rates,
Which range from split-second atomic frequencies
To multi-billion year astro-physical lags
All of which cyclic event reoccurrences
Are guaranteed to humanity as absolutely reliable
By the exclusively science-discovered
Cosmic behaviors' integrity.

Despite the industrial revolution's
Momentary fumbling and mess---
As occasioned uniquely by the myopia
Generated by 'this year's accounting' limitations---
It now is discernible scientifically---
That unwitting Earthians
Gradually are being shifted
Over an epochal threshold,
Successful crossing of which,---
If not totally frustrated by reflexive inertias,---
Will witness the successful gearing of all humanity
Into the eternally inexhaustible, energy system
Of omni-self-regenerative celestial mechanics.

Humanity is as yet acquiring
Its many human support increasing
Techniques and practices
For all the growing reasons
We only expand wealth production
Under mass-fear mandates of war.
We could acquire, peacefully and directly
A total humanity supporting productivity
And comprehensive enjoyment of our whole planet
By simply deciding to do so
Whatever we need to do
And know how to do
We can afford to do!
This is the cosmic law
Now in clear scientific evidence,
And the more love,
The more satisfactory the wealth augmentations.
Whether history entrusts you or others

With progressively greater responsibilities
At this crucial-to-Earthians'-survival moment
Depends upon whether you, they, or both of you
Comprehend these epochal transitional events.

The State of Maine's Bay-of-Fundy's
Twice-a-day, fifty-foot tides
Are pulsated by Sun-compensated, Moon-pulls,
Those tides will be pulsated twice daily
As long as the Moon and Earth co-orbit the Sun.
Fundy provides more economically harvestable,
Foot-pounds of energy daily
Than ever will be needed by all humanity
While attaining and sustaining ever-higher
Standards of living,
Greater and more healthful longevity
Than heretofore ever experienced.

It is economic ignorance of the lowest order
To persist in further surfacing and expenditure
Of the Earth's fossil fuels---
It is even more ignorant and irresponsible
To surface and transport oils
Of Arabia, Venezuela, Africa and East Indies
To refineries and storages on the Coast of Maine
Thus putting into ecological jeopardy
One of the world's
As yet most humanly cherished
Multi-islanded, sea coast wildernesses.
In view of Fundy's tidal energy wealth
Such blindness is more preposterous
Than "carrying coals to Newcastle."
It is accelerated human suicide.

On the other hand we must recall
That Passamaquoddy's semi-completed
Tidal generating system
Was abandoned on the officially stated
Ignorant, political-economics assumption
That electricity could not be transmitted
Beyond 350 miles
And therefore could not reach
Any important industrial centers.

It is known in political actuality
That Passamaquoddy was discontinued
Through the combined lobbying efforts
Of Maine's paper pulping and electric power industries
Whose political policy logic was persuasive
Despite that those two industries
Have together succeeded
In polluting Maine's prime rivers
To kill all but a pittance
Of the Maine coast's once vast fishing wealth.

Space-effort harvested
Scientific know-how and the computer capability
Have together made possible
The present inauguration
Of one million volt transmissions
And a 1,500 mile delivery range
Of underground, electric power network systems.
Many Passamaquoddies could be plugged
Into the invisible underground,
Transcontinental, time-zone spanning
Electrical energy network integration
And thence relayed to Alaska
While picking up Canadian Rockies water power
Along the way.
The integrated North American network
Could not only be trans-linked
Through Mexico and Central America
Into an Amazon-to-be-powered
South American network
But also across the Bering Straits
From Alaska to Russia
To join with their now completed
Eastern extension of Western Russia's network
Powered by northward flowing, into-the-Arctic
Siberian river systems.
This now feasible, intercontinental network
Would integrate America, Asia and Europe
And integrate the night-and-day, spherically cycling
Shadow-and-light zones of Planet Earth
And this would occasion the 24-hour use
Of the now only fifty per cent of the time used
World around standby generator capacity
Whose fifty per cent unused capacities
Heretofore were mandatorily required

Only for peakload servicing of local non-interconnected energy users.
Such intercontinental network integration
Would overnight double the already-installed and in-use,
Electric power generating capacity of our Planet.

And lying well within
The progressive 1,500 mile hookup reachability
From an American-Russian power integration
Are the intercontinental networks of China, India and Africa.

It is everywhere around the world
Incontrovertibly documented
That as the local kilowatt hours
Of distributed electrical energy increase
The local birth rate
Is incommensurably diminished and longevity increases.
In respect to any of its specific geographical areas,
The birth rate of that area
Trends in inverse proportion
To electrical energy generation and distribution,
The sudden world population bulge
Which has occasioned
Dire population increase predictions
Was occasioned first by the failure to die
Of those who used to die
And secondly by the continued new birth acceleration
Only within the world's
As yet non-industrialized countries.
As world industrialization will be completed
By twentieth-century's end
The ever-diminishing birth rate
Of the industrial countries
Will bring about world population stabilization
By 2000 A.D.

Universe has no pollution
All the chemistries of the Universe are essential
To its comprehensive self-regeneration.
The ninety-two regenerative chemical elements
Associate, disassociate and intertransform
In a wide range of time-lag rates.
All the dumped chemistries
Spoken of ignorantly as "pollution" or "waste"
Are always needed *elsewhere*
In the intelligent integration

Of World-around energy renerating economics.
All the sulphur emitted annually
From the world's industrial chimneys
Exactly equal to the amount of sulphur
Being taken annually to keep industry going.

And while the by-product chemistries
Are in high concentration
Before going out the stacks or nozzles
They can be economically distributed
To their elsewhere-needed functioning.
After leaving the stacks or nozzles
The byproduct chemicals are so diffuse
As to be economically unrecoverable
In their diffuse state the byproducts
Often become toxic
To various biological species,
The ultimate overall costs of which
May easily be cessation of terrestrial life.

Yesterday's preoccupation with major energy harnessing
Primarily for the killing of humans by humans
Now can be comprehensively redirected
To intelligent and responsible production
Of a total-humanity sustaining system.
Swift realization of all the foregoingly considered
Epochal transition of human affairs
From a "might" to a "right"
Accounted and inspired
World economics
Is now scheduled for swift realization
By inexorable evolutionary events
To be accompanied by maximum social stresses
With only one alternative outcome
To its total human advantaging---
The alternative is human extinction
Aboard our Planet.

All thinking humanity young or old
Not only will condone
Reversal of public position taking
When it is predicated upon
Better and more inclusive information
Than was at first available
In fact it will think even more favorably

Of the integrity
Of those who admit error for humanity's sake
At the risk of losing previous political support.
So well informed is the young society
Which now is taking the world initiative
That only such integrity of long distance thinking
And unselfish preoccupation
Can win its support.

I pray you will make your stand
Swiftly and unambiguously clear
As being against any further incursions
Of petroleum into Maine
Or of pipelines in Alaska.
I pray that you will concurrently
Initiate resumption of Passamaquoddy
Together with initiation of a plurality
Of such Fundy tidal energy convertors
With combined capacities
Sufficient for celestial-energy support
Of all human life aboard our Planet
To be maintained successfully
Until Earth-based humanity
Has successfully migrated
Into larger cosmic neighborhood functioning.

Richard Grossinger

A Winter's Tale

1.

We have engendered a plague without a name. We falsely ennoble ourselves by calling it The Lie.

We lie to create our gross national product, even as we whitewash routinely the primacy we give to race and caste. We burn and chainsaw forests, hide our toxic overloads in oceans and streams, sell starving children into armies and prostitution, all the time pretending to be benign caretakers of those in our charge. Bottomless debts and paramilitary units mark our reign.

We are no longer lying just strategically to achieve certain ends but lying in the sense that it is impossible to discern the truth. It is this larger Lie that deludes political hacks into their petty lesser mistruths: they presume that Truth itself has become a meaningless commodity.

Ronald Reagan "lied" about visiting Nicaragua, about being among the troops liberating Europe; he also pretended at times not to be able to hear or remember. In the guise of reducing the national budget his administration created deficits with millennial consequences, engendering mafia-level theft in the Savings and Loan industry, the Department of Housing and Urban Development, and the preexistent Pentagon procurement scam. In a petty afterthought, Reagan even had Jimmy Carter's solar energy devices removed from the roof of the White House. While dedicated ideologically to a war on crime, Ron's good old boys actually sponsored multibillion-dollar global white-collar graft, with the U.S. Treasury as guarantor. And, while apparently paying (with the promise of Israeli arms) to keep Americans hostage in Iran, they sabotaged any investigations into the big-business arming of Saddam Hussein. In fact, patrons of the Republican Party were the most significant capital beneficiaries of the Iraqi war machine. Then, while declaring Khadafy's Libya a den of killers (and, with patriotic sanctimony, bombing Tripolis), Reagan gave routine blessing to Iraq's chemical annihilation of thousands of Kurds, to say nothing of daily cynical murders carried out by right-wing military bands in Central America and, less publicly, Asia and Africa.

It little matters anymore whether Man lies or God lies because Man now speaks for both. He routinely lies about the Bible, the prophecies of Jesus and Mohammed and Divine Right in the Holy Land. The voice of God would have no way of penetrating the media cabal that engulfs the world with billboards, slogans, and sales kitsch.

The Lie is no longer a fugue; it is our entire logos.

The depth of our political crisis is such that Soviet bureaucrats, who made strategic lying into an art during the post-War era, have now instituted doctrinal truth-making called *glasnost*. It is as though they awoke suddenly from a trance and discovered a threat to their own existence. The Lie had become even more powerful than the Bomb and held civilization at its mercy.

For decades we collaborated with the Soviets on the charade of an ideological death clinch. It is not clear what either of us gained other than a generation of recreational wars, sterile industries, and a permanent legacy of radioactive waste. When Saddam Hussein finally dumped oil in the Persian Gulf and set the Kuwaiti oil wells on fire, he may have been acting from pure spite ("So I have to leave?—well, DIG THIS!"), but he also gave East and West a precise mirror of their disingenuousness. Like the Chinese at Tiananmen Square, he took the palliative chatter of global politics to its natural conclusion.

We too act without motive, without honor. Our waters and fields are ravaged with oil and poisons. We have no baseline ethics or concern for the lives of other species or our children. We destroy the planet slowly from addictions that are morally equivalent to spite. Hussein's most effective "Scud" launch was to mirror the behavior of a phony civilization that tried to condemn him as its Other. Would that our own liberation were as simple as Desert Storm.

Drug money piles up in Swiss banks beyond plan or need while the children of the bankers beg and die in Zurich's Needle Park. Genocidal armies rape Cambodia, Haiti, and Somalia, while we pretend not to be implicated (or to care, except in socially responsible ways).

It is not because people do not understand the consequences. It is because there is no yardstick or standard of allegiance. There is no integrity that is not a sales pitch, no ethical commitment to the dispossessed, no planetary code to treat soil, water, and air as the only true currency rather than something to be exploited for profit no one needs. There is only waste which hides terror which only further waste and profligacy will symptomatically assuage.

To an American generation after the one that greeted the sixties as salvation, there is nothing left but to suspect every guru of sexual and monetary indiscretion, every politician of mafia or defense connections (or some other sellout), every scientist of professional cynicism, every renegade "new scientist" of commodization and narcissism, every Marxist of a secret bank account—and everyone in general punching in and punching out, getting paid, and even if not shaving points or pilfering, looking the other way, most of the planet unemployed or dumbstruck, addicted or enslaved. Even the various realms beyond death—nirvanas, bardos, and hells—are marketed by Advocacies like adventures through cosmic theme parks. Our Great Lie wants to wrest Death too from its shadow beneath an old tree and put it up for sale, with devotional ikons, visualization techniques, and future lives bought and sold at self-help, positive-thinking global-culture expos. Only the intellectually elite need apply.

The serial murders committed by Yahweh and Krishna cults (or freelancers like the L.A. strangler) have no motive or explanation anymore. They don't need them. They need only emptiness to fill. Once upon a time Hitler had an agenda, however diabolic. The rationale of contemporary mass killers is a banal literalization of our unexamined pornography, a fantasy of the dark side of instinct (of what lies beneath the shadow of the tree) which conceals more than it represents either in Nature or Psyche. Meanwhile we suffer the callous endgames of junk-bond gurus and addiction-generating "therapists." We invent (and lithium-suppress) anorexias and megalomanias born of defunct cannibalisms and hysterias, while Donald Trump and his imitators buy and sell companies, buildings, and lives beyond motive or need also.

Clearly the nations of Eastern Europe represent not our past but our future, for we have yet to face the task of kicking out our tyrants. We are in more of a collective trance than they ever were, for at least they faced a burlesque of Gothic dictators and party officials hiding in palaces. We face only a barrage of superstars, promoters, self-promoters, reassurers, and bosses, pouring tar, plastic (and worse) into rivers and tissues, building up the illusion of equity in deficit, all the while convincing us that our system is just and serves the future of the world.

In just one decade the call of our shadow has driven us from even the pieties that allowed special prosecutors to pursue the illusion of crime and punishment in the seventies and made the Kennedy assassination a puzzle within a puzzle within a puzzle. If John Kennedy was a sham of Camelot (dealing with and dealt out by the mob or Pentagon mafia), if Richard Nixon floated a mediocre fib of misdemeanor level—Ronald Reagan told whopper after whopper of gargantuan proportions, tossing out imaginary scenarios that no one would have suggested even approximated truth. Whereas we retain the fantasy that someone even bothered to connive (and cover up) Kennedy's death .... and Nixon forfeited his Presidency, Reagan thrived in adulation while he sold the U.S. to Japan, Kuwait, and whomever could put on a suit and come to the table.

No need any longer to steal brains, substitute bullets, or doctor film. No need even to erase archival tape. There is nadia minding the store.

If we track Nixon and Kennedy back one sitcom to their famous debate, we can measure the increasing scale of our self-deception. The Vice-President—who was being outflanked and (ultimately) upset by his opponent—not only was gracious during the exchange between them but acknowledged that both he and Senator Kennedy shared the same hopes and goals for the nation and both were qualified men with reasonable differences of philosophy for Americans to choose between. Nixon and Kennedy agreed that reducing federal debt while maintaining important programs would be difficult and they collaborated in presenting the populace with a realistic picture of the national "crisis." They presumed the seriousness of the occasion and neither tried to trick the audience into either inflated views of themselves or negative caricatures of the other. As one commentator recently remarked in *The New Yorker,* "Watching [a rebroadcast of] the debate brought home not so much the wit and poise of J.F.K. or the nascent malevolence of Richard Nixon as something far more surprising and disturbing—the almost unbelievable debasement of American political discourse in the intervening thirty years." Today we are contemptuously tossed a Popeye-Donald Duck dialogue. Cartoon images are invoked mainly to enlist and polarize; photographs of aborted embryos, naked children, gay eros, and black murderers are routinely paraded as incitements. The presumption is of course that people will give mindless allegiance to slogans and symbols. So the distinction between actually cleaning the air and rivers, on the one hand, and inventing rhetoric to make the public think you are doing it, on the other, has become almost irrelevant.

Whereas, at the time of the Nixon-Kennedy debates, merchandising and propaganda were almost self-spoofs, now they have become precise technologies. They are designed (at a collective level that transcends individual motives and sales pitches) to hypnotize viewers and cut them off from the sources of their own humanity and power.

Marxists and their successors once argued the pathology of commodization in such a persuasive manner that it has become fashionable to blame our fiscal and moral bankruptcy on the conversion of everything—goods, symbols, people, emotions—into products. If this prognosis is correct we are facing a brief flicker of the universalization of capitalism before the real dark ages. (In fact, we live in a dark age already—a fact that any outing along the streets of a major city should reveal. That's the reason for all the glitter, the language plastered to stone and steel facades, even the graffiti—to make us think the lighting will be bright enough.) Our most ironic self-deception in the West now is to flatter ourselves that we represent a Truth the Eastern Bloc is turning toward. The commoditization process—the mania to convert nature into products for which desire must be created, has led—first to an illusion about the simplicity and accessibility of nature (such that existence itself seems to become raw material without limits), and second to an acceptance of video-synthesized desire. No wonder some would rather sit in rags in the wind. We watch car, perfume, and jeans ads which propose "the good life," meaning life itself. While many of us may not buy into these images, few of us can challenge them at a profound enough level to escape the miasma of products and clichés of relationship they provoke, so we find ourselves adrift among vague unfulfilled states and mirages that this pounding desire mill continues to churn out. And we feel smug before Eastern Europe?

2.

While we are in obvious need of new paradigms, seemingly liberal scientists like Carl Sagan and Jonas Salk beat the drums nationally for the MacArthur Foundation to give its distinguished awards to debunkers and cynics in order to hasten the marginalization of those attempting to add so-called paranormal energies to our potential repertoire—not to study this matter critically and objectively, but to expurgate the researchers, just in case they might tap some unsanctioned resource for the future of our planet. A recent award went to the clown of debunkers, the self-named Amazing Randi. (Carl and his colleagues may know celestial mechanics and cosmos marketing, but when it comes to the actual karmic and conditional forces that move the universe, he is still in kindergarten.)

Cynical scientists deny anomalous effects in experiments not so much because they are committed to a mode of quantitative data as because their whole guild is involved with not discovering certain things.

Back in the early seventies large numbers of people questioned a Moon-landing by astronauts. By the late 1980's NASA itself was vociferously denying that it had *even photographed* an object resembling a human face on the surface of Mars. The agency's implicit rationale speaks for our time: "It can't be there; therefore, it isn't there." And anyone who has since suggested rephotographing the site merely for further discussion has been ostracized from the space community. The implications of considering the possibility of the Face (and a cosmic humanoid connection) are considered so subversive that they aren't even condoned for scientific speculation.

Professional skeptics who debunk telekinesis and homoeopathic medicines as well as UFOs and shamans are equally liars, but their lie is one that pretends to protect the last vestige of truth—the so-called objectivity of science. There can be no objective science in the face of the kind of mind-matter relationship suggested by spontaneous paraphysical episodes.

A more open-minded scientist, John Todd (founder of the New Alchemy Institute), has routinely found inexplicable powers in living systems and integrated these into self-sustaining technologies. He is presently being "taught" by communities of plants, sunlight, bacteria, mollusks, and fish he introduced to one another in successive gravity and solar orchestrated cylinders. These weave unexpected synergies, sorting raw sewage and septage, removing even dioxins and heavy metals and ending in pure streams. This, however, according to official standards, is not "water"; to be acceptable for release, it must go through conventional toxic tanks.

These same congeries of organisms, when set loose in polluted ponds, have spread beyond all projected boundaries and reorganized life forms to the outermost shores. Homoeopathic physicians likewise have a remarkable record of cure using remedies containing microdoses of vital energies, but these doctors produce only actual cures, not theoretical and fundable models of cure—so the overfunded Randi is rushed to France to debunk a well-publicized seemingly successful homoeopathic experiment. Why? So that no cancer victim will be tricked into remission?

Our existence now flounders for the lack of any verifiable measure at all. From the universalization of capitalism and commoditization—and their spiritual counterparts in religious and scientistic fundamentalism—to their unconscious negation in various forms of addiction and narcissism, we have come to a collective existence devoid of any context in a universe of the blackest nights against an infinity of anonymous stars that even radical physicists like Stephen Hawking and Rupert Sheldrake cannot set right (though they tantalize us through their false oppositions of metaphysical materialism and quantum bio-physics). When mind and matter are so evidently at war we are far more subject to the tyranny of an unnamed and uncompensated truth than we are heir to any pleasantly speculative realities that bubble up through consumer civilization like so many more Commodities in the guise of Ideas. Even the voice in which I speak is such a commodity, for anything produced with words now is trapped in a marketing process. There is no diatribe, or the negation of one, that leads out of our morass.

How can past and future lives have any meaning when this one is timelessly waiting? Why "acquire" lives, mantras, and dakinis when the ground of experience is in freefall and human beings casually deal out both life and death in episodes of mass machinery . . . when our aggrandized species turns animal existence into laboratory experiments, mass burger and plastic-wrapped organ selects? Why even cherish incarnation—or desire reincarnation—when bodies are routinely trashed, aborted, and iconicized?

The problem is that we can no longer imagine the alternative. Hence, UFOs in hangars and "men in black" badgering citizens (plus a host of unidentified objects and spirits) are bogey occupants of our world—not as things but also not as phantasms. They exist and do not exist, and that is our dilemma.

Recently released Freedom-of-Information-Act documents appear to confirm a Government cover-up (during the 1950's) relative to incidents of not only general alien contact but specifically the recovery of a crash-wrecked UFO and extraterrestrial bodies from a site outside Roswell, New Mexico. The same documents also explicitly describe a clandestine agency (Majestic 12) set up under the Truman administration for the sole purpose of making deals with aliens. Ostensible witnesses have since come forth to claim treaties with extraterrestrial humanoids granting them underground bases and even official approval for human abductions and cattle mutilations. This makes denial of deals with ayatollahs and a statue of a Face on Mars seem tame indeed. But are the documents themselves "real"? Were they planted in Government files—and if so, to protect what deeper, more dangerous secret? The witnesses, who come and go like yetis, likewise. . . .

The same fake sincerity lies at the heart of all our fabled controversies: Does an ego dwell in the embryo? Who was opening his umbrella on the Zapruder film on that sunny day in Dallas? What crashed in Roswell, New Mexico? I am not denying these controversies have actual solutions. I am saying that the stubborn fictions espoused by opposing parties transcend any dialogue, let alone consensus.

What about accounts of supposed UFO abductees? Usually these have been reported as excruciating episodes in which luckless victims have been coerced as lab specimens, sometimes for straightforward examination, sometimes for the breeding of mutant embryos that have then been appropriated by the aliens, and (if the darkest rumors are to be believed) sometimes for permanent imprisonment, dismemberment, and experimentation. The large number of such reports and the ubiquity of their occurrence would seem to preclude any conventional form of conspiracy or fabrication: it is unlikely that so-called abductees are "lying."

However, once we consider that these abductions are actual events we must also presume an ingenious, trans-solar confederation of antipathetic aliens far more resembling the works of Hollywood and pulp science fiction than the realm of cosmic space with its actual immense distances between suns. According to those who monitor such matters, these "creatures" may be malevolently deceitful—engaged in the theft of biological material from the Earth and the subjugation of its inhabitants, turning victims into cyborgs, etc.—or they may be benevolently guiding us into a paradigm shift. Abductees with otherwise similar experiences have surmised both scenarios. Likewise, we could imagine the babies stolen embryonically from their mothers returning to Earth as either avatars leading us into the next utopia or tyrants enslaving us. We can also extend our imagination to the horror of their use as raw material for some alien robotics. Any of these scenarios has apocalyptic consequences, but the mere images of these and other cataclysms, raptures, and endgames are mainly *falsely* apocalyptic, as though death were only our invention of degrees of oblivion, heavens and hells, fortunate and unfortunate rebirths, and had no reality or consequences of its own. We have promoted a spiritual life without doubt and with only the psychotronic implant of pain and love.

Regardless of interpretation, these aliens and death demons, if they exist, are lying to us, and, if they don't exist, the abductees and channels and priests are lying to us, and if the aliens don't exist and the abductees and channels are not lying to us, then we are lying to ourselves in a complex way that reveals just how stuck we are at this crossroads.

3.

In *The Winter's Tale,* Leontes, King of Sicilia, is entertaining his boyhood friend Polixenes, King of Bohemia. The visit has already been extended more than once, but as Polixenes prepares to leave, Leontes asks for just one more "gentle reprieve." Initially Polixenes is firm in his resolve to go but is finally convinced by Queen Hermione to linger.

For some obscure reason this innocent exchange between his friend and his wife haunts Leontes so that he gradually weaves a fantasy of an affair between them. The more he dwells on this imaginary event, the more evidence for it he seems to find. The more irrational he becomes in his behavior, the more his own counselors begin to act suspiciously in defense. A tailspin of doubt and jealousy sucks everything into itself until Polixenes must flee with Camillo, the senior Sicilian counsellor, in fear of their lives. Then Leontes imprisons pregnant Hermione. Her newborn daughter is ultimately condemned to abandonment "in an uncivilized place outside of Sicilia." A courtier bears the infant away in a ship.

Leontes has disassembled his entire life, his entire reality, at the bidding of a trivial paranoid fantasy.

Watching this play from our outpost of modern sensibility we recognize a drama quite different from what Shakespeare's audience saw. If there is one thing we appreciate fully, it is suicidal obsession. In fact paranoia has become fashionable because it is so often warranted. The CIA and KGB could be spying on anyone, assassinating anyone; the man with the umbrella is everywhere, rain or shine. Even those who died of conventional tumors—like UFO investigators (after coming out of the closet) and witnesses to the Kennedy killing—are possible victims of viral warfare. Even AIDS has a shadowy origin. And if the aliens are manipulating our politics, slaughtering and mutilating cattle as well as kidnapping citizens later listed as missing and stealing embryos, then paranoia is the least of our required responses. Cosmic episodes aside, in a time when people are starving in the streets, and banks lend billions without collateral, and the planet is said to be losing its protective layer and developing greenhouse conditions, when the ravages of habitation are already undermining the physical basis of life, what trivial subterfuge is George Bush playing when he sends Stealth bombers on his invasion of Panama, or denies ozone deterioration, or takes over the oilfields? Does he still believe that the weapons programs can save the planet from the type of attack that will come from Saddam II or the Greys in the nineties, the year 2000, and after?

Is our planet becoming Venus? Does the HIV virus cause immuno-deficiency effects, or is it simply one opportunistic virus preying on depleted immune systems, its notoriety a fiction of drug companies and governments selling AIDS paraphernalia, anti-AIDS life-styles, hostile aliens, single assassins, threatened democracies, and general disinformation? Will Mikhail Gorbachev go to work for Exxon, or Stanford, or the Common Market? Have UFOs crashed in the U.S. and does the Government hold alien crafts? Is there a Sphinx on Mars with a message for us? Did the Russians lose a satellite to a UFO near Phobos? What was the secret discussed but not revealed at Malta or Helsinki?

Either these things are or they are not. There may be middle grounds of interpretation but not of fact. Hermione answers:

> "Since what I am to say must be but that
> Which contradicts my accusation, and
> The testimony on my part no other
> But what comes from myself, it shall scarce boot me
> To say 'not guilty': mine integrity,
> Being counted falsehood. . . ."

But Leontes had a real option: he dispatched messengers to the oracle of Apollo, which even innocent Hermione was willing to accept. They returned with the judgment of gods.

"You here shall swear upon this sword of justice,
That you, Cleomenes and Dion, have
Been both at Delphos, and from thence have brought
This seal'd-up oracle, by the hand deliver'd
Of great Apollo's priest, and that since then
You have not dared to break the holy seal
Nor read the secrets in't."

Of course they haven't. Nowadays we would bet the opposite.

The oracle affirms the truth as we have seen it enacted, exonerating Hermione and Polixenes, naming the babe as truly begotten, identifying Leontes as a jealous tyrant.

The King's initial response is to challenge even Apollo: "There is no truth at all i' the oracle . . . this is mere falsehood."

But after Hermione falls into a coma—which will last sixteen years—Leontes finds "his rational mind" and undertakes a penance.

There is no point in overplaying the connection between the text and our modern era. We have our oracles too, whether they be computers predicting climatic effects, channels reporting from spirit realms, or Fundamentalist preachers quoting the books of their faiths. When we are an audience for *The Winter's Tale* we trust its oracle not only because we have seen the inside of the play unfold, but because Shakespeare's sensibility allows for no further intrusions, no mind-altering drugs or counter-espionage, no aliens, no lying courtiers or Congressmen. There are not even "separate reality" Third World peoples (they rest on the bare edge of *Cymbeline* and *The Tempest*) to confuse the Western economic truth or the breeding of nobles: the son of Polixenes will find Perdita, for she is the daughter of Sicilia, even when raised by a Bohemian peasant. The gods require destiny and resolution (and shine on these noble lords if not on dispossessed Apache chiefs and princesses of Mesoamerica). Our nostalgia cannot be for the romance; it must be for the Oracle, which we can no longer consult.

Apollo, are there aliens? Must we stop producing fluorocarbons? Or is it too late? Does that mean the end of all life on this planet?

The oracle is silent. When the junkie in Needle Park is asked for the outcome of his own addiction he is not even as remotely hopeful as Hermione, imprisoned unjustly. His jailer is larger than his existence and certainly than any moral order. What higher authority is there if, as some cosmic explorers claim, we are merely the experiment of the aliens: "I have seen them. They are the watchers. And it is horrible!"

Consider the deconstructionist implications as Leontes denies Camilo's reassurance that the glances of Polixenes meant nothing:

After listing all the imagined indiscretions between the lovers and querying, one by one, if they are nothing, he concludes, "Is this nothing?/Why, then the world and all that's in't is nothing;/The covering sky is nothing; Bohemia nothing;/My wife is nothing; nor nothing have these nothings,/If this be nothing."

In England the audience could chuckle at the play on words. In California, Christmas, 1989, one hears only the echo, not even the harbinger, of *Godot*.

Is our condition nothing? Our modern crisis nothing? Is all this nothing?

In truth, our global ecological crisis cannot end by a benign mechanical solution like water fuel or a Wall Street-sponsored clean-up. Our trauma cannot be healed by syntax and subtext. We are stuck, as both Whitehead and Jung would have had it for different reasons, in the shadow of the background of a fake civilization, perhaps capping millennia of fake civilizations since the Phoenicians and Vikings sailed out of the megalithic culture complex of the late Stone Age.

Throw off the Soviet Union and what is left is Russia. Throw off America and what is left is Europe and the Apache-Tahitian archipelago. Throw off Russia and Europe utterly, and perhaps we will find Sufi-Hindu relics in Uzbekistan or beyond.

In order for language to regain any validity it has to go back well before Homer. The words must be concrete, unhedged, reflecting the depth of an unknown world in layers, a commitment that water be water, stars bear spirits, trees and their roots speak, animals practice mind . . . every plant and stone carry either a medicine or a poison. A world still retaining some archaeozoic power when translated into Anglo:

> "The bird fell in death to the ground, its feathers strewing the earth.
> The people hastened to the bird
> And spake to one another, saying: O, elder brothers.
> It is a swan, O, elder brothers,
> A white swan, O, elder brothers,
> A bird fit for a symbolic article.
> We shall use it for our ceremonial article.
> Behold its feet are dark in color.
> The tip of its bill is also dark.
> Its feathers are white.
> From this bird also
> We shall take personal names, O, elder brothers, they said to one another."

The Osage made of the white swan a standard, and of the puma too, and the flint knife, and of the radiant star a ceremonial object. In the House of Mystery, the Rite of Vigil.

"This shall be the name of the little ones as they travel the path of life."

102

Revolutionary Letter No. 63

Free Julian Beck
Free Timothy Leary
Free seven million starving in Pakistan
Free all political prisoners
Free Angela Davis
Free Soledad brothers
Free Martin Sobel
Free Sacco & Vanzetti
Free Big Bill Hayward
Free Sitting Bull
Free Crazy Horse
Free all political prisoners
Free Billy the Kid
Free Jesse James
Free all political prisoners
Free Nathan Hale
Free Joan of Arc
Free Galileo & Bruno & Eckhart
Free Jesus Christ
Free Socrates
Free all political prisoners
Free all political prisoners
All prisoners are political prisoners
Every pot smoker a political prisoner
Every holdup man a political prisoner
Every forger a political prisoner
Every angry kid who smashed a window a political prisoner
Every whore, pimp, murderer, a political prisoner
Every pederast, dealer, drunk driver, burglar
poacher, striker, strike breaker, rapist
Polar bear at San Francisco zoo, political prisoner
Ancient wise turtle at Detroit Aquarium, political prisoner
Flamingoes dying in Phoenix tourist park, political prisoners
Otters in Tucson Desert Museum, political prisoners
Elk in Wyoming grazing behind barbed wire, political prisoners
Prairie dogs poisoned in New Mexico, war casualties
(Mass grave of Wyoming gold eagles, a battlefield)
Every kid in school a political prisoner
Every lawyer in his cubicle a political prisoner

Every doctor brainwashed by AMA a political prisoner
Every housewife a political prisoner
Every teacher lying thru sad teeth a political prisoner
Every indian on reservation a political prisoner
Every black man a political prisoner
Every faggot hiding in bar a political prisoner
Every junkie shooting up in john a political prisoner
Every woman a political prisoner
Every woman a political prisoner
You are political prisoner locked in tense body
You are political prisoner locked in stiff mind
You are political prisoner locked to your parents
You are political prisoner locked to your past
Free yourself
Free yourself
I am political prisoner locked in anger habit
I am political prisoner locked in greed habit
I am political prisoner locked in fear habit
I am political prisoner locked in dull senses
I am political prisoner locked in numb flesh
Free me
Free me
Help to free me
Free yourself
Help to free me
Free yourself
Help to free me
Free Barry Goldwater
Help to free me
Free Governor Wallace
Free President Nixon
Free J Edgar Hoover
Free them
Free yourself
Free them
Free yourself
Free yourself
Free them
Free yourself
Help to free me
Free us
DANCE

Roy A. Rappaport

Sanctity and Adaptation

I

Man is facing an adaptive crisis because he seems to be unwilling or unable to regulate the ecological systems which he has the ability to alter. A number of factors have contributed to this state of affairs, and have perhaps even made it inevitable. For one thing, the technology of alteration and the empirical knowledge upon which it is based is simpler and more straightforward than that of regulation. It is also the case that alteration is usually in accord with the purposes of men while regulation often is not. Bateson (1968a) suggests tht it is not merely the nature of some of his purposes which have endangered man, but purpose itself. Conscious purpose, which aims toward the achievement of specific goals, does not usually take into account the circular structure of cause and effect which characterizes the universe, and this cognitive failure leads to disruption.

This is a gloomy analysis, for surely purposefulness, which I take to be a concomitant of consciousness, must have been strongly selected for during much of the 3,000,000 years of man's span on earth. Man's purposefulness could hardly have endangered most of the ecosystems in which he participated as a hunter and gatherer (although hunting by fire may have been disruptive in some areas). Moreover, the foresight which forms a component of his purposefulness must have contributed substantially to his survival. A trait that has been adaptive for so long cannot easily be renounced; indeed if purposefulness is a concomitant of consciousness, its renunciation is impossible.

It was probably with his elevation to the role of ecological dominant, a role assumed with the emergence of plant and animal cultivation perhaps 10,000 years ago, that man's purposefulness became seriously disruptive. Cultivation demands that complex climax communities of plants and animals be replaced by simpler communities composed of smaller numbers of species selected by man according to criteria of apparent usefulness and arranged by him in limited numbers of short food chains of all of which he himself is supposed to be the terminus. Needless to say, such communities are likely to be less stable than the climax communities they replace. The relatively degraded nature of these anthropocentric ecosystems is in part a function of their simplicity, in part a function of the nature of constituent

This paper was prepared while the author was a fellow at the John Simon Guggenheim Foundation and a Senior Specialist at the Institute of Advanced Projects, East-West Center. The author is grateful to both sponsoring institutions.

species: often poorly adapted to local conditions, often helpless, frequently unable even to reproduce themselves without some assistance. And man himself is a poor dominant. It is interesting to note that dominants in non-anthropocentric ecosystems are almost always plants. They are well suited to the role, for by their mere nonpurposeful existence they fulfill the demands of their associated species. Men, on the other hand, must maintain their dominance through behavior. And since their behavior is less reliable than the existence of oak trees or algae, and since they are capable of making mistakes, and since the purposes which inform their behavior may not coincide with the requirements of the systems which they dominate, the conditions set by men tend toward instability.

But Bateson has suggested that the purposes of some men, at least, are tempered by wisdom, an awareness of the circularities of cause and effect operating in the universe, and of the interrelatedness of apparently separate things, and that wisdom resides as much in the non-discursive aesthetic sensibility as it does in knowledge (1969). He thus argues that the aesthetic sense is important in human adaptation as part of a mechanism by which man can transcend his own purposefulness. Later in this paper I shall take up the possible place of the sacred, which I believe to be related both formally and systemically to the aesthetic, in human adaptation. But first, I shall discuss the place of actors' understandings in the structure of adaptation and some possible malfunctions of adaptive structures. After a discussion of sanctity, the part that it perhaps has played in human adaptation and the ways in which its operation has been disrupted by the development of technology, I shall offer some brief general suggestions concerning theories of action.

II

I take the term adaptation to refer to the processes by which organisms or groups of organisms maintain homeostasis in and among themselves in the face of both short term environmental fluctuations and long term changes in the composition and structure of their environments.

Homeostasis may be given more or less specific, if not always precise, systemic meaning if it is conceived as a set of goal ranges on a corresponding set of variables abstracted from what, for empirical reasons, we take to be vital or indispensable conditions of the systems under consideration.

The simple cybernetic model suggested here has the advantage of possible empirical specificity on the one hand and broad applicability on the other, and it provides us with a set of systemic and biological criteria which permits us to assess in the same terms the adaptiveness of ontologically dissimilar phenomena. For instance, we can compare the adaptiveness with respect to population dispersion of particular religious beliefs, rules of filiation, courtship practices, social hierarchies and rituals of men with territoriality among wolves, epideictic displays among starlings and the

106

endocrinological responses of rats to changes in population densities. It has the additional advantage of reminding us that man is a species among species, that he is free from none of the requirements of organisms in general, and that he is subject to the same general limitations as other animals.

Of course, there are serious difficulties with such simple notions of adaptation and their application to the activities of organisms, parts of organisms or groups of organisms. For one thing, we are aware only dimly or not at all of some of the survival needs of social and organic systems, and even when we can identify such needs metrical difficulties may be such as to vitiate whatever predictive or even analytic possibilities the conceptual formalization would seem to promise. As far as group phenomena are concerned, at least, it is probably the case that in the present state of metrics and of ecological and biological knowledge this view of adaptation, as simple as it is, is more heuristic than operational.

But to declare that a formulation is heuristic rather than operational is not to derogate it, nor is it sufficient grounds to remove it from criticism. Conceptual models which are less than operational form an important, perhaps even the major, portion of the intellectual equipment with which men, including scientists and social critics, operate. It is surely the case that some of these models induce behavior which is more appropriate to the world's structure than do others, and it is therefore useful to underline the heuristic deficiencies in the proposed model of adaptation, although they may be obvious. Commoner called attention last year to the deficiencies of the atomistic models with which scientists have long operated. We may note here that simple cybernetic models of adaptation may themselves be atomistic, and that concern with the homeostatic maintenance of some variables may distract us not only from other variables, but from a consideration of the structure of the larger system from which they have been abstracted. Thus, although we may represent the homeostasis of a system as a set of goal ranges on a corresponding set of vital variables, it would be a mistake to represent adaptations as, simply, a collection of more or less distinct corrective feedback loops. When we refer to the adaptation of any system in a general sense we imply much more than the sum of its special adaptations (some of which may be, in part, contradictory), for these special adaptations must be adapted to each other in structured ways. Adaptations, human and otherwise, must take the form of enormously complex sets of interlocking corrective loops, perhaps arranged hierarchically, which incude not only mechanisms regulating material variables, but regulators regulating these regulators, others regulating them and so on.

The notion of control hierarchies is hardly a new one, and it has been employed with considerable success in the construction of machines and the organization of industries. Analogies of "natural" systems to such "artificial" systems may be misleading. Since we devise the artificial systems we know how they are put together, and have fairly accurate ideas of how they work. But since we don't consciously construct natural systems we must discover their structure. And their structure will surely differ from those of machines in a number of ways. For one thing, they are bound to be much more complex than any machine or industrial organization devised for a much more limited range of functions. Organisms not only need to do things, they must be able to stay alive. For a second, they are likely to be much messier than artificial systems. The construction of an artificial system is likely to reflect the elegance of reasoned design, but the natural system will always reflect the opportunism of evolution (Kalmus 1966). Third, artificial systems are likely to be much more tightly coupled than some natural systems, particularly social and ecological systems.

Because of their complexity, their messiness, and the relative incoherence characteristic of at least some of them, it may well be that we shall never be able to describe the hierarchical organization of natural systems in manners which approach exhaustiveness, and the notion of hierarchical regulatory structures, like that of the feedback loops of which these structures are made, remains heuristic. But it is a heuristic that emphasizes the operation of whole systems, the interrelation of functions, without sacrificing attention to specific functions. Moreover, the very inadequacy even of holistic models as descriptions has an important metaheuristic function. It suggests to us that we are participating in systems whose workings, although crucial to us, we are not, and probably never shall be able to analyze in sufficient detail to predict with precision the outcome of many of our own acts. We must, therefore, investigate the possibilities for developing theories of action which, although based upon incomplete knowledge, will permit us to participate in such systems without destroying them, and ourselves along with them.

III

As Vickers observed in his contribution to last year's conference, there still exist here and there economically primitive communities that apparently do not disrupt, and even maintain, the homeostases of the ecosystems in which they participate. It may be that the equilibria of such systems are a function of the relative inability of the human participants, because of their lack of powerful technology and their small scale social organization, to do much damage. But the damage that can be done by small groups of people equipped with nothing more than digging sticks, axes, and fire should not be underestimated, and I believe that at least in some instances the equilibria they maintain is in part a consequence of their understandings of the world, and the behavior which they undertake in the light of these understandings. Yet surely these understandings are likely to be even less accurate than our own.

I found that among the Tsembaga of the New Guinea Highland, a recently contacted group of bush-fallowing people among whom I have worked, relationships both with other local groups of Maring speakers and with the non-human species with which they shared their territory are regulated by protracted ritual cycles. Although the rituals which constitute these cycles are undertaken to maintain or transform the relations of the living with supernaturals, I have argued elsewhere (Rappaport 1968) that their operation helps to maintain an undegraded biotic environment, limits fighting to frequencies which do not endanger the survival of the Maring population as a whole, adjusts man-land ratios, facilitates trade and marriage, distributes local surpluses of pig throughout a wide region in the form of pork and assures to members of the local group rations of high quality protein when they are most in need of it.

I found it convenient, in attempting to comprehend the place of native understandings in Tsembaga adaptation, to invoke two models, terming these the "operational" and the "cognized."

The operational model is that which is constructed by the analyst through specified operations consisting of observations and measurements of phenomena and their covariations. This model, despite its likely deficiencies, is taken by the analyst to represent the material aspects of the group, and its physical and social environment. In the Tsembaga case the environment was represented as a complex system of relationships composed of two major subsystems, distinguished from each other by differences in the materials exchanged in each and by partial discontinuities in coherence, but affecting each other through mechanisms available to direct observation. The relations of the Tsembaga with the other species with which they shared their territory, were represented as the local or ecological system. Their relations with other Maring groups occupying other territories were represented as the regional system. Both of these major subsystems could have been analyzed into subsystems of a lower order.

Such operational models are constructed without reference to the conceptions of their environments and themselves entertained by the actors. They are simply abstract models adopted by observers to establish, as best their operations permit them, the nature of a portion of the material universe in which the actors act. But it is homeostasis in the operational model, expressed as the maintenance of critical variables within empirically defined goal ranges, that we take to indicate adaptation, regardless of the understandings, values, or wishes of the actors.

On the other hand, it is necessary, if we are to understand the role of native understandings in adaptation, to construct models of these understandings. I refer to these as "cognized models." Many difficulties, methodological, epistemological and ontological beset the construction of such models and it is well to mention before proceeding that anthropology has by no means solved them. Much of what follows, therefore, is highly speculative, and should be taken as such, although this will not always be indicated by my language.

It is obvious that cognized and operational models are likely to be overlapping but not coextensive. An operational model is likely to include material elements, such as nitrogen-fixing bacteria, of which the actors may not be aware, but which affect them in important ways. On the other hand, cognized models often include elements, such as supernaturals, whose existence cannot be demonstrated by observation or measurement.

It is sometimes the case that elements peculiar to one model are isomorphic with elements peculiar to the other. For instance, the behavior of certain spirits, whom the Tsembaga say occupy the lower portions of their territory, and the consequences of their behavior, correspond closely with that of the anopheles mosquito whom the Tsembaga do not understand to be a malaria vector. But elements, and relationships among elements, in the two models need not always be identical or isomorphic. The two models may differ in structure as well as in content.

This is not to say, of course, that cognized models are merely less adequate representations of reality than the operational models we attempt to construct. The accuracy of cognized models, although by definition they must be taken by those who entertain them to be accurate representations of the world in which they live, is really a secondary matter as far as adaptation is concerned. The primary question concerning cognized models is not the extent to which they conform to "reality" (i.e., are identical or isomorphic with operational models), but the extent to which they elicit behavior appropriate to the material situation of the actors. The appropriateness of behavior may be assessed by ascertaining its effects upon the homeostasis of one of more of the vital variables included in corresponding operational models. We are dealing here with what Pask (1968) has called hybrid systems composed of "word systems" (native understandings as we are able to ascertain them) and "thing systems" (operational models).

It is certainly the case that accurate representations of material conditions often form one of the bases for appropriate, or adaptive, behavior. But not always. In some cases, indeed, it is unlikely that people would do things that need to be done if they knew what they were doing, that is, if they understood the material contexts and consequences of their actions. It is not merely that adaptive behavior may be associated with understandings which do not accurately reflect material conditions, but that some adaptive behavior may be elicited only by such understandings. To call them misunderstandings or inaccuracies would be to misinterpret them. Cognized models are to be understood as part of populations' means for adjusting to their environments. They are guides to action and should be assessed as such, and some of their apparent inaccuracies may be demanded by their function. For instance, Maring local groups may initiate warfare only once during their protracted 10–20 year ritual cycles. During a major portion of the cycle a truce, both commenced and terminated by spectacular rituals, is in force. While it might to be to the advantage of a strong local group to attack a weaker neighbor in violation of the ritual truce, such attacks seldom occur. Although there have been exceptions,

Maring local groups are unlikely to violate ritual truces because their members fear that should they do so they would not receive the support of their ancestors and their bellicose enterprise would fail. It may be argued that ritual truces are advantageous to the Maring as a whole because through them the occurrence of warfare is limited to frequencies which do not endanger the survival of the population as a whole but which do permit ecologically and demographically more successful or more pressured groups to expand at the expense of those which are less so. This advantage is secured by masking from some local groups an awareness of where their own immediate material interests lie and by providing them with an awareness of non-existent entities. Awareness, as Pask has noted, involves a correlation between word systems and thing systems, but it is not necessarily the case that a relationship of direct representation is the most advantageous form of correlation.

IV

I have suggested elsewhere that the place of cognized models in the material relations of populations is analogous to that of "memories" in the controls of automated systems of material exchange and transformation. In an automated system, signals concerning the states of variables are received in the memory where they are compared to "reference" or "ideal" values or ranges of values. In response to discrepancies between the values of the signals and the reference values, programs are initiated which tend to return the value of deviating variables toward states approximating reference values or reference ranges. These corrective programs are, ideally, discontinued when the discrepancy between the signal emanating from the system component and the reference value is eliminated (Powers, Clarke and McFarland, 1960).

It is reasonable to assume that people also compare the states of components of their environments, as these states are indicated by signs, with their notions of what these states should be (reference or ideal values or ranges) and initiate corrective programs in response to discrepancies. For example, the timing of Maring ritual cycles is a function of the dynamics of pig herds. A local group signals that it is entering into a truce by sacrificing all but its juvenile pigs to its ancestors in partial payment for their assistance in the hostilities just concluded. It may not again initiate hostilities until it has completed payment to the same supernaturals through another series of large-scale sacrifices. The number of animals required for such sacrifices is not specified. There is prestige to be gained in the eyes of members of other local populations by sacrificing large numbers of pigs and this prestige can, to some extent, be converted into military support. But large pig herds are burdensome because they must be fed, and nuisances because the beasts invade gardens. When women's complaints concerning the labor they must expend in feeding pigs and the nuisance of garden invasions by pigs exceed a reference value, the limits of tolerance of a sufficient number of people to shape a consensus, a corrective program in the form of a pig festival is staged, during which the pig herd is drastically reduced. Garden invasions and women's complaints about pigs are reduced to zero or nearly so, and at the same time obligations to ancestors are fulfilled, permitting the celebrants to initiate hostilities once again.

The strategy of regarding the relationship between cognized and operational models to be that of controls to material systems has the advantage of providing us with a framework for inquiring in detailed ways into the adaptiveness of ideology. Among the questions we might ask are the following:

1. What is the relationship between (culturally recognized) signs and the environmental processes they are taken to indicate? Is it the case, for instance, that soil depletion is indicated by signs (detected) where there has been only a slight change in soil structure or composition, or only when the process is well advanced?

We may also ask about the sensitivity of the operations through which such signs induce responses. Among the Maring, for instance, it is necessary for a consensus that there is error with respect to pig herd size to develop before corrective actions are initiated. On these grounds alone regulatory operation is likely to be sluggish. In contast, a Polynesian chief can respond to signs of error or deviation without waiting for the formation of a consensus.

2. What is the relationship between reference or ideal values, which are likely to reflect directly people's wants or "values" rather than their needs, and the actual material requirements of the local population, the larger regional population, or the ecosystem as a whole? More formally, what is the relationship between the reference values or ranges of values in the cognized model and the goal ranges of the corresponding operational model? Is it the case that reference or ideal values lead a people to exceed the goal ranges of the operational model or do they lead them to initiate corrective programs before goal ranges are exceeded? It may be noted here that measurements undertaken in the field suggest that neither the desire for prestige nor their fear of ancestors lead the Maring to raise more pigs than their territories can support.

3. We may ask if corrective programs, whether they are undertaken with respect to an awareness of actual material relationships or of goals, do in fact correct the deviations in response to which they are initiated. If it were not for the fact that the very fluctuations in the size of pig herds are important in the regulation of warfare frequency, it might be said that Maring pig festivals over-correct, reducing the herds from too large to too small.

We may nevertheless note that there is considerable room for malfunction in signal detection, in the setting of reference values, and in correction, to say nothing about the lag between detection of error and correction, distortion of signals and so on.

V

Our illustrative material underlines the point made earlier that it would be erroneous to take the general adaptations of social groups to be nothing more than the maintenance of homeostasis among heaps of discrete variables. The relationships among special adaptations, that is to say among mechanisms regulating these variables, must be regulated and general adaptations must take on the form of hierarchies of regulatory mechanisms.

There may be some ambiguity in the notion of control hierarchies, and it is well to make explicit that I am referring, simply, to controls at various levels in hierarchies of inclusiveness, that is hierarchies of systems, subsystems, subsubsystems and so on. For example, if a primitive horticultural community together with its territory were taken to be a system we might be able to discriminate within it, by virtue of partial discontinuities in systemic coherence and by the existence of discrete regulatory mechanisms, a number of major subsystems, such as an enculturation subsystem, a military subsystem and a subsistence subsystem, and so on, and within these we perhaps could identify subsystems of lower order. For instance, the subsistence subsystem might include production, distribution and consumption subsystems, each composed of variables in more coherent relations with each other than with those in other subsystems and each possessed of more or less discrete regulatory mechanisms.

In the previous section we suggested that each of these regulatory mechanisms consists, at least in part, of a cognized model which includes an image of the regulated domain, corrective programs and a mechanism sensitive to error as well as reference values. The domains of controls of the lowest order include the concrete variables of biology and environment. The domains of higher order controls include the outputs of the controls of next lower order for which it sets output reference values. For instance, a production quota (an output reference value) is not likely to be set within a production system, but to emanate from the controls of a more inclusive system (here labelled a subsistence system) which regulates regulations among the outputs and demands of its several subsystems.*

*I have already noted that no natural social-ecological system is likely to be as neat as the illustrative scheme offered here. It is not always the case, for one thing, that all of the variables of a particular class (garden variables, consumption variables) will be regulated by the same mechanism. Conversely some mechanisms may regulate variables of a rather disparate sort. Institutional analyses (in Malinowski's sense) or even the use of labels associated with institutional analyses (subsistence system, commissariat, educational system, etc.) tend to make the world appear to be more rationally structured than it in fact is. We may be further misled into believing that we already know what we need to discover, namely what the systems and subsystems in the phenomena under investigation are composed of and how their components are related to each other. Natural systems and their subsystems are not to be identified through a priori classifications of variables or by particu-

Perhaps we could discriminate in controls at all levels immediate, working and long term memories (Pask 1968), and also what Bateson has called learning II or deutero learning and in some cases learning of an even higher order. But it is not with hierarchies in this sense that I am concerned at the moment. I am concerned, rather, with relationships between controls at various levels in hierarchies of inclusiveness. There are several characteristics of control hierarchies that are of interest to us here.

1. Coherence

It is likely that higher order controls operate more sporadically than those of lower order. Such sporadic, and perhaps lagging operation allows lower order controls to do what they can to correct error before more inclusive systems are brought into operation. For instance, among some primitive horticulturalists the population of a local community is continually redispersed over available land in accordance with rules of filiation, land tenure and usufructory rights. All of these conventions can be regarded as the corrective programs of low order controls operating with respect to some reference value. While this value may be a notion of the "proper" man-land ratio, it may also be tolerance for some possibly density-dependent irritation, such as intra-group bickering or witchcraft accusations (Vayda and Rappaport 1967). It is only when these low order controls are no longer capable of reducing the discrepancy between the deviation signals and reference values that expansive warfare is triggered by higher order controls acting as back-ups. In more general terms it may be argued that the hierarchical arrangement of regulatory mechanisms, operating with increasing lag and sporadicity, may inhibit the communication of local disruption to wider portions of the system. So far as I know no measure of systemic coherence, the extent to which a change in the state of one variable effects changes in the states of others, has been devised, but it may nevertheless be suggested that too great a degree of coherence can be as lethal as too little, and that systems of different sorts, machines, organisms, societies, ecosystems, are viable within different ranges of coherence. I would suspect that the degree of coherence necessary for the proper functioning of a machine or an organism would be lethal for a society, and that within societies or communities lower order systems are, and perhaps must be, more coherent than those of higher order. Along these lines it may be the case that controls in lower order systems not only operate more con-

lar kinds of output (foodstuffs, warfare), but by partial discontinuities in coherence between clusters of highly coherent variables and by the domains which particular mechanisms regulate. I have presented an overrational hierarchy merely for the sake of simplicity. Simplicity also requires that we merely note, but do not discuss, the likelihood that in any body of social-ecological phenomena there will coexist a number of control hierarchies relating to each other in extremely complex ways. It is surely permissible to attempt the analysis of one or a limited number of these hierarchies. Indeed, much more ambitious undertakings may not be feasible.

114

tinuously than higher order controls, but with narrower reference ranges, that is, less error is tolerated before corrective programs are initiated.

It seems to be the case that increasing coherence in more inclusive systems is a concomitant of evolution, and it may be that the degree of coherence in contemporary affairs is approaching the lethal. As Vickers (1968) wisely noted in his contribution to last year's conference, our problem isn't that we are not one world, but that we are, that we can neither regulate the world system nor decouple from it and that, therefore, disruptions are both more likely to occur and more likely to be transmitted with great speed from their points of origin to remote places. But such obvious dangers seem hardly to have been recognized. Increased coherence has often been regarded as a good in itself and policy making frequently seems to aim deliberately toward the achievement of states of "hyper-integration." It is well known, for instance, that colonial powers have almost invariably sought, often in the name of "development" or "modernization," to couple previously autonomous systems to a world economic system. In some instances such policies have been pursued even in the absence of economic justification, and thus seem gratuitous. At any rate, the resulting replacements of local homeostases by dependence upon world markets have sometimes been disastrous. It could be argued, of course, that the envelopment of local systems by the worldwide system has been inevitable, but it can nevertheless be asserted that the managers of this process have generally been guilty of shortsightedness or indifference concerning the outcomes of the policies they have put into play and have done little to preserve any aspect of local homeostases against the danger of disruptions of remote origin. Indeed, some aspects of colonial policy seem to be almost deliberately designed not only to couple local systems to the world system, but to destroy local homeostatic mechanisms. The unimpeded access to native peoples granted missionaries is an example. The religious practices of many primitive peoples seem to play an important part in maintaining both social and ecological equilibria. These practices should be presumed to be well adapted to these functions inasmuch as they are in most instances the products of continuous evolutionary development. Christianity, a product of advanced civilization, can make little or no contribution to the adaptation of most native peoples. Indeed, it can only disrupt them.

2. Simplicity of Higher Level Controls

We have noted that the regulatory operation which takes place in higher order controls is not the regulation of the many variables comprising the lower order systems, but simply of the outputs of the lower order systems and the relation of these outputs to each other. This suggests that in primitive societies at least the phenomena directly subject to higher order controls are likely to be less varied and complex than the phenomena subject to lower order controls. This in turn implies that cognized models forming the memories of higher order controls are likely to be simpler in structure and contain fewer components than cognized models associated with lower order controls. For instance, whereas the cognized model of the production system of a horticultural people will surely include detailed knowledge or putative knowledge of a wide range of such phenomena as soil, weeds, crops, weather and horticultural techniques, and some theory concerning the complex relations among these phenomena, the cognized model of the subsistence system, the system of next higher order, need only include knowledge or putative knowledge of the outputs and capacities and necessary conditions of existence of the production and other of its subsystems, and the simpler relations prevailing among these fewer variables.

To fulfill its functions adequately a higher order control need not "know" all or perhaps very much about the operations of the lower order systems subject to it. It need be aware only of their outputs, capacities, and within broad limits the conditions necessary for their continued existence. But it also must presume that within these limits lower order control mechanisms do operate, and it must rely upon them. We may be reminded here of Bateson's green thumb metaphor. Great gardeners, political leaders and psycho-therapists operate at high control levels. They are successful not because they are aware of all the details of the lower order systems with which they deal, but because they understand that their own high level control operations (which are directed toward maintaining coherence among a number of lower order systems) presumes the operation of lower order homeostatic mechanisms, and because wisdom or knowledge leads them to respect or even to fulfill the conditions necessary for the continued operation of these lower order control mechanisms.

Increased knowledge of the elements regulated by lower order controls, and the relations among them, does not necessarily, or perhaps even usually, lead to more effective regulation. The temptation to meddle, to subject directly to a higher order control the variables ordinarily regulated by lower order controls, probably increases with increased knowledge. But a little bit of knowledge is a dangerous thing. An awareness of the principles of homeostasis does not supply the details of any particular homeostasis, and knowledge of some of the details does not provide knowledge of all. A number of attempts at ecosystem regulation by men informed by some, but apparently insufficient, knowledge of the systems to be regulated have ended disastrously. It could be argued that increased knowledge of ecosystems results in decreased respect for them, and thus leads men to be guilty of, and subsequently to be punished for, what might be called ecological hubris. It is perhaps the case that knowledge will never be able to replace respect in man's dealings with ecological systems, for, as we have already observed, the ecological systems in which man participates are likely to be so complex that he may never have sufficient comprehension of their content and structure to permit him to predict the outcome of many of his own acts. Any theory for acting in systems which the actor doesn't understand must include a large measure of respect for endogenous regulation.

3. Systems, Social Groups and Purpose

Our discussion of control hierarchies has taken systems and their subsystems to be composed of clusters of variables discriminated from other clusters by partial discontinuities in coherence. But at one level of inclusiveness or another systems become coextensive with particular individuals or social groups, and special problems concerning purpose arise.

Some years ago Karl Deutsch (1949) suggested that we may be able to distinguish several orders of purposes, and that these might be associated with systems on all levels of inclusiveness. First order purposes are to be associated with systems composed of variables together comprising less than total organisms, and are identified by such terms as reward, adjustment, and so on. Second order purpose is individual self-preservation, while third order purposes are to be identified with the preservation of social groups of increasing magnitude and inclusiveness. Beyond these we might, according to Deutsch, note fourth order purposes associated with, perhaps, the preservation of life in general, or of order in the universe. The preservation of ecosystems could be regarded as either a third or fourth order purpose.

It may be suggested, then, that hierarchies of purposes are characteristic of control hierarchies, and further, that there is considerable opportunity for regulatory malfunction when higher and lower level systems are coextensive with inclusive and included social groups.

It would seem to be the case, in other than extraordinary circumstances, that as far as informing the behavior of participants is concerned, the purposes of the most immediate system are more cogent than the purposes of more inclusive but more remote systems. A higher wage for themselves was more cogent to New York's garbage collectors in their decision to strike recently than the possibility that garbage accumulating on the streets would encourage epidemic in the city, and the possibility of higher profits has been more compelling to steel management in the United States than the effects that increased prices might have on inflationary trends in the general economy.

From where anyone sits the world looks like a zero-sum game and it is thus likely that relations between various groups subject to the same regulatory mechanisms (for instance, labor and management) are always characterized by some conflict. One of the goals of such conflicts is usurpation, the elevation of the purpose of one's own subsystem to a position of preeminence in a more inclusive system. The attitude that justifies usurpation is nicely summed up in the phrase "What is good for General Motors is good for the United States." A similar attitude has generally been characteristic of recent man in his relations with his physical and biotic environment, for as social groups have become larger and more differentiated ecosystems have become more and more remote and their purposes less compelling. But needless to say, the world is not a congeries of zero-sum games, and what is good for General Motors is not likely to be good for the United States for an indefinite length of time. The major subsystems of complex societies have become sufficiently powerful to capture and subsequently subvert or destroy the larger social and ecological systems of which they are a part, and any social system must develop mechanisms through which its imperialistic subsystems can be "kept in their places." But the problem of developing such means is fraught with contradiction. In societies such as our own it may seem that we need to devise more elaborate political and economic regulatory mechanisms, but experience informs us that such mechanisms, for instance federal regulatory agencies, are likely to become the instruments of the very subsystems they were meant to regulate.

It may be suggested that the more discrete such agencies are, that is the more closely they are identified with particular bodies of personnel, the more vulnerable they are to capture by one or another of their subsystems. But the better they have been insulated against possible capture the more invulnerable they are should they be captured. It also seems to be the case that control mechanisms, when they are identified with particular bodies of personnel, bureaucracies, develop purposes of their own. These are likely to become rigidly defined, and are unlikely to be identical with those of the systems being regulated. The development of elaborate special control mechanisms may open unparalleled opportunities for disorder, even chaos.

In summary, we may be reminded that Bateson has suggested that it is not inappropriate to refer to man's purposeful degradation of the systems in which he participates as immoral, especially when such degradation seems to be willful, or almost so, and that immorality seems to have a structure. The three types of malfunction described in this section, "hyper-integration," "meddling" and "usurpation," can be regarded as three varieties of structural immorality. There are doubtless others, as for instance attempts to reduce coherence below viable levels. The states' rights and neighborhood school movements, attempts to preserve local patterns of segregation by partial decoupling from the larger system, might serve as examples.

VI

From immorality we may turn to sanctity. Before proceeding to the part that sanctity may play in human adaptation, a discussion of sanctity itself is necessary.

I have argued elsewhere (in press) that sanctity is to be understood in the light of the peculiarities of human communication. Human communication is symbolic communication, that is, in human communication signals are not intrinsic to their referents, but only conventionally related to them. The advantage of symbolic communication, that it frees signals from the constraints of the here and now and permits discourse on past, future, distant, imaginary and wished-for events, has been widely discussed, some scholars even claiming that the emergence of the symbol can be compared in importance and novelty to the emergence of life. But considering the fundamental importance of symbolic communication in human affairs little attention has been paid to a problem concomitant to its very virtues: Any mode of communication that employs symbols can accommodate lies. Lying seems possible if and only if a signal is not intrinsic to its referent. Lies are thus transmitted by symbolic communication and symbolic communication only. Although there seems to be some limited use of symbols by infra-human animals, man's reliance upon symbolic communication exceeds that of other animals to such an extent that it is probably for man alone that the transmission of false information becomes a serious problem. His very survival may be involved. It is plausible to argue that the survival of any population depends upon social interactions characterized by some minimum degree of orderliness and coherence, and that social orderliness and coherence depend upon communication. But communication is effective only if the recipients of messages are willing to accept, as being in at least some minimum degree true, the messages they receive. If they are unwilling or unable to give credence to received information, it is plausible to assume that their responses to particular stimuli will tend toward randomness. To the extent that actions are random they are unpredictable and are thus likely to elicit further apparently random responses on the parts of other actors. Randomness begets greater randomness, and orderliness and coherence could be reduced to such a degree that a population could not fulfill its biological needs. Credibility gaps are extremely dangerous, and societies which rely upon symbolic communication, that is to say all human societies, are faced with the problem of assuring some minimum degree of credibility and credence in the face of the ever present possibility of falsehood.

It is true, of course, that some messages present no problems. Some contain logically necessary truths and others can be assumed to be true from experience. But the preponderance of messages upon which social actions rely are concerned with systemic states and their changes and are likely to be neither logically necessary nor subject to validation from experience. Furthermore, it is often, if not usually, the case that that recipient of a message upon whih action must be taken is not in a position to verify the message even if means of verification exist, and for many messages important in the working of societies they do not. For instance, Maring men communicate their commitment to assist another group in future warfare by dancing at its festival. Hosts thus judge the extent to which they will receive military support by the size of the visiting dance contingents. But there is no procedure by which they can verify the message which the visiting dancers constitute. How then can they base weighty policy upon such messages?

It is interesting to note that messages concerning military support are transmitted by the Maring in the course of religious rituals, rituals that have a purpose, to honor dead ancestors, distinct from the messages transmitted within them. Since this is the case it is plausible to assume a belief, on the part of at least some of the participants, in the existence of deceased ancestors. Indeed to assume otherwise would be to make nonsense of the proceedings. We can thus say that fundamental to Maring religious beliefs are such propositions as "Deceased ancestors persist as sentient beings."

Now such statements are neither logically necessary truths, nor are they subject to empirical confirmation or disconfirmation. Yet they are taken to be *unquestionably* true. Indeed, paraphrasing some theologians and philosophers (Bochenski 1965, Hick 1963) I regard this characteristic, rather than substantive content, to be criterial of religious discourse, and since religious discourse is sacred discourse I take this characteristic to be criterial of sanctity as well. I am asserting that *sanctity is the quality of unquestionable truthfulness imputed by the faithful to unverifiable propositions.* As such it is not ultimately a property of objects, or putative objects, but of discourse about them. It is not, for instance, the divinity of Christ, but the assertion of his divinity, which is sacred.

While the sacred inheres ultimately in such non-material propositions as "The Godhead is a trinity," setting them above legitimate doubt, it penetrates (sanctifies) sentences concerning material objects and activities. Theological discourse may serve as the vehicle for transporting sanctity from an ultimate sacred proposition such as "The Lord our God the Lord is One" to sentences such as "Eating pork is evil," or "Pork may not be eaten," but the connection may be merely an association in time and space in rituals. Thus, such messages as "we will lend you military support" when they are transmitted in religious ritual, and thus sanctified, are taken to be true, or at least sufficiently true to serve as the bases of social action. In other words, sanctity, although it inheres ultimately in unverifiable statements, is socially important as a meta-statement about statements of a partially material nature, such as "eating pork is evil," or a fully material nature, such as "we will lend you military support." Statements all of whose terms are material may logically be amenable to verification, but as we have already observed, the recipients may be in no position to verify them. However, *to sanctify statements is to certify them.*

It would be naive to assert that sanctification insures the truth of messages, although it may help. But it can be argued that people are more likely to accept sanctified than unsanctified messages as true, and insofar as they do their responses to sanctified messages, responses likely to involve the coordinated action of social groups, will tend to be non-random and therefore predictable. That messages be at all times in fact true is not necessary. What is necessary is that social interactions be in some minimum degree orderly, and the acceptance of messages as true, whether or not they are, contributes to this orderliness. Indeed, it may make this orderliness possible. Following a lead of Bateson's (1951) it may even be claimed that belief, insofar as it results in non-random actions which lead to predictable responses, creates orderliness by creating truth. To put this differently, many of the messages crucial to the maintenance of social orderliness and coherence fall into the class of messages the validity of which is a function of the belief in them (Bateson, ibid.) Belief in them, we have argued, may be a function of their sanctification, and we might claim as far as informing behavior is concerned, sanctity forms an additional member of the set which also includes the necessary truth of logic and the empirical truth of experience.

VII

Let us return to control hierarchies. We have already noted that the sanctification which flows from ultimate sacred sentences containing non-material terms can envelop sentences consisting entirely of material terms. There are probably some general constraints upon the substance of sentences that may be sanctified, and I shall touch upon them later. But it is surely the case that sanctity can and does invest the sentences of which cognized models and their corrective programs are composed.

In this regard it may be suggested, although no studies, so far as I kow, have been made in just these terms, that cognized models in higher order controls are likely to contain more abstract and fewer concrete terms than do those of lower order controls. While this feature of control hierarchies is probably more evident in primitive societies it is to be noted in modern societies as well. The terms of economics, for instance, which may include such notions as "free enterprise" and "corporate ownership" are less concrete and carry a stronger moral connotation than those of agronomy, and the contents of the cognized models with respect to which community coherence is maintained within viable limits are likely to include yet more abstract terms, such as honor, prestige and freedom, gods, ghosts and demons. In other words, the higher the level of control, the greater the importance of moral and mythic terms in the cognized model.

Such a progression from the concrete to the abstract is expectable on several grounds. It could be argued simply that the relations among such concrete things as soils, plants and agricultural techniques put more constraints upon their conceptualization than does coherence among systems place upon its conceptualization. But more important, and more germane to our present discussion, is a matter that we raised earlier. The range of differences possible in the regulation of the components of a low order system, such as a production system, is probably narrower than that which is possible in higher order systems. The physiological requirements of cultigens, for instance, probably put greater restraints upon agricultural practices and the cognized models associated with them than the necessity to maintain coherence between production and consumption systems places upon procedures of distribution, etc., and the cognized models associated with them. Thus, to use an example from modern societies, Soviet wheat agriculture probably resembles American wheat agriculture more closely than the Soviet economic system resembles the American economic system. Since there is greater latitude or freedom in the maintenance of coherence between systems than in regulation within systems, it may be suggested that the higher its level the more arbitrary the particular control mechanism. That is, the particular control mechanism that does operate is only one of a number of possible ways in which the proper degree of systemic coherence can be maintained. However, any society must choose only one or a limited number out of the possible range if chaos is to be avoided. But the arbitrariness of the selection is possibly available to the understanding of the actors, i.e. they can conceive of other ways to maintain comparable levels of systemic coherence, and those who are subject to a control are not likely always to feel that it is operating in their immediate interests. Arbitrariness invites criticism and recalcitrance. However, to phrase regulation in moral or mythic terms, that is, to sanctify it, is to place it beyond criticism and to define recalcitrance as sacrilege. Sanctification, in other words, transforms the arbitrary into the necessary, and regulatory mechanisms which are arbitrary are likely to be sanctified.

A related point may be made in terms of another sense in which we may speak of sanctity and abstractness in control hierarchies. The systems with which we are dealing are "hybrid systems" in Pask's (1968) terms, for they consist of (*a*) bodies of discourse, which we have labelled cognized models, (*b*) material objects, and (*c*) the activities undertaken with reference to the cognized models but affecting the material objects. It thus seems to be the case that the structure of control hierarchies is "heterarchical," to use another of Pask's terms. The implication is that the level of discourse embodied in cognized models is likely to correspond to the level of control.

This possible feature of control hierarchies is of considerable significance with respect to a point already mentioned: the establishment of the output reference values of a regulatory mechanism is not a function of that regulatory mechanism but of one of higher order. It suggests that these reference values cannot be derived from the function or logic of the systems in which they operate. But since the reference value of a lower order control is an output of a higher order control it presumably may be deduced from the cognized model and input of the higher order control. In other words, reference values either are, or are something like, theorems in the higher order systems from which they emanate but either are, or are something like, axioms in the lower order systems in which they operate. Thus, the higher order controls, which we have discriminated in terms of the greater inclusiveness of the domains subject to them, may also be what Bateson (1968b), following Whitehead and Russell, has termed "of higher logical

122

type," and Gödel's theorem, or something like it, may operate between controls on different levels. (I have used the phrase "something like" because the logic of the discourse with which we are concerned may not be amenable to rigorous formalization.)

This obviously can result in problems when the lower order system into which the reference value enters from above is coextensive with an individual or social group with purposes of its own. Whereas most men are willing to accept such axioms as "the shortest distance between two points is a straight line" as the basis for certain of their behavior, they are likely to be more dubious about accepting calls to fight in distant wars or production quotas the rationale for which they do not understand and do not believe to be in their own interest (i.e. in accord with their own purposes).

Sanctification again plays an important role. On the one hand recalcitrance may, as we have already noted, become sacrilegious, and sacrilege implies punishment. But no society thrives on punishment, and sanctification also operates positively here in a way which I believe to be both more interesting and more important. We may recall an example already presented in a different context. It will be remembered that Maring groups, even when they are more powerful than their enemies, rarely launch attacks in violation of ritual truces. Although their material advantages might be well served if they did so, they do not take this to be the case because they believe that their deceased ancestors would not assist them, and that their undertaking would therefore fail.

This peace-keeping operation depends upon the non-material nature of such components of higher order cognized models as spirits of deceased ancestors. Through the invocation of unquestionable propositions concerning spirits whose very existence cannot be verified, which is to say cannot be falsified, the purpose of a higher level system, the entire Maring population, is made to appear to be the purpose of one of its subsystems, a local territorial group. The societies of ancient Mesopotamia, organized economically around the temples of gods whose well-being was conceived by their servants, the entire community, to be a necessary precondition for their own prosperity, could serve as another example, as could those archaic societies in which there was conceived to be a correlation between the health and prosperity of the king and the state of the crops. In more modern societies such morally laden and sanctified terms as "honor" may function in a similar way. In general terms, then, through sanctification the purposes of higher order systems may be injected into lower order systems. As such, sanctification operates as a counterthrust to attempts on the part of subsystems which are also social groups to promote their own purposes to positions of dominance in higher level systems. In slightly different terms, sanctity helps to keep subsystems in their places.

VIII

It is necessary, before taking up other aspects of sanctity's possible role in adaptation, to consider the foundations upon which sanctity rests.

We needn't take up the question of the origin of sanctity. Suffice it to say that on the grounds of distribution among living peoples, and on the grounds of clear inference from archaeological remains of great age (Neanderthal), the idea of the sacred must be of great antiquity. Indeed, I have suggested, following arguments advanced by Erikson (1968) and Waddington (1961), that its emergence and elaboration was bound in a relationship of mutual causality to the development and elaboration of symbolic communication (Rappaport, in press). But if it is true that the operation of control hierarchies is dependent upon their sanctity, and if this sanctity flows from ultimate sacred statements, there is a more important question for us here. Upon what does the unquestionable status of sacred statements rest and how is this status maintained?

In some societies force is employed. But I wish to delay the consideration of such societies. Where coercion is relied upon it is coercion, and not sanctity, upon which the operation of the control hierarchy depends. I wish to confine discussion at this point to systems which are distinguished by the absence or virtual absence of institutionalized differences in coercive ability between individuals or social segments, a state of affairs not uncommon among horticultural and hunting and gathering peoples.

It is in such egalitarian societies that the importance of religious experience in providing both an epistemological basis for sacred propositions and a mechanism for maintaining their unquestionable status is clearest.

Although secular information of direct social import is transmitted within many religious rituals, it is also the case, as we have already observed, that religious rituals (virtually by definition) are undertaken, implicitly or explicitly, with respect to sacred propositions. While participants do not always experience strong emotion in the course of a ritual, it is probably the case that ritual participation does affect the emotional states of the faithful at least some of the time. While some religions emphasize ecstasy, others cultivate serenity and yet others involve "feelings of awe." All that seems to be common to religious experience generally is that it is ineffable, that is to say, non-discursive.

The importance of the non-discursive aspect of religious experience cannot be exaggerated. Inasmuch as the experience is non-discursive it cannot be falsified. The truth of such an experience is sufficiently demonstrated by its mere occurrence. Moreover, it cannot be discredited by the discourse of the conscious mind. It happens and it is felt, and it therefore carries with it a subjective quality of truth. And since the experience is a response to the enunciation of a sacred proposition, or occurs in a place or in a ritual associated with such a proposition, that proposition partakes of the same sense of truth. I am suggesting, in other words, that ultimate sacred propositions are taken to be unquestionably true because their enunciation in ritual or in the symbols kept in holy places elicits from the faithful a non-discursive, and therefore unfalsifiable, affirmation. Moreover, when this affirmation is given by participation in a public ritual it is thereby transformed into a discursive statement (which might be rendered "I or we affirm the sacred proposition") amenable to transmission to other participants. We have already argued that the latter are likely to accept such messages as true because of the sacred context in which they are transmitted. The circularity of this operation needn't trouble us because it doesn't trouble the faithful. Indeed, they are unlikely to be aware of it. Ritual, thus, not only invokes in the participants private religious experiences, it provides a mechanism for translating these private experiences into messages of social import and also a means for certifying these messages.

We may now suggest the outlines of an encompassing cybernetic loop. Inasmuch as the religious experience is an intrinsic part of the more inclusive emotional dynamics of the organism, and inasmuch as the emotional dynamics of an organism must be closely related to its material state, it is plausible to assume that religious experiences are affected by material conditions. But the latter are, particularly in primitive societies, in some degree a function of the operation of the control hierarchy which the religious experience itself supports. Thus, the willingness, indeed the ability of the members of a congregation to affirm through religious experience the ultimate sacred propositions which sanctify the control hierarchy may be in considerable measure a function of the effectiveness of the hierarchy in maintaining equilibria in and among those variables which define their material well-being in the long run, and thus adaptation.

IX

In the last section I employed the phrases "in some degree" and "in considerable measure." In part these expressions merely indicate the speculative nature of this formulation, and the vagueness of some of its terms, but they are also meant to carry a heavier burden.

First, I wished to suggest looseness of coupling between the states of variables defining adaptation on the one hand and willingness or ability to give non-discursive affirmation to sacred propositions on the other. Such coupling has to be loose, and lagging in operation, if the system is not to succumb to disruptions attendant upon over-coherence, that is, if it is not to be responsive to short-run parochial discontents. Sanctification must be allowed to support programs apparently detrimental to the low order purposes of some, or even all, of those subject to them for more or less protracted periods if higher order purposes are to be served. Lag permits distinctions to be made between short-term hardships required by the fulfillment of higher order purposes and those resulting from the effects of deep-seated regulatory error, such as environmental degradation. It may be that the duration of the lag is related to the type and intensity of hardship, but as time goes on more and more of those subject to the hierarchy will find conditions sufficiently intolerable to make them, first, unable to affirm through private experience the sacred propositions, and perhaps later, unwilling even to participate in ritual. Thus sooner or later regulation itself must be adjusted if men are not to seek new gods.

It is, of course, possible to make such adjustments without challenging ultimate sacred propositions. Since these propositions *are* propositions, and since they are likely to contain no material terms, they do not constitute specific directives nor are they irrevocably bound to particular social forms. This means that their association with particular directives or institutions is not intrinsic, but is, rather the product of interpretive acts. Any product of interpretation allows reinterpretation, but reinterpretation does not challenge ultimate sacred statements. It merely disputes previous interpretations.

Reinterpretation possibly occurs in all of the cognized models in the hierarchy. Since reinterpretation can be considered to be learning it becomes important to inquire into the extent to which such models are capable of learning of higher type (Bateson 1968b). Surely they must differ in this respect.

A possible malfunction in sanctification should be noted in this context. It seems sometimes to happen that sentences directly involved in regulation (thus containing material terms and sometimes cast in the form of explicit directives) are taken not merely to be sanctified by ultimate sacred propositions but to *be* ultimate sacred propositions. When this occurs regulation becomes highly resistant to adjustment through reinterpretation with, perhaps, disastrous results. A possible modern example of such confusion in "level of sanctity" which a sentence is to be assigned is the resistance of the Catholic Church to birth control. To an outsider it appears that the legitimization of birth control could be accomplished through reinterpretation, that is, without any challenge to dogma.

There was a second important reason for introducing indeterminate language into the general cybernetic scheme. Our discussion so far has implied that the function and nature of religious experience plays little or no part in shaping other components of the system which it helps to regulate. I don't believe this to be so.

What I have been calling religious experience is, I think, at the very least a species of what Bateson and others would call aesthetic experience. In fact, Bateson, in his prefatory paper and elsewhere (1967, 1968a), and Susanne K. Langer (1953) have both argued or implied a connection between the aesthetic and the sacred and both have implicated in this connection non-rational, non-discursive, processes. Bateson argues that art is part of man's quest for "grace." He tells us that Aldous Huxley used this term to designate a quality of naiveté and simplicity inhering in both his concep-

126

tion of God and in the behavior and communication of animals. This behavior and communication, being dominated by primary processes, is free of deceit and purposefulness, products of reason. To Langer art is "significant form," and its significance is "that of a symbol, a highly articulated sensuous object, which by virtue of its structure can express the forms of vital experience which language is peculiarly unfit to convey" (p. 32). She means by "vital" to refer to the "dynamism of subjective experience" (p. 31), which she then identifies with feeling and emotion. Later, following Cassirer, she suggests, as have many others, that the "powers" that personified inhabit myth and cosmology are constructed out of these non-rational processes, but adds that their existence in the unconscious is brought to awareness through the experience of art, particularly participation in dance which she believes to have originated in religious ritual, and which remains an important part of the religious rituals of many peoples (p. 182).

It may be inferred from Langer's argument that not all discourse is equally amenable to sanctification, and that if discourse is to be sacred, that is, if it is to be non-discursively affirmed as such, its structure must be in some degree compatible with the structure and dynamics of the non-rational. To put it differently, the structure of sacred discourse is subject to constraints imposed by the requirements of social and ecological regulation on the one hand, but also by the structure and dynamics of non-rational processes (and perhaps *their* regulation) on the other. Questions are then raised concerning the extent to which discourse which is compatible with the structure and dynamics of non-rational processes is appropriate to social and ecological regulation, and vice versa.

Bateson suggests that the two constraining forces are compatible. Whereas we may infer from Langer's discussion of Cassirer and other sources that the stuff of the unconscious and affective is imposed upon sacred discourse, Bateson suggests that this imposition has, at least in the past, conferred adaptive advantages with respect to social and ecological factors by permitting men to use their total organisms, and not simply their consciousness, as analogues in their attempts to understand nature. The narrowly defined and often destructive purposes which are to be found in consciousness are thereby, if not overcome, at least "put in their places" by being included in a larger structure which includes materials drawn from non-rational as well as conscious processes. While the unconscious does not contain information concerning ecological systems, the structure of the total mind, of which the unconscious and affective are parts, resembles that of ecological systems, whereas the structure of consciousness alone does not. Thus analogues of ecological systems constructed from the materials of the non-rational as well as the rational have a "structural wisdom" that analogues built from consciousness alone would not be likely to possess.

Against this it might be argued that as the reason has purposes so does the heart, that these, as Freud and others have claimed, may also be destructive, and that their representation in the discourse through which men seek to understand the social and ecological systems in which they participate must be disruptive. But we have been learning in recent years that the non-rational may not be as demonic as Freud, who dealt mainly with pathological cases in a perhaps pathological civilization, believed them to be. However, even to grant the existence of demons in the unconscious is not to argue that they have not served as adequate metaphors for the destructive forces of nature.

I am inclined, then, to agree with Bateson conerning the compatibility of the forces constraining the structure and substance of sacred discourse, and I think that ethnographic materials justify such agreement. We can be confident, I think, that myths and other forms of sacred discourse do include figures and relationships drawn from the unconscious, and we can also note, among many primitive peoples, that the selfsame discourse is important in the effective regulation of social, ecological or demographic variables. It is thus possible to argue that among some primitive peoples, at least, non-rational processes do not disrupt but strengthen the operation of the encompassing cybernetic loop that I earlier sketched.

X

The sacred, we have argued, has played an important role in the adaptation of technologically simple communities to their social, biotic and physical environments. But the role of the sacred changes with changing political circumstances, and these changes, in turn, seem to be in considerable degree a function of technological development.

We have noted already that the sacred is highly adaptable and a great variety of sentences concerning a wide variety of regulatory mechanisms may be sanctified. Among the Maring, for instance, most sentences are instructions for corrective programs, sentences such as "the ancestors demand the slaughter of all adult and adolescent pigs during the festival." In other societies sanctification seems to invest sentences concerning authorities or regulatory agencies, rather than specific programs, sentences such as "the chief has great mana."

It may be noted that although we, and perhaps the faithful, cast such sentences in the declarative, they imply that the directives of the regulatory agencies, or authorities, to which they allude should or must be obeyed. If political power is taken to be the product (in an arithmetic sense, much as force is the product of mass times velocity) of [men] × [resources] × [organization] (Bierstadt 1950), we might argue that as far as securing compliance with directives is concerned, sanctity operates as a functional alternative to political power among some of the world's peoples. Indeed, if authorities are taken to be loci in communications networks from which directives emanate we may be able to discern in history and ethnography a continuum from societies, such as the Maring, that are regulated by sacred conventions in the absence or near absence of human authorities through societies in which highly sanctified authorities, such as Polynesian chiefs, have little actual power, to societies in which authorities have great power but less sanctity. It would be plausible to expect this continuum to correlate roughly with technological development, for advanced technology places in the hands of authorities coercive instruments that are not only effective, but also likely to be unavailable to those subject to them.

Our argument implies that the development of technology disrupts the cybernetics of adaptation. In the technologically undeveloped society, authority is maintained by sanctification, but sanctity itself is maintained by religious experience which, I have argued, is responsive to the effectiveness of the control hierarchy in maintaining the variables defining adaptation in viable ranges. In the technologically developed society the authority is freed, to the extent that technology has provided it with coercive instruments, from the constraints imposed by the need to maintain its sanctity and therefore from the corrective operations that the maintenance of sanctity implies.

This is not to say that authorities even in technologically advanced societies dispense entirely with sanctity. It is to say that the relationship between sanctity and authority changes. Previously a characteristic of the discourse associated with the regulation of the entire system, sanctity comes more and more to be concentrated in the discourse of a subsystem, "the church." When it is so confined sacred discourse is likely to continue to ratify authority, but it tends also to become decreasingly concerned with the environment of the here and now and increasingly concerned with ethics and with the environment of the hereafter, the promise of which stirs the meek, the good and the orderly to religious experience. But religious experience, and the rituals in which it occurs, previously part of an encompassing corrective loop, are eventually left with little more than those functions long recognized by students of society: they reduce anxieties produced by stressors over which the faithful have little or no control, and they contribute to the discipline of social organization (see, for example, Homans 1941, p. 172). To the extent that the discourse of religion, religious ritual and religious experience contribute to the maintenance of orderliness and the reduction of anxiety without contributing to the correction of the factors producing the anxiety and disorder they are not adaptive but pathological. Indeed, their operation seems to resemble that of neuroses (see, for example, Freud 1907).*

Whereas in the technologically undeveloped system authority was contingent upon sanctification, in technologically more developed societies sanctity becomes an instrument of authority. Compliance and docility are cultivated more efficiently and inexpensively by religious experiences in-

---

*This is not to say that religion *is* a neurosis, nor that to practice religion is a symptom of neurosis. Moreover, like neurotic symptoms it may be preferable to available alternatives.

spired by hopes of post mortem salvation than by the coercion of police and inquisitions. But although force may remain hidden, and although religious experience may be encouraged, it is nevertheless the case that in some systems the unquestionable status of the discourse for which sanctity is claimed rests ultimately upon force. In such societies authority is no longer contingent upon sanctity; the sacred, or that for which sanctity is claimed, has become contingent upon authority.

In the last paragraph I used the phrase "discourse for which sanctity is claimed" rather than "sacred discourse." I earlier argued that (a) sacred discourse rests ultimately upon propositions whose unquestionable status is contingent upon affirmation in religious experiences which (b) link these propositions, and the rest of the control hierarchy, adaptively to living processes in both the faithful themselves and the ecological systems in which they participate. It may be misleading, then, to use the term "sacred" to refer to discourse (a) the unquestionable status of which rests ultimately upon force, and (b) which is pathologically linked to the living processes of the faithful and not linked at all to the ecological systems in which the faithful participate.

It is interesting to recall here a distinction de Rougemont (1944) made some years ago between ordinary lies, the transmission of messages known by the sender to be untrue, and those lies which tamper with the very canons of truth. To these, in consideration of the devil's putative proclivity for appearing to be what he is not, de Rougemont applied the picturesque label "diabolical lies." It may not be inappropriate to place in this category assertions of sanctity for discourse the unquestionable status of which rests ultimately upon force while appearing to rest upon non-discursive affirmation, and which forms part of a pathology while appearing to confer advantages upon those who give it credence.

XI

It is not only the ultimate corrective loop that is disrupted by the degradation of sanctity. We earlier suggested that within the control hierarchy itself sanctity operated to prevent the promotion of the purposes of subsystems to positions of predominance in more inclusive systems. This function is also endangered, distorted or destroyed by the emergence of authorities with a technologically based capacity to secure compliance through force. Whereas the charge of sacrilege as well as rebellion can be levelled against recalcitrant segments or subsystems of the system, it is also the case that any segment or subsystem possessing sufficient manpower, resources and organization to capture the mechanisms regulating the more inclusive systems is in a position to claim that its own purposes are sacred. In short, when sanctity becomes contingent upon authorities whose ability to secure compliance rests upon force it becomes irrelevant to the maintenance of the hierarchical ordering of purposes.

It is not only by making possible the capture and degradation of the sacred that technology disrupts the self-corrective tendencies of natural ecological systems. Technological development, obviously, is also correlated with increased coherence, increased ability to alter environments and increased ability to meddle comprehensively in the regulation of systems which are incompletely understood. Somewhat less obviously technology develops purposes of its own.

Galbraith (1967) and others before him have argued that the products of modern industry are so complex and so much lead time and investment is required to produce them, that industry could not function if it were subject to traditional regulatory mechanisms, such as the market. Industrial firms have, therefore, grown to a size which permits them to become independent of the money market for funding their investments, to set demands for their own products through mass communications media, and to control prices charged them by their own suppliers.

It is important to note that despite differences in ownership arrangements there is little difference in the organization of industrial firms in the U.S.S.R and the U.S., according to Galbraith. In both the complexity of the technology is such that effective management must inhere in hierarchies of experts. The mature corporation, even in capitalist societies, is no longer operated for the benefit of the owners, who have become anonymous, but for the purposes of the firm itself. These organizational purposes, with which the members of the managerial technostructure identify, are neither more nor less than the survival and enlargement of the firm; the fulfillment of these purposes merely requires that its output be maintained and increased.

Since these firms are enormous and their products are specialized their effective operation becomes central to the economy of the industrial state. They therefore develop special claims on the apparatus of government. Indeed, the organizational boundaries between governments and industrial firms become increasingly vague, and the purposes of industry more and more usurp positions of preeminence within the society as a whole. "What is good for General Motors is good for the United States." In what amounts to a further degradation of sanctity, unquestionable status is claimed for such propositions, which also often include such non-material terms as "freedom," "individualism," "private enterprise," and so on.

Man's ecological dominance is thus replaced by the dominance of industry, and as climax ecosystems once gave way to anthropocentric ecosystems, so anthropocentric ecosystems give way over wider and wider areas to concentrations of machinery and conrete from which most living things are excluded.

It would be absurd to rail against the existence of industry. It will not, and perhaps cannot, be abolished save by a cataclysm that might also abolish everything that lives, and it ought not to be. The problem is one of preserving life even in the presence of industry, or better, to return industry to the service of living.

Science of course has a role. While it is surely the case that much of science has been devoted to the development of technology and has thereby made substantial contributions to environmental disruption, the partnership of science and technology is recent, uneasy, and incomplete. It is of course true that the "scientific and educational estate," to use Galbraith's term, has grown enormously in response to industry's need for trained men to serve it. But some men are also educated and, becoming aware of the circular structure of the universe through such disciplines as ecology, physiology, cybernetics and even anthropology, become critical of the industry for which they or others have been trained. Knowledge, encouraged by industry for its own purposes, sometimes achieves an ancient wisdom which leads it to devise means for controlling that which nurtured it. Such disciplines as ecology and cybernetics are themselves part of a cybernetic mechanism.

Not unrelated, there is still sanctity. Although sanctity may become degraded in the churches, throughout history revitalistic movements have again and again emerged in the streets and in the fields among men sensing, and perhaps suffering from, the malfunction of control hierarchies that cannot reform themselves. Depending upon the propositions to which they accord sanctity, these movements have sometimes been corrective, sometimes more disruptive than that to which they are a response. Some of those that have apparently achieved success have, in the course of becoming institutionalized, themselves reduced the sacred to the status of authority's instrument. It is, perhaps, seldom clear in the early stages of such movements whether they will be pathological or adaptive, or whether, adaptive at first, they will later become pathological.

There is again in the streets and on the campuses a movement among youth who, rejecting subjugation to the purposes of machines, are in search of new sets of sacred propositions. The outlook for this movement, which is perhaps singularly amorphous, is not yet clear. Certainly in some of its aspects it seems destructive. But there are also indications that at least some of those participating are ready to accord sanctity to those propositions of ecology, physiology, anthropology and cybernetics that once again assert the circular structure of a world composed of a multiplicity of living things. Indeed, one of its prophets not only calms his followers with mantras during confrontations with the police, on quieter occasions he quotes Bateson and Commoner (Ginsberg 1969).

Whether such movements are sufficient to the tasks confronting them it is too soon to tell, but their strength is not to be underestimated. The anti-war movement, for instance, was able to drive a president from office. But I do not cite the youth and anti-war movements to suggest that with them, necessarily, lies salvation. I mention their emergence, and the emergence of the biological, social and cybernetic disciplines only to underline the obvious: that corrective, or potentially corrective forces emerge through

132

unplanned evolutionary processes, and to suggest that theories of action should be predicated upon the existence and continual generation of such forces. Indeed, if such a theory is to avoid the dangers attendant upon meddling in the regulation of highly complex and poorly understood systems, it should focus upon spontaneously emerging corrective forces and upon their nurturance. No clear line can or need be drawn between planned intervention on the one hand and the nurturance of spontaneous forces on the other, but emphasis in a theory of action should be on the latter. Such a theory of action should aim toward defining those actions which encourage the development of regulatory mechanisms as a class, rather than attempting to specify the corrective actions to be undertaken in various circumstances. Such work is better left to ecology, urban planning or the social sciences. To be somewhat more specific, the theory should provide a framework for (1) identifying spontaneously emerging forces as potentially corrective or disruptive with respect to specific conditions and, hopefully, systems as wholes; (2) understanding the processes by which such forces are generated, maintained, and directed: (3) specifying the conditions which encourage their development; (4) understanding the processes or conditions which tend to channel emerging but inchoate forces into corrective or disruptive courses of action; (5) understanding the processes by which such forces are or may be transformed into more or less durable regulatory mechanisms, i.e., "institutionalized"; (6) discovering or inventing the procedures by which regulatory mechanisms may be prevented from becoming rigid and unresponsive.

Both science and sanctity will surely have places in the substance of such a theory, and perhaps in its epistemology as well. In the arena of action itself I believe that it is the task of those disciplines which are concerned with the necessary interdependence of living things to provide viable propositions to which men can accord sacred status.

References Cited

Bateson, Gregory. 1951. Conventions of communication: where validity depends upon belief. In Jurgen Reusch and Gregory Bateson, *Communication, the social matrix of psychiatry*. New York: Norton.
———. 1967. Style, grace and information in primitive art. Paper presented for Wenner-Gren conference "Primitive art and society."
———. 1968a. Effects of conscious purpose on human adaptation. Paper prepared for Wenner-Gren symposium "The effects of conscious purpose on human adaptation."
———. 1968b. The logical categories of learning and communication and the acquisition of world views. Paper prepared for Wenner-Gren symposium "World views: their nature and their role in culture."
———. 1969. The moral and aesthetic structure of human adaptation. Paper prepared for Wenner-Gren symposium "The moral and aesthetic structure of human adaptation."

Bierstadt, Robert. 1950. An analysis of social power. *American Sociological Review* 15:730–38.

Bochenski, Joseph M. 1965. *The logic of religion.* New York: New York University Press.

Commoner, Barry. 1968. The cybernetic organization of biological systems. Paper prepared for Wenner-Gren symposium "The effects of conscious purpose on human adaptation."

Deutsch, Karl. 1949. Some notes on research on the role of models in the natural and social sciences. *Synthese* 7:506–33. Reprinted as "Toward a cybernetic model of man and society" in Walter Buckley, ed., *Modern systems research for the behavioral scientist.* Chicago: Aldine, 1968.

Erikson, Erik. 1968. The development of ritualization. In Donald Cutler, ed., *The religious situation: 1968.* Boston: Beacon Press.

Freud, Sigmund. 1907. Obsessive actions and religious practices. *Z. Religionspsych.* 1:4–12. Trans. in James Strachey, gen. ed., *The standard edition of the complete psychological works of Sigmund Freud,* vol. 9. London: Hogarth, 1959.

Galbraith, John. 1967. *The new industrial state.* Boston: Houghton-Mifflin.

Ginsberg, Allen. 1969. Playboy interview: Allen Ginsberg. *Playboy,* April 1969.

Hick, John. 1963. *The philosophy of religion.* Englewood Cliffs, N.J.: Prentice-Hall.

Homans, George. 1941. Anxiety and ritual: the theories of Malinowski and Radcliffe-Brown. *American Anthropologist* 45:164–72.

Kalmus, H. 1966. Control hierarchies. In H. Kalmus, ed., *Regulation and control of living systems.* New York: Wiley.

Langer, Susanne K. 1953. *Feeling and form.* New York: Scribner's.

Pask, Gordon. 1968. Some mechanical concepts of goals, individuals, consciousness and symbolic evolution.

Powers, W. T.; R. K. Clark; and R. L. McFarland. 1960. A general feedback theory of human behavior. *Perceptual and Motor Skills* 11:71–88.

Rappaport, Roy A. 1968. *Pigs for the ancestors.* New Haven, Conn.: Yale University Press.

——. In press. Systems and sanctity. In T. Harding, ed., *Creative anthropology.* Chicago: Scott, Foresman.

de Rougemont, Denis. 1944. *La part du diable.* Nouvelle version. New York: Brentano's.

Vadya, A. P., and Roy A. Rappaport. 1967. Ecology, cultural and non-cultural. In James Clifton, ed., *Introduction to cultural anthropology.* Boston: Houghton-Mifflin.

Vickers, Geoffrey. 1968. A theory of reflexive consciousness. Paper prepared for Wenner-Gren conference "The effects of conscious purpose on human adaptation."

Gary Snyder

On Geography
Interview conducted by Richard Grossinger and David Wilk
9 November 1971

GROSSINGER: I'll ask you to talk first about regions. What sorts of things you've done in your own region. Or regionalism in general.

SNYDER: Well, the first thing is establishing the criteria for defining a region, a set of criteria, and that in itself is very interesting... since, even though we know better, we are accustomed to accepting the political boundaries of counties and states, and then national boundaries, as being some kind of regional definition; and although, in some cases, there is some validity to those lines, I think in many cases, and especially in the far West, the lines are often quite arbitrary and serve only to confuse people's sense of natural associations and relationships. So, for the state of California, which is the only area I'm capable of talking about really right now, what was most useful originally for us was to look at the Kroeber maps in the *Handbook of California Indians*, which showed the distribution of the original Indian culture groups and tribes (culture areas), and then to correlate that with other maps, some of which are in Kroeber's *Cultural and Natural Areas of Native North America*... and just correlate the overlap between ranges of certain types of flora, between certain types of biomes, and climatological areas, and cultural areas, and get a sense of that region, and then look at more or less physical maps and study the drainages, and get a clearer sense of what drainage terms are and correlate those also. All these exercises toward breaking our minds out of the molds of political boundaries or any kind of habituated or received notions of regional distinctions.

There's a lot of background, of course, to such an interest: like why would people arrive at a point of trying to see things in that way. Without going back over all that, because I think we know that, really, I'll just say there are two things behind it. One is political; the other is ecological. The political side of it is a long-range, a long-term feeling we've all had that political entities are not real. Simply that. A political anarchist position: that the boundaries drawn by national states and so forth don't represent any sort of real entity. But that kind of perception's been around for a long time, and it's been a more or less academic perception, a theoretical perception, whereas what gives reality to this kind of thinking now is the realization—in terms of efficient and elegant associations of natural systems, the sort that men are going to have to, and want to, live in in the long run (if there's going to be a condition of harmonious growth rather than outrageous growth)—that people have to learn a sense of region, and what is possible within a region, rather than indefinitely assuming that a kind of promiscuous distribution of goods and long-range transportation is always going to be possible . . . since the energy resources apparently won't be there, quite likely won't be there. And that brings you back into thinking more in terms of your human scope and your human scale: what can you do in an area that you can ride a horse or walk on, and what are the things that you rely on in that case, what resources do you develop. And that gives you a very strong, concrete sense of how regions and then subregions and sub-subregions work, and makes a study of aboriginal native peoples' ways of life more than just an academic exercise.

GROSSINGER: How has that worked in your region?

SNYDER: Well, in our region, which is the Nevada County west slope of the Sierra drainage of the Yuba, South Fork, Middle Fork, North Fork of the Yuba River, in our region, white settlement was determined almost entirely by the Gold Rush, and so it has no relation to anything which is on the surface; it has relation to that which is under the surface, or was under the surface, and is of almost no value now in making any sense. Other things happened, such as, because of early logging and fire, there was a period of grazing, ranching, that was made possible, which, as it turned out, was a very short-term phase; and the grass succession was rapidly replaced by the manzanita and forest succession again, and so the tendency of that whole area is to go into forest; old farms are abandoned and are turning back into woods. Consequently, nowadays any of us who think about any gardening or farming think about it in very limited terms as something which is possible in special areas but not desirable to the region as a whole (since the region produces a great deal of life without human interference, enough life to support human beings, in small numbers, in reasonable numbers). All this is part of defining—California.

GROSSINGER: What clue does American Indian demography give to the present state of culture in California?

SNYDER: The Indian cultures give you a sense of what California probably in some sense—quote—*is*. That is, the way it divides up people's habitats and the things it makes them dependent on still holds, but there have been some profound changes in the state. The greatest single change has been the draining of the Sacramento Valley and the San Joaquin Valley, the draining of the tule swamps. You see, the great central valley of California was originally a vast area of swamp; tule is a type of reed or rush that grew in abundance in the swamps. The state has been profoundly altered, first with the Spanish grazing and ranching, and then later with the deliberate agriculture, the draining of the swamps of the great central valley. The great central valley itself was never a place of much habitation. Indians lived on the margins of it, in the eastern margins and the western margins, in zones between the hills and the valley, the hills and the plains, where they would be able to draw up higher into the hills in the winter and be above the rather chilly tule fogs, and move out into the tule swamps in the summer and other times of year when it was convenient for varieties of wild plants that were edible and out there, and for hunting the tule elk, and for snaring and netting and trapping the millions upon millions of water fowl that pass through, and also there are large herds of prong-horned antelopes in the central valley. And the grasses of the plains and hills were different from the grasses you see now; they were all perennial bunch grasses... whereas the grasses now are all European grasses, mostly annuals, all annuals, a lot of cheat grass, which has reduced the quality of the range. So all of that great biological richness of these enormous swamps, plains, was drained, and the water fowl were all shot off and so forth, and it's been turned over to tractor agriculture; that's a major change. And the tule elk is virtually extinct: that's the first great impact of man in California, which modern Californians know little of. The draining of the swamps and the destruction of the water fowl flocks all took place in the same period, in the 1850's and '60's, and that was a period of intense market hunting where what would now be considered game birds were sold in the marketplace, in large numbers, at dirt cheap prices, by people who went out and shot them commercially, with giant shotguns that would kill three hundred at one blast. And that's what Raymond Dasmun has described as, that single period between 1850 and 1865, the greatest single destruction of wildlife for its period of time in the history of the world... taking place right there in California.

GROSSINGER: How do you get your information on local soils?

SNYDER: What we do with finding out about local soils is go to the local soil conservation bureau, and those fellas come out and spend a couple of days with you, very relaxed, and very helpful, and take a soil auger along and bore profiles of the soil at different ponts, and tell you what's going on out there, and it's all free.

GROSSINGER: You were saying something about Sauer and local agriculture.

SNYDER: Yes, I was just reading that the other day. Sauer says the Mediterranean is the best model for California agriculture because we have summer drouth and wet winters, which is not typical of the rest of the country. The rest of the country gets rain in the summer; you see, California doesn't; it's a different plant zone; it really is.

GROSSINGER: And you were speaking earlier of that signature with the mushroom and the deer.

SNYDER: I was simply saying that with the rains, and the snows in the high country, the higher country, the deer move down, and, as it happened this year, the rains brought the deer down, and brought the deer mushroom out at exactly the same period of time, so that the deer arrived and began to eat the deer mushroom, which was there waiting for them, which is called deer mushroom because deer love it so, and they smell it under the oak duff, and they kick back the oak leaves, and find it and then eat it.

GROSSINGER: Is the fact of the nation being so large and complex part of the inevitable spur toward regionalism?

SNYDER: I'm not saying that the continent as a whole, or even the planet as a whole, cannot be, in some sense, grasped and understood, and indeed it should be, but for the time, especially in North America, we are extremely deficient in regional knowledge—that as invaders here, who have never stayed in any one place long enough to develop a sound sense of what the system of a given region is; it is like a prior exercise almost, to have a really strong sense of how things work and to be able to move through the seasons with fairly accurate knowledge of what's going on within a given region at any given time of year and to know how your own life and food production is related to that. Rather than being limiting, that gives you a lot of insight into understanding the whole thing, the larger systems.

Let me say something on top of that. We had some people stop by last summer who wanted to videotape a whole lot of what some of us and my neighbors were doing, and everyone said they weren't interested in being videotaped; and their response, because their intentions are certainly good ... their response was: don't you want to participate in the spreading and dissemination of knowledge with other people and serve a communications role; and the natural reaction to that on the part of a number of people, and myself included, was—at this point there is no use in disseminating knowledge of this order to people who are not in any way equipped to grasp it; and what we would be interested in doing is to share knowledge with the people who have similar knowledge of their own territory, because we'll understand what they have to say and they'll understand what we'll have to say; but to put it out into the mass media, even like intellectual or avant-garde mass media, is simply to titillate and to arouse a lot of intellectual notions without giving anyone any grounding in it. Consequently, you could say, roughly, there is a world network of urban centers, all of which are relatively similar, and any urban person can be put down in any other city and he'll know how to find his way around; and that network has extremely swift information and communications systems. There is also a much older network of country, rural, traditional cultures that have been in contact for millennia, that share basic ways of dealing with things, and they too know each other and recognize each other whenever brought into contact; and there is an internationalism possible on that level which is not generally recognized. But what I'm driving at is simply this: from getting more skills where I am I know how much better I could talk to a Tibetan

138

nomad now, and I understand more of what Japanese farmers were doing, and I expect that that kind of depth and potential communicability will go on on a level which really hasn't been seen much.

GROSSINGER: This leads me to ask you to say something again about the lost technology, the one we've lost in taking on this one.

SNYDER: There's a lost technology, and there's a ghost technology that was never developed that always existed like a ghost somewhere off to the side . . . and they are similar; they are both technologies of independence and decentralization, and decentralized energy sources. Aldous Huxley used to talk about that, you know; in one of his novels, *After Many a Summer Dies the Swan,* I think he talks about it. First of all, with our present technology, we tend to forget that there were a number of very workable and, in some cases, downright elegant solutions to our problems, our daily problems, of life on the farm, in the eighteenth century, which was kind of like the high point of that, that we've forgotten about, and we tend to exaggerate the problems human beings would have if . . . there were no fossil fuels simply because of our ignorance of what the other ways of doing it were, that those methods are there . . . like waterwheels, who uses waterwheels anymore to grind flour, and yet it's evident that waterwheels are non-polluting and non-resource-destructive, and very workable. Or an even more interesting example is the Pelton wheel. The Pelton wheel was developed by a mining engineer named Pelton who lived in Camptonville, California, only 25 miles from where I am, in a town that only has a population of about 30, as a maximal efficiency waterwheel. He specifically designed the shape of the little cups on the wheel, put the wheel on bearings, balanced it in a very perfect way, and instead of running off of a flow of water, you have to have maybe a 200-foot head, and then a very small jet, that is, it's nozzled right down, and the jet hits the cups at right angles, and the cups spin on a low-friction bearing, and turn a shaft . . . and a Pelton wheel can be made in any size. Now the Pelton wheel served in the northern mines, the northern mines district of California, for a number of years, and served remarkably well, only to be replaced ultimately by electricity . . . so that the Pelton wheel technology has been forgotten about, but they ran a huge deep-shaft gold mine called the North Star Gold Mine . . . it ran for several decades entirely powered by Pelton wheels operating air pumps that compressed air; the Pelton wheels compressed air and it ran all the equipment down in the mines thousands of feet deep, compressed air, no electricity whatsoever. I've heard about this; I haven't seen it, but I've heard about it: a fellow in the next county north, Plumas County, who has a Pelton wheel about eleven inches in diameter running off a jet of water which is only an eighth of an inch in diameter, with which he powers his whole house; it makes enough electricity to run a house, just a little water wheel this big . . .

WILK: What does he use for a generator?

SNYDER: He runs an electric generator off of that wheel... and like an eighth-inch jet of water, which means: one small creek, with enough head on it, which you do with plastic pipe, PVC pipe. That's what I mean by a ghost technology, a technology that is part of the industrial revolution but is off to the side a little bit and never gets quite developed... because everything in the technology which did get attention was in the direction of centralization and proliferation of products and so forth, and the other angles, that would, say, liberate men to live in a decentralized way, just like all the ideas that the Department of Agriculture was circulating in the '30's in the direction of self-sufficient homesteads, under Roosevelt, when there was a period that the government and Department of Agriculture actually thought that self-sufficient homesteads were the coming thing. All that information is set aside somewhere and forgotten about; that's the ghost technology. The combination of that alternative decentralist self-sufficiency technology plus the technology that was forgotten, that is just like around the corner, is a great potential sensible living capacity for use in some other time... in some future time... even right now if you want to use it. That whole Pelton wheel's fascinating to me; I'm going to develop a Pelton wheel myself... or like what Allen Ginsberg's got on his farm, a hydraulic ram pump, a nonelectric, self-propelling water-pump system, that will pump any amount of water if you just have time; it will fill up a huge water tank. I'll send you a picture of a Pelton wheel; they're very beautiful things. They have them on display and so forth in little parks around the county...

GROSSINGER: Like they was history.

SNYDER: Yeah, like they was history.

GROSSINGER: What would you say to someone who didn't want to do farmwork, who, in fact, wanted to be liberated from it because it's back-breaking?

SNYDER: It's only backbreaking if you're trying to maintain a standard of living that's out of proportion to who and where you are and is dictated by the tastes of the city rather than the tastes of the country, which is what nineteenth-century American farm tastes were dictated by: the Sears Roebuck catalogue; look at the 1908 Sears Roebuck catalogue... and that whole trend of the nineteenth century was for everyone to live as though they were in the capital... like if you were out in India as a British civil servant, nevertheless you dress for dinner and eat in the English fashion, which I guess would be five p.m., whether you're in Madras or Afghanistan ... that whole nineteenth-century notion, which was an interesting kind of cosmopolitanism, forced people into outdoing themselves at farming, and that of course was combined with the fact that by the late nineteenth century agriculture was almost all market agriculture anyway, and they were growing single-crop, or certainly limited crop, cash crop kinds of things, had gotten away from self-sufficiency and diversification and, in many cases, had not even been in the region they were in, like, say Nebraska, or the wheat farms of eastern Washington, they hadn't been there long enough, one generation only, to develop the sophistications that would have made life easier for them; it takes perhaps a long time to get to know how to live in a region gently and easily and with a maximal annual efficiency, to know when to do what through the passage of the year, when to make the most out of every opportunity in the passage of the year, and also to know when to rest during the process of the year, and that back-breaking farm work of our Anglo-forebears out on the Plains and in the homesteading counties of the Midwest and so forth was because they were both ignorant and greedy and competitive and forced by a capitalist system from behind. They were so forced that in most cases they were trying to pay off debts. They went into hock to do their farm thing. They were into hock for tools and for seed. And a lot of them never got out of hock. There's a whole capitalist and mercantile thing which goes with the frontier that people don't generally know about. The alternative thing to look at, if you're curious, are the Spanish-American farms, farming communities, that developed in the Upper Rio Grande Valley and the tributaries of the Rio Grande Valley, that had been there for almost 300 years, that developed a what you might call Western-derived, Spanish-derived, Mexican-derived agriculture system in North America on a stable basis, and although they can certainly be said to be poor, their backs were not broken and they were never alienated or in a position of having no culture ... where they had for a long period a strong stable Spanish-American Catholic culture, which, for a good period, was in relative harmony with the surrounding Indian cultures too. Then the American Indians certainly are a case of, the Pueblos are a case of an agricultural stability that allows plenty of time and does not break the back. I mean they can work very hard, but they also can have festivals two weeks long.

GROSSINGER: What would you say to people who say that they're isolated?

SNYDER: In relation to what is always the question. Nobody is really ever isolated. The question seems to be whether or not they're able in whatever, say lonely region they think they're in, to have a cooperative or semi-cooperative community function ... or to what degree sharing takes place with neighbors, and in that process, to what degree that circle of neighbors is able to establish a sense of its own center, its own knowledge, its own magic ... or it remains dependent on news from outside, and thus feels continually in a cultural backwater. This is one of the strangest problems of this century ... is that business of whether or not you can feel you're at the center or whether or not you feel you're in a backwater. It's paradoxical that Portland, Maine, feels like it's a backwater, but maybe some hippie commune deeper in the hills doesn't feel like it's a backwater. I saw something like that happen on Suwa-no-se Island in southern Japan just as a real case in point: a Japanese island subculture, the Amami Islands subculture, having one branch up on this tiny tiny volcanic island . . . the people on the island, 40 people at most, living almost totally self-sufficiently by fishing and sweet potato growing, with their own songs, their own way of brewing alcohol, their own kinds of musical instruments, and customs like tattooing the backs of the hands on the women, and so forth, and their own designs and fabrics, feeling completely at ease in their world and completely centered in their world, and then the expansion, post–World War II, of the Japanese city culture, radio and then television coming in, and the television comes in because the national television system of Japan, a national monopoly, gives the island a television set, like installs it for them, so they can watch it, and it's installed in one of the little buildings off of the school building, and the whole island for a while goes down in the evenings to watch the television, except the reception is poor; the combination of these things is within, say, ten years, to shift their perception of themselves from what I've just described to a perception of themselves as a miserable backwater people, out of the stream of things, and what they do is start wearing badly-fitting and poorly-conceived imitations of what the people on the mainland wear, so they just look like they got no style, you know, and thinking that Tokyo must be the most wonderful place in the world, and losing all of the style that they had, and this is what's happening all over the world, and we know all about it, but it's that profound little switch that takes place there between thinking, we have a validity of our own, we are authentic, we're real people, to that other thing of thinking, we're third class people, and there's such a subtle switch in there where that happens, wherever that line is . . . but it's reversing that in some ways that we're interested in; it's in putting the center of authenticity back within local communities, and removing them from a dependence on some kind of centrally-dictated model . . . which I think can be done, without creating a climate of simple provincialism, a climate which is not even interested in what goes on in the world at large. It seems to me that there's no reason why you can't have an intelligent and formed way of seeing a large world without losing your own sense of local vitality.

WILK: What happened with the small Japanese island happens in the ghetto.

SNYDER: It happens everywhere; it happens with every American Indian group; it happens with ghettoes; it happens with small towns; it happens with people in New Guinea, and Port Moresby and so forth. It's what the impact of the modern world has done to the rest of the world; it's given everybody else an inferiority complex, and bad taste, theoretically, since they can't match the central model, quite; and something like that's been going on a long time. In the Roman Empire it talks about the backwardness of the people of the provinces as against the people who are true Romans; and so I see that as going hand in hand with the development of the state, the city, and imperialism, and it's certainly one of the most insidious and effective means of political imperialism, to demoralize and enslave the people it's out to get, because that's what it amounts to, an enslavement.

WILK: I wonder why people are prone to that, why it's so easy for them to have their equilibrium disturbed like that.

SNYDER: Well, that's another thing: some people are less disturbable than others; some have more resistance than others, and that's a very interesting anthropological question, because some of those who have the most resistance are not necessarily the ones who have the greatest surface strength. There's a whole study there in what gives a culture resilience and inner strength, and what makes a country collapse: why did Mexico collapse in front of the Spaniards in ten years?; how did that happen?... whereas in Sonora how come the Yaqui have still not collapsed?; in essence they still resist Mexico. India is very interesting because you have an area there where for two, for three thousand years, civilization, that is to say, class structure, writing systems, money economy, markets, various kind of governments, have dominated the plains, iron technology and so forth, iron tools, have dominated the plains for three thousand years, and yet a dozen miles away, up into the hills and through the woods, there will be cultures that have been aware of that whole civilized thing and have traded with it for these three thousand years, but have essentially kept intact, haven't really been disturbed by its presence. And yet those people on the plains represent an earlier assimilation of a number of other primitive cultures... but the hill people hold on.

GROSSINGER: I'll switch to another topic and ask you some questions about the limits of technology, which I'd like to put in the context of a quote. It is part of a discussion of the conceivable extents of technological civilizations in Carl Sagan's *Intelligent Life in the Universe:* the hyperbole of all this can direct us away from some more localized questions and problems and focus us on something like the cosmic scale that is always implied:

> Let us now return to the subject of the material resources available to a developing society. After reaching a high state of technical development, it would seem very natural that a civilization would strive to make use of energy and materials external to the planet of origin, but within the limits of the local solar system. Our star radiates 4×10^{33} ergs of energy each second, and the masses of the Jovian planets constitute the major potential source of material. Jupiter alone has a mass of 2×10^{30}

grams. It has been estimated that about 10^{44} ergs of energy would be required to completely vaporize Jupiter. This is roughly equal to the total radiation output of the Sun over a period of 800 years.

According to Dyson, the mass of Jupiter could be used to construct an immense shell which would surround the Sun, and have a radius of about 1 A.H. (150 million kilometers). How thick would the shell of a Dyson sphere be? The volume of such a sphere would be $4\pi r^2 S$, where r is the radius of the sphere, 1 A.U., and S is its thickness. The mass of the sphere is just the volume times its density, ρ, and the mass available is approximately the mass of Jupiter. Thus, $4\pi r^2 S = 2 \times 10^{30}$ grams. Thus, we find that $\rho S \simeq 200$ gm cm^{-2} of surface area would be sufficient to make the inner shell habitable. We recall that the mass of the atmosphere above each square centimeter of the Earth's surface is close to 1000 gm. If the over-all density of the shell were 1 gm cm^{-3} or slightly less, the thickness of the shell, S, would be a few meters. Man today, for all practical purposes, is a two-dimensional being, since he utilizes only the surface of the Earth. It would be entirely possible for mankind in the future —say, in 2500 to 3000 years— to create an artificial biosphere on the inner surface of a Dyson sphere. After man has accomplished this magnificent achievement, he would be able to use the total energy output of the Sun. Every photon emitted by the Sun would be absorbed by the Dyson sphere, and could be utilized productively. The inside surface area of the Dyson sphere would be approximately 1 billion times greater than the surface area of the Earth.

SNYDER: The burden of the argument remains with the man who presents the argument, as to why this is necessary, or what it serves. He only once uses the word "the development" ... of our society [*note: looking back to just before the section quoted*]; he doesn't give what his assumptions are about the development that would make this kind of thing serve man's best interests. And so it remains unanswered, perhaps because he's naive, or perhaps he doesn't want to talk about it, and this is really the point where you must come up front and say *what is* in man's best interests: what amounts to actual growth, actual development, actual expansion of the human possibility.

GROSSINGER: There's a certain blindness. Not only are the ends and means confused, but the relation of this sort of extravagant statement to either is uncertain.

SNYDER: Well, of course, there's blindness, but at least one can try to express, as far as he thinks of these things at all, what he has in mind. Otherwise such an argument is useless. Because all he's saying is that we can have more people, and that we can use the energy of the sun efficiently. That's no more than ... qualitatively that's no different than saying: we should populate all of North America and have lots of electric generators. And we *know* that that isn't satisfactory to us at this point, so why should populating the entire inside of a sphere and getting all of the energy of the sun be of any more interest, *unless* there can be another dimension that's brought out in that.

GROSSINGER: I suppose he might claim that that could be possible.

SNYDER: ... which could be possible without doing that too.

GROSSINGER: Well, that's the biggest suggestion I know of.

SNYDER: Yes, that's a big suggestion, but psychologically it's no larger than the suggestion of doing the whole trip of industrial U.S.A. would be to a Natchez Indian. [*Long pause.*] In essence, you know, we already have done what he describes there. And what he does is just explode it larger.

GROSSINGER: I think the idea came from a kind of planetary think tank.

SNYDER: Well, those guys are paid to sit around and smoke expensive dope and think things up.

GROSSINGER: I'd like to ask you to say something about Rappaport's "Sanctity and Adaptation," which you've just read.

SNYDER: Well, the key thing that would seem to hold up for the whole essay is right at the back, in fact the final sentence: "In the arena of action itself I believe that it *is* the task of those disciplines which *are* concerned with the necessary interdependence of living things to provide *viable* propositions to which men can accord *sacred* status." [*Italics denote Synder's emphases.*] And I think that's a really beautiful proposition to put in front of us, and very pregnant, because it puts in the hands of the biological sciences, biochemistry, biophysics, as well as in the hands of, say, poets and priests, to really look at what they're doing and to come out up front with the holy truths of it, which a number of people have intimations of, but we haven't been able to make those statements so clearly so far.

GROSSINGER: How does it speak to a priest?

SNYDER: Well, it throws it back on a priest in a very nice way, because he has to ask himself: gee, does my religion deal with the interdependence of things? And if he can't see that in his tradition, maybe his tradition is off-base. If it doesn't show *that,* then his religion has not, at least in these terms, served mankind as well as it should and cannot, perhaps, serve mankind so well in the future. And I shouldn't say just mankind: I should say: serve all sentient beings. And so in a sense you can say it's limiting if it does not have a bodhisattva function for all sentient beings. But that very function is not out of harmony with the concept of the void ... because those two things really go hand in hand, and to leap over what would be a lot of rhetoric in between, I'll say that: to serve mankind's interests well and to make the greatest possible development of the creative potential available does not require either numbers of human beings or a complex society. That something with the sophistication and the richness of the traditional transmission of knowledge in Rinzai Zen . . . in a tradition such as that there is such richness, such subtlety, such continual surprise and excitement . . . it's so fundamentally grounded on the actual facts of existence and at the same time has all of the suggestions of other realms, other possibilities . . . it keeps bringing them back, over and over again, to the center. The exploration of consciousness itself and the unfolding recognition of the same principles which are at work in our own minds as being the exact principles that are operating around us is the most beautiful of possible human experiences, at least for some time to come yet, and something of that order is what is—quote—what the development of human society should serve . . . because, among other things, that teaches you that you're not alone, or that you cannot act simply for yourself . . . that teaches you that you are in an interdependent condition with other beings, and it teaches you the sanctity of life, and also how to take life; it solves, not exactly solves, but makes meaningful and beautiful the primary paradoxes that human beings have to live with, like: the food of Eskimos is souls . . . how to deal with that, how to make that into real poetry . . . and so I say my experience has been within the Zen tradition.

I invoke Rinzai Zen because that's been my experience; the Hopis will invoke their tradition; Tibetans will invoke their tradition; other traditional people will involke their traditions, insofar as they have the courage of those traditions left. But the sum of those traditions, which is the sum of a body of wisdom and a body of lore, which would explore consciousness and would explore nature from within, rather than from without, that would assert, ultimately, as the American Indians, as the Pueblo assert, that we are in a transition phase right now: between having lost our capacity to communicate indirectly, intuitively, and to understand the life force, and the return to that condition, and we are doing hard practice, hard yoga on Earth for these thousands of years because of some errors we made. But our hard yoga, our hard practice, will win us back that skill, that capacity, that direct knowledge of the forces and energies of the universe. Those cannot be won by any matter of scientific inquiry or tools; those can only be won by the most complex and sophisticated tool there is, the mind.

Section IV

EVOLUTION AND COSMOS

Edward Dorn

THIS IS THE WAY I HEAR THE MOMENTUM

having touched the Slaughter Stone
            of the Henge of Stone
                    Rock
                in the memory of
                Memory Rock

        in the memory
    of Brittany Dolmen and then across
        the return into a people
            woe to them who eat too much
        from a people who eat
                too fast as
                tho it were an exercise

        yet
    well being arose
            from
    the emptiness
            of the stomach
        from the universe
            every change of placement
    the shift of every leaf
        is a function
        of the universe which
    moves outward from its composed center
            40 bilynyrs.   Then returns
                            the pulse
                    and location will have changed
                The location free of reference
            except this obvious measurement because you can feel
            completely a straight 5 B. years
                from some moment now which is not
                an apparent edge
            but as mappa india anna
                as the source of speech
            is no simple explosion

                    our given pulse
                                    hits inside this
            everymoment we live
                                    to hear this
                    COSMOS
                the soul of the universe
            calls indifferently the populations
                to proceed
                    from the tincture
                to the root of the natural
                in the present effort
                        to arise into the light
                ness of these limbs
            these parts of the universe having growth

            So the foot of this book
        is grown at last for the book to stand upon
    thrown from myself as my life was given to me
        with sharp aim
                right across the quality/quantity question

                When I reached the Tor
                and walked up to
            be elevated
        enough to sense the zodiac
            of its configured presentations
            of itself the lit
                and distant hills simply
                    the joy of expansion
                which is what we've experienced
        for 35 billion years
            and can take in
                        the moment
        approaching when all of it
            will be stilled in a shimmy
            of its own distance
            as the thing holds so
        with the delicacy of water tension
    to avoid dispersal
            of all thats here   the wholly
            beautiful seizure of the co-
    ordinates of its distance
        the scansion of its trip
                as we come around again to feel wide open
            on the arc

Jule Eisenbud

Interview
Conducted by Richard Grossinger, 8 Jan. 72

GROSSINGER: What do you understand from the interest in and response to the Serios phenomenon?

EISENBUD: There hasn't been any particular interest in Serios, I would say, except on the part of a very few people. It was a great disappointment to the publisher, although I warned them. I warned them at the time that they were going to publish that they were going to be in for trouble. They had hoped to see another best-seller out of it, like *The Gift of Prophecy,* or something like that; I told them that it was impossible, that they would meet nothing but resistance.

GROSSINGER: Why did you think that?

EISENBUD: Because I knew that this would provoke the deepest, essentially cosmic resistances in people: the fear to reach out and apprehend the cosmos.

GROSSINGER: Why that book rather than some other book?

EISENBUD: Because it was most dramatically focalized in the ability to visualize anything you see, and mirror far-off things, for a moment, and catch it, freeze it. The point is: I think that people do apprehend the essential truth of this, and defend themselves against it; they have to, because of the way that we live and because of our culture. And it was interesting to see the way different reviewers handled this. There was always, in each review, a sneaking admission of the truth of the thing, and the rest of the review was an onslaught, and displacement, you see, of the fear, an essentially cosmic fear. Also, there are paranoid fears involved, as I explain in the book itself. In fact, the book says why it couldn't be received. I say plainly in the book what the nature of the resistance will be against this. It's partly cosmic; it's partly a resistance to the acknowledgment that we kill each other, that thoughts can kill, that we're dangerous creatures, that we don't really need extensions of or implementations of our aggressions with guns, or bows and arrows, or knives, rocks, spears; we don't need it at all; we do it without these things. That, if the universe comes into Serios in this way, he can also go out to the universe, and create it. I say this in veiled ways. I don't put it on the line. But in one chapter I put out the nature of the resistance; it's a resistance to our own murderous aggression. And this was apparent to me, and I told the publishers of this.

Don't expect that this book can have a great popular sale; it just won't. They didn't believe me, much to their chagrin.

GROSSINGER: I guess they thought the phenomenon itself was interesting enough.

EISENBUD: Well, they thought: Look what *Bridey Murphy,* and what *The Gift of Prophecy* did, and look what the Cayce books did, you see, in terms of sales. I *assured* them; I remember telling John Wiley on the way down from the mountain; again and again, I said, you're wrong; I don't care what you do, how many you print, but I want you to know in advance that you'll be shot down, and secondly that you won't have the great popular interest that you think there will be, because it evokes too many resistances. People don't want to know what the essential nature of mind is, or what our relation to the cosmos can be.

GROSSINGER: How does the Serios experiment fit into your total work?

EISENBUD: My whole insight into this whole way of approaching the human mind and its relation to the universe comes from the psychoanalytic data, essentially from telepathic dreams, and the kind of behavior that can be tied together by means of the psi hypothesis. In other words, the psi hypothesis makes a good deal of sense within the psychoanalytic context's method of observation. There are many, many data that simply cannot be understood without postulating psi factors in human interrelationships. Now, after having brooded on this for about twenty years, I was primed for someone like Serios, although I didn't believe the first reports I heard. But when he started to perform, it was very exciting, and it was exciting for as long as he performed, which was about three years, because everything was just right on target. He almost did what he needed to do to fill in various parts of a comprehensive theory, which I'm still working on, because precognition is part of it. He couldn't precognize, but he provided one of the main tools in the theory of precognition. And all of this will come out if I live long enough and have enough energy.

GROSSINGER: In what way was Croisset different than Serios?

EISENBUD: Well, each has his thing. Croisset can't put pictures on film. Serios can't precognize the future. Croisset can. He can *pinpoint* it in a very specific and remarkable way, and he's done this for over twenty years in his very extraordinary chair tests. He will put down statements about people who, two or three weeks later, on a given specified date, *will* occupy a space. And his statements will be correct, within certain limits, but certainly far beyond chance expectations. For instance, in the experiment we did, he was in Holland; on January 6, he said, some man who will take the ticket (you know, with a certain number; the ticket-dispensing thing was randomized) will be a man 5 feet, 9½ inches tall, who works both in science and industry, who has a gold tooth in his lower jaw, who has something wrong with his big toe, a mark or a scar, who has something to do with roulette, who lives in a house where someone plays the record player so loud that it's a nuisance and he can't stand it, and so on, and about half a dozen more statements, each of which were true. The man wandered in that night; he had never heard of Croisset in his life; he was a physicist, who took the ticket for this specific hot seat; he was a physicist for Dow Chemical, which is both science and industry; he was 5 feet, 9¾; he's the only physicist there in a department of 11 physicists with a gold tooth in his lower jaw, who wears a steel plate because of bad surgery on an ingrown toenail; this was the 23rd of January; the statements were made on the 6th of January in Holland; who on the 19th of January drew a picture of intraatomic forces in his notebook, which looked just like a roulette wheel; and his particular hobby, this one was the change from the active to the passive, it isn't somebody in his house who plays the record-player too loud and continuously; *he* does, because he's addicted to bag-pipe music; he turns it up as loud as he can, and the people at home can't stand it; it drives them up the walls. There were other details too; for instance, somebody laughed at him because he measured something with a ruler and was wrong. There were two people there he hit on the nose. The first one he described was a lady, 5 foot, 6, on the nose, who was wearing dark hair or a beret; she wears her hair like a beret, and it's an optical illusion; people think she's wearing a beret. One of the most interesting statements was: she has something on page 64 of a book, which is emotion-ally charged for her. According to her statement, when she got home she went to the sideboard where she had things to send to her daughter in Japan, and there was a book lying there, and it was open to page 64, and she was considering tearing it out because she wanted to send the book to the girl, but on page 64 was the subheading: "When It's Time To Go," what to do with a pet when you have to put the pet to sleep; the book was *The Cat You Care For;* she was considering tearing this out because they had put their own fourteen-year-old siamese cat to death some months before, and the daughter didn't know it, and now she would have to confess to the daughter. Now here we get into something that Jung would call synchronicity; Croisset had had frequently what are known as "reso-nance factors" between him and the target person he precognizes about. Now Croisset's wife was going blind, progressive intractable blindness; and when we visited them last summer, she was totally blind; in fact, her two eyes were enucleated; at the time he made his precognition one eye was enucleated, and the other was totally hopeless. Now the woman who was this target person was a past president of the Colorado Association for the Blind, and this was her major activity; secondly, Croisset had had to put a family pet to death, a dog, because his wife kept tripping over the dog. Now this is a resonance factor, and Jung would call it synchronicity, but there's another way of working it through. That it's not synchronous at all;

it's very very causal. But, you see, to me, this type of thing, the ability to simply step over time, as if there were no barrier at all, is of such metaphysical, philosophical importance as to render everything else patent pending actually, until you understand. Everything else is almost trivial until you begin to understand what the hell goes on to enable a person to do this. All the work of physics stops at this point, and in fact, because of this, physics, in its present form, is through. I remember, a number of years ago at the University of Freiburg, when they were describing another chair test of Croisset, someone in the back of the hall saying, *"Ein kleiner Gott. Ein kleiner Herr Gott!"* A small God. And, indeed, he gives the impression of being a small God . . . because the curious damn thing is, you see, that I was unsatisfied, for a certain reason, with the randomizing that was done the first time, so I called the randomizers back again; they included a physicist, a professor at Denver University, an electrical engineer, a professor at Boulder, and so on, two psychiatrists here in town; I called them back and said, "We must go through the randomizing again." It involved a shuffle, and a weather cut, which is simply an arbitrary cut at a certain point (after five people shuffle, you take what they call a weather key, the difference between the maximum and minimum of different cities in the paper that day); it's window-dressing. But you go through a pretty damn random cut, and the same guy came out again, the physicist from Boulder, number 28. Now this begins to take on elements of a weird fantasy. Everybody's been ducking the whole phenomenon of precognition. Science is obviously set solidly against it; and the resistances to this are so strong that even in Shakespeare's day, as you know from one of his Henry plays, *Henry V* I believe, there were laws against attempting to do this; if you were caught doing it you could be put to death. The way they framed Margaret in one of those plays was to see that she went to see a witch who would precognize the future, and then they had the king's men come in and catch her there, and that was the end; she escaped with her life by banishment; that's all. But, you see, one of the precognitions given (Shakespeare knew so much that he knew even how these damn things were displaced) . . . when the witch said, "Let Somerset shun castles on the plains . . ."—he was killed under the sign of the Castle Inn in St. Albans, by Richard, you see.

I have a theory here. You see, I don't think Croisset foretells the future; I think he creates it. He draws his people; you see, he scans the community for people with certain characteristics; he draws them there; he is able to control the shuffle; there is such a thing, you know, as a psychic shuffle; curiously enough Serios was able to do it; he could make you shuffle, and he would name the card that you would come up with.

GROSSINGER: That's one of the reasons why I'm sometimes scared of going near those people. When I was given a review copy of the book on Peter Hurkos by the Portland newspaper and read it, my immediate sense

154

was that there were a highly disproportionate number of disasters associated with the people he himself associated with.

EISENBUD: There's no question about it.

GROSSINGER: I simply figured he was doing it.

EISENBUD: On two or three occasions that I met with Croisset over the years... every time I've been with Croisset I feel I've escaped with my life if I didn't see a cloud come over his face, a veiled look as he was talking to me. Well, I felt, I can live another year. Because these guys do come up with strange precognostications, you know; Eileen Garrett was that way too, but not so good as Croisset by any means. I feel that he produces the future.

GROSSINGER: What sort of image does this give you of the space the Earth lies in?

EISENBUD: I don't have a perception there. I have simply a logical construction, that space and extension is just an irrelevant non-applicable parameter when it comes to the mind. It has nothing to do with the mind, any more than space has to do with a concept, like beauty, or with a tone, you see, F or A, or anything like that; I don't think it has anything to do with space. Any quality. And it has nothing to do with the mind, and the mind's capacity. Space just isn't there. There is no space. Theory of probability has nothing to do with space. Chess has nothing to do with space. You see, you can play chess on a cosmic scale, you know, of cosmic space, or you can play it on a thumbnail. The logical moves are the same. Mathematics has nothing to do with space, the logic of mathematics, it makes no difference. ½ has nothing to do with space . . . at all. Pi has nothing to do with space. Well, what has to do with space? Space is the objectification of something. This guy who visited me today; he was rather logical, compulsive, not a guy who would have depth perceptions. He arrived logically, philosophically, at the notion that you can construct the universe out of thought. The whole universe. And again, the problem is, how we all manage to construct the same universe more or less, and get consensual agreement out of our constructions. But then he went into this strange experience with a yogi, who put him into this sort of trance, a Castaneda thing, and he saw it all, he was correct; he was all over the goddamn place. Insofar as he was he. But there was a complete decomposition of self and reality.

I got into this by saying: that Serios provides one of the essential mechanisms whereby we're able to do this, because he shows we have perfect information from the far corners of the Earth, if we have a mind to get it. Because his information is extremely precise. And, of course, you need perfect information in the present before you can do anything with the future. You see, I'm approaching this somewhat mechanistically, rather than globally, mystically, poetically, with reservations as to the mechanistic kind of approach. I'm aware that it's abstractive, that it lacks the thing that makes experience experience. Yet it's the only way I can grapple with it at the moment, and it's the way I prefer to grapple with it rather than saying interesting things about precognition that I can't put in relationship to a lot of other things in science. I am committed to science and the scientific approach, with all my awareness of the thin-ness of the scientific approach with life experience, you see. It's a way of zooming in and sharpening focus, recognizing that you haven't got the whole picture; that's all. It's something I can do, and if I live long enough, I'll draw a picture of how this all happens.

GROSSINGER: Does it have moral implications for you?

EISENBUD: Everything has moral implications. I feel that everything I do is to find a better place in a lumpy bed; that's all. And also, I find out I've been a moralist ever since I was a neurotic child, and this is the derivation of my moral stance, and it all came back to me when I went through an LSD experience; I did nothing but weep for mankind, in general, and a lot of individuals in particular. And I went through a phase of what the Hindus call . . . some sort of compassionate identification; and I realized that I am driven to . . . I don't know quite how to put it . . . you see, this is my thing; I can't go to Alabama to march with Medgar Evers; that's not my thing. This is my thing. This is my garden in the Voltairian sense; and this is the thing I do well, like Anatole France's legend of the juggler, the virgin who smiled on him; this was his thing; it was aces high. This is my thing, but basically, I know, it's a moral thing with me. My hope is that, somehow, it will make things better for people. I think people are miserable. I don't agree with you about developing consciousness at all. I think of every soldier who's killed in the war, every civilian who's killed in Vietnam . . . it's a terrible tragedy. And it's all well and good to say that the tragedy is that they didn't live fully enough. I don't think so. I think the tragedy is that they died, under such circumstances. Have you ever been so close to death that you don't know whether you're going to live or not? Well, that's quite an experience. And when I look at these mangled bodies in Vietnam, and when I look at these poor slobs in America who are getting the shaft all through life, economically, sociologically, it's very hard for me to think that they have this hard gemlike flame, you know, in their consciousness. I think of them more as the feral children, who have been deprived of awareness and perception and consciousness. When you talk of the balance of things in the cosmic sense, like a kind of bookkeeping, frankly it doesn't make much sense to me. I think of the millions of people who have always suffered, who have been killed or maimed or starved, and I can't take the Shavian point of view that there's only one stomach to be hungry and the rest is pure multiplication. And also, the mystic point of view, which, again, can see the incidents and events and actualities of human experience

156

as a nothing in the cosmos, and they say it all evens out in the end, there's no good, there's no evil, there's one beautiful cosmic light, you see; I can't help seeing this as a defense against the terrible pain of identification. I think we do identify, however this comes about, and we're there; we *are* them; we're right there, and that a lot of the cosmic insight, a lot that passes for cosmic insight, is a defense, against this feeling painful identification. We are exposed every day to things we simply cannot live with were we to feel them head on. We can't see each of the dead as a loved one, but I think something in us does, and we defend ourselves against it; our defenses are largely the things we're doing. I don't take the attitude of a Lord Cavendish: I do it because it's a game, and it's fun; it has no moral significance whatsoever. I wouldn't do it if I didn't feel it had moral significance, that in some way I would add to the possibility of man being somewhat less miserable. I know all love and laughter, and sex, and it's good, but on the whole man has been a miserable bastard. Why? It's a cosmic tragedy, huh? You can see the cosmos as Blake saw it, and Boehme, and Walt Whitman, this great big song of myself; that's one way of looking at it. And maybe it's right. I don't know. Whitman walked about among the maimed of the Civil War, and he wrote about the cosmos as this great big beautiful thing. I see man as an ecological tragedy, a philosophical tragedy (he hasn't got half the sense of a rabbit running from a fox, or half the beauty, or fitness). How can you even think we make a cosmic tremor?, or someone like Dorn write about feeling the pulse?

GROSSINGER: You seem to think somehow that he's talking about something beautiful as separate, or justifying the poetic structure by something outside of existence; yet that very poem says we merely experience what is; we experience the experience. It's pure Darwinian. We are part of that universe which moves out of its composed center forty billion, or however many years away. He's not talking about ecstasy, or big beautiful things; he's simply talking about measurement, and that's what Blake is doing too. It's not mysticism, or poetry, opposed to trauma. If there's a structure at all—and I don't see how there couldn't be, because what could you argue outside of it—then they're bound to that structure together. We don't cause a cosmic tremor by going out to the stars; the long Darwinian tunnel we're at the end of, from stars to planets to bio-worlds to thought-patterns, takes care of that. We *are* the cosmic tremor; and to blind ourselves to part of the experience because it might be repression of some infinitely deep pain is, in some sense, actually to damage the fine structure of being, and to cut off the one part of our relationship with a vast and terrifying universe that seems to be at home with us. I mean, for all the hell, we do exist at this distance of things; we're still in touch, despite the violence; one doesn't exploit this to deny the starving millions or the reality of suffering, as you imply. One simply attempts to make a statement about where we are, to locate us, to give us reference points in the whole affair which has brought us to such a place; and in this sense, at its clearest, its least solipsistic and introspective, is visionary, and I'm not going to try to tell you why. You ask how an artist could justify doing his little thing in the face of all this slaughter, when he doesn't even leave a mark on the cosmos. But that's just the point; he doesn't have to *make* a mark. The mark he does make is irrevocably tied into a forty-plus-billion-year passage out of the stars that carries all those suffering bodies in its pulse too, for better or for worse. I don't think that's bullshit, or getting off too easy at all...

EISENBUD: Well, I guess I should say you've made a fine apologia. I just don't happen to buy it.

GROSSINGER: Well, I'd like you to pick up anyway and say why you think it all got fucked up in the Darwinian tunnel between here and the stars.

EISENBUD: I have no idea. It's beyond me. But you see my own feeling is that we have a lot of false development to attempt, in some way, to back-track on, in much the way, although this isn't a preconception, in much the way most people have a lot of backtracking to do to get over hang-ups, bad development in childhood, the accidents of the way they happened to develop, and I think that mankind has a lot of backtracking to do too, to get rid of its ways of looking at things, its ways of feeling and *not feeling* things, its peculiar denial of complicity in each other's lives. I was saying before: thoughts alone can kill; bare, naked thoughts; isn't all this armor of war, this machinery, these bombs, aren't they all gross exaggerations. We don't even need them. We kill each other without them, as the Serios experiment implied.

GROSSINGER: Would things be better if we had such knowledge, if we didn't repress what you call the psychic, or the telepathic ability? Does Serios suggest to you anything about a possibility in mankind?

EISENBUD: I don't think that there's very much there to be optimistic about. I think it gives us a glimpse into the possibilities we could achieve as individual consciousnesses, but I don't know whether we're ever going to make it, and I don't know the place of this in evolution. I don't know whether this is a forerunner; a vestigial thing. I have no way of placing it. But, you see, I think it's tied up with the way we go about killing ourselves. I see our need to destroy ourselves and each other. You have no idea. It can come out anywhere, at any time. We could have Hitlers in America. Neighbors who you think are nice guys. They'll destroy you. Yet these are the possibilities in humankind, and all this is, to some extent, in some way that I cannot yet quite comprehend, a defense against these other capacities in us that we don't wish to realize. To put it schematically, and simplistically, and almost absurdly, because we don't wish to realize that we can just kill with our minds, we go through this whole enormous play of killing with such, of overkilling with such overimplementation; it gets greater and greater and greater as if . . . It's a caricature of saying: how can I do it with my mind; I need tanks; I need B-52 bombers; I need napalm, and so on, and so on, which is a caricature of: I have examples of people who died this way. Not that I could see them do it, but if I put together the jigsaw, it looks as though this one was responsible for that event. I have a paper in press now which says this, and nobody's going to like it, and I present the data, the clinical data. Of course, I say, we have to entertain this hypothesis.

GROSSINGER: You know Cannon's article: "Voodoo Death"?

EISENBUD: Yes, of course, of course. But the whole point is: that there a man deliberately said: I'm going to kill you. We mask it. It goes on unobtrusively. Which doesn't make a damn bit of difference. What's the difference whether I do it or streptococci do it. We have cover stories, you see. All science has produced cover stories for the deaths we create; it's streptococci; it's accidents, and so on. But, what I'm trying to say is: there must be, I feel, a relationship between this truth, which we will not see, and this absurd burlesque of aggression that goes on all around us, as if we're trying to deny that the other is possible. It sounds crazy, but it's a way of looking at things. The Jesus myth, our myths, you can kill someone and worship him for 2000 years and atone for it, as if we're making amends. This is a focalization of blood-guilt, essentially. But it's a big story and a long one, you know. And again, had I your selectric typewriter and your age and your mind, I would write ten volumes on it. It has so many facets to it. It's a vast project that I don't think I any longer have the kind of energy to do.

Jule Eisenbud

Evolution and Psi

It may seem curious to many of you that I have again been invited to talk on a topic which is widely felt to be without scientific merit. I am referring of course not to evolution but to psi phenomena, more widely known as telepathy, clairvoyance, psychokinesis, and the like. But many things that have ultimately proved worth while in science have had questionable beginnings, so I do not feel too apologetic in asking you once more to entertain provisionally the notion that it is possible for information to be conveyed and apprehended apart from any known physical means of so doing, which is what is meant when we talk about psi phenomena.

Let me remark right off that saying something of significance on the evolution of psi abilities (or at least of those that manifest themselves overtly) is much more difficult than saying something of interest about the possible role of psi in evolutional processes. The reason is that we are shorter on hard data bearing upon the former than we are on theoretical considerations conceivably relevant to the latter.

To begin with, we know virtually nothing about the genetic aspects of psi abilities, despite the widespread notion that these seem to run in families. No valid studies have been made in this area and no such are likely to be made, when the tremendous difficulties encountered in getting reliable data on the heritability of even normal cognitive abilities are considered. Nor are there any artifacts or paleontological data to help us place psi abilities within the evolutionary scheme. Thus, although we have records of what today we would call psi occurrences for as long as there have been written records of man (which is anyway merely an instant on the scale of human evolution), we have nothing that gives us a hint on the question that seems to interest a great many people: which way are our psi abilities going? Are they, like our molars and our body hair, likely to disappear in time, or are they, like our burgeoning cerebrums, likely to continue to increase in magnitude and complexity so long as nature and providence allows the human experiment to continue? If we could only say something definite about the relation between psi abilities, the enigma of consciousness, and the physical attributes of the central nervous system, we might be able to infer something about this question; but here too, unfortunately, hard data are lacking.

With such a paucity of data, and small possibility of performing pertinent experiments, one would think that the problem could be laid to rest as one of nature's great unsolved mysteries. But such is not the case. Forecasting trends in human evolution, including evolution of the psychic side of man, has long been one of the fringe benefits available to anyone who has had anything at all to say about the human condition. As far as the psychic side of man goes, two points of view may be said to sum up the situation: In one, psi abilities are seen as residua of archaic modes of functioning which will probably disappear as the brain becomes cleverer and consciousness expands; in the second, these abilities are forerunners of things to come and will probably become more important as the brain becomes cleverer and consciousness expands. The first point of view is apt to be held by those to whom the existence of psi processes is an embarrassment; the second by those to whom human depravity is an embarrassment. Neither point of view is supported by facts, and there is in any case no guarantee that were psi abilities to become more available they would be used for good and not for evil. However that be, all we seem to be left with in regard to the question of whence and whither psi abilities in evolution, after the smoke of much tendentious speculation has lifted, are man's ceaseless fears and fantasies about his own nature.

II

But this does not end the question of the possible relation of psi to evolution. According to several biologists, if psi didn't exist something like it might well have to be invented to account for still outstanding puzzles in the field. The situation is this: No one quarrels with the importance of mutations (spontaneous random variations in the germ plasm) and natural selection (the selection by the environment of those features most favorable to reproductive superiority) in producing evolutionary changes. Doubts about the importance of these processes were laid conclusively to rest decades ago by brilliant experiments on protective coloration and countershading in moths, butterflies, and fish, and by a variety of experiments with that stellar experimental performer, *Drosophila,* the little fruit fly. The only question that remains is whether mutation and selection is the whole picture.

Numerous biologists, exemplified by Nobel laureates Monod (1971) and Luria (1973), believe that these dual processes are quite adequate, given enough time and a sufficient number of chances in the mutational lottery, and aided perhaps by certain types of guiding pressures on selection which may develop (still by chance) en route. Others (Lillie, 1945; Koestler and Smythies, 1969; Polanyi, 1958; Whyte, 1965) feel, however, that it is not simply a matter of time and lottery tickets but basically a question of how and to what degree the lottery is rigged as, according to them, it necessarily has to be. These hold that the evolutionary development of complex structural and behavioral characteristics of different populations would seem to depend on the confluence of combinations of factors requiring a degree of ordering of events—at the very least some highly efficient feedback and control mechanisms—impossible to ascribe to pure chance.

But the problem, as seen by many who argue for something beyond simple mutation and selection, is not merely that of the enormous complexity of even the most elementary biological structures (let alone the marvels of design which characterize more advanced forms), but is one of how selection can work on behaviorisms and structures that have not yet arrived at the point where there can be anything like a clear payoff in terms of differential death and reproductive rates. The most frequently cited instance is that of the eye, where eons would have had to elapse before the light-sensitive spot or disc became an optical system with enough efficiency to sense food or predators. (The fact that eyes have developed independently in more than a dozen species doesn't make the problem any easier.) But examples can be given in the hundreds: almost any moderately complicated animal courtship or nest building or ritualized predatory activity (from protozoa up) will do, to say nothing of the delicately integrated behavior of conglomerates, from colonies of protozoa which carry out complicated building activities to the well-known group behavior of termites, bees, and ants. What happens during the hundreds of millions of years before these complex instinctual individual and group behaviorisms —that work, as the ethologists tell us, on an all-or-nothing basis—get to the point where they can work at all? Darwin himself was well aware of the difficulties that some of these points made for his theory of natural selection. (The eye and the instincts, both individual and conglomerate, particularly disturbed him.) If we add to problems of this sort questions as to how constancy of patterns as well as of species is maintained, the seemingly contradictory question of why complexity of organization and structure so often proceeds to a point far beyond what is necessary for adaptation (again a headache to Darwin), the occurrence of virtually identical anatomical and biochemical structures (e.g., enzymes) from widely dissimilar gene pools, and finally, the development of structures when the genic factors responsible for them have been experimentally removed, as in the case of *Drosophila,* whose eyes reappeared after inbreeding 60 generations of an eyeless strain (T. H. Morgan, 1929), it would appear that a major theoretical mutation might indeed be required for all the facets of evolutionary fact to be satisfactorily accounted for.

One might imagine that a few comparatively simple probability computations would be able to show whether or not the biosphere could have evolved to its present state with mutation and selection operating purely on a chance basis. But mathematicians and biologists differ widely on just about every step of the way (Moorhead and Kaplan, 1967), resulting in a theoretical free-for-all that seems to allow every investigator to maintain the position he probably always had anyway. To some the very fact of life itself remains the height of improbability, to say nothing of everything that has happened since the first organic molecules learned the highly unlikely trick of replicating themselves; others seem ready to go to the stake with unshaken faith that simple dice casting, if carried out long enough, is equally capable of producing the marvels of sexual reproduction, where DNA is parceled out to various populations "after their kind" (as Genesis has it), and the highest distillation of human consciousness in a Shakespeare, a Mozart, or a book with the intriguing title *The Origin of Species.*

It isn't as if all investigators committed to a mechanistic approach fail to appreciate the magnitude of the problem on their hands. Attempts to deal with at least some of the difficulties mentioned go back to the end of the last century. Around this time Baldwin (1896) in America and C. L. Morgan (1896) in Britain introduced the notion of "organic selection," which they thought might provide a kind of shortcut to the evolution of certain characteristics. Their idea, then and subsequently hotly disputed, was that animals develop changes in habits in response to environmental changes (e.g., in climate or food supply) and then tend to seek out those environments where these changed features are more or less constant. Mutation would in time bring about the genic changes that, by selection, would tend to perpetuate the adaptive behavior. (This scheme was subsequently put on an up-to-date ethological basis by Thorpe, 1945.)

In 1957 C. H. Waddington, of Edinburgh University, introduced the notion of the tendency of genes and gene combinations to stabilize out by means of what he calls "creods," after the Greek words *chre,* meaning "it is fated or necessary," and *hodos,* meaning "path." A creod seems to be not unlike what our local farmers and ranchers call a gully which, once formed, tends to perpetuate a channel for runoff (and unfortunately for erosion too). Waddington holds that such gullies in the genescape, which he thinks can develop from purely random initial conditions, might go far in explaining outstanding puzzles like the exposive separation and fanning out of species in the Mesozoic period, the resistance of species to change, once formed, and other problems. Waddington (1961) also invokes a principle he calls genetic assimilation, which states that genes which are favored in what amounts to the process of organic selection (for which he uses the term "canalization") are able then to stabilize those alterations in the creodic gullies that will further increase the chances of certain inherited characteristics persisting in the genetic structure.

Others see these amendments to the classic Darwinian scheme as not providing nearly enough of a catalyst to evolutionary development to account for problems of the magnitude of those mentioned earlier. Without more powerful shaping pressures, it is held, these dubious shortcuts provide at best merely a few more tickets in a gigantic lottery, increasing the chances of getting some of the prizes from virtually zero to near zero. The late great theoretical biologist Ludwig Bertalanffy (1952) saw the beginnings of an answer in General Systems Theory, a manifoldly derived discipline dealing with the properties and principles of hierarchical systems as wholes, irrespective of the nature of their components. L. L. Whyte (1965), also accepting the necessity for "internal factors in evolution," postulates a set of "coordinating conditions" by which a "St. Peter of internal selection" acts to pass or reject genes depending on the requirements of the evolutional situation. And the mathematician Ulam (1967) sees organizing instructions and rules as conceivably carried in the gene itself. These and other questioners of classical Darwinism appear to feel, nevertheless, that although the laws and principles of the organizational forces required to shape evolution are insufficiently known, they are still ultimately rooted in (even if not wholly reducible to) the elementary forces known to physics.

A biologist who does not accept this article of faith is Sir Alister Hardy, of Oxford University. In his Presidential Address to the zoology section of the British Association (1949), he drew attention to the data of psychical research and their possible role in filling some of the still existing gaps in the modern synthetic, so-called neo-Darwinian theory of evolution. He further elaborated his ideas in *The Living Stream* (1965), a detailed, lucid, and provocative treatment of the types of data that present evolutionary theory seems unable satisfactorily to account for. Curiously (or perhaps not so curiously in view of the earlier mentioned absence of a mathematical yardstick in these matters), Hardy accepts the classical hypotheses as adequate to account for such complex processes as camouflage and mimicry (his special area of expertise), and even for such a remarkable development as so-called coincident disruptive coloration, where a pattern (e.g., lateral stripes) that is carried across an animal's (e.g., frog's) limbs folded close to its body in the resting position (as if painted on) disintegrates when the animal extends its limbs in motion. What boggles him are the variegated data of homology—the development of similar structures in different species (like the fin and the limb) from totally different gene pools and, along somewhat different lines, the occurrence of virtually identical structures not only from widely dissimilar gene pools but from widely separated regions (e.g., the Tasmanian wolf, a pouched marsupial, and the Siberian wolf, a placental). To illustrate the difficulties involved for classical selection theory, Hardy gives extensive citations of the data of Sir D'Arcy Thompson, who had wrestled with these problems in his great work, *On Growth and Form* (1917/1961). Thompson demonstrated the morphological intertranslatability of disparate species and showed "that forms mathematically akin may belong to organisms biologically remote." In *The Living Stream,* after reviewing some of the data of psychical research, Hardy speculates on how extrasensory communication between animals might lead to some answers. The existence of telepathy, according to him, "may be a clue to a much more fundamental biological principle." Holding it "most unlikely that so remarkable a phenomenon should be confined to just a few individuals of one species of animal," he believes that the psychic side of animals, independent though it may be of the DNA code that governs the form of the physical frame, "may interact with the physical system in the evolutionary process." Postulating an unconscious telepathic

164

communication between members of the same species of animals, he sees such a process as aiding organic selection ("or genetic assimilation—whichever term you prefer") by providing "psychic blueprints" that would stabilize common behavioral patterns until they gradually became converted through favorable genetic changes into well fixed instinctive patterns. Although a firm believer in organic selection in its own right, Hardy feels that instead of changes in behavior coming about solely through external selection acting separately in each individual animal (aided at the most, perhaps, by some imitative tendencies, or possibly the tendency of some animals to follow one another as they browse and graze and fall into similar habits through trial-and-error exploratory behavior) the changes would tend to spread through the population and be canalized by psychic sharing of experience on a telepathic basis. "There would [then] be two parallel streams of information—the DNA code supplying the varying physical form of the organic stream to be acted on by selection—and the psychic stream of shared experience—the subconscious species 'blueprint'—which *together with the environment* would select those members in the population better able to carry on the race" (p. 258). Most instinctive behavior, he feels, ultimately comes about in this way—changes in behavior preceding changes in structure and ritualized function. Hardy also feels that the psychic blueprint idea might go far in explaining the secret of homology. It may be, he conjectures, "the group 'mind' which indirectly *selects* those gene complexes presenting (in development) its best expression."

Throughout *The Living Stream* Hardy carefully avoids any suggestion of direct psychic action on the gene or gene complex. Indirect selection comes about through changes of habit, and it is only this, which may later become structuralized through genetic changes which in themselves are purely fortuitous, that is facilitated through "psychic sharing" or the "psychic blueprint."

The possibility of direct action on the genetic material of a more broadly conceived psi factor was suggested in 1971 by another British biologist, John L. Randall, who sees in both the origin of life and in its subsequent evolution "a tremendous increase in information content which cannot be satisfactorily accounted for by any mechanistic theory." Citing the work of Grad (1967), Smith (1968), and others on the effect of psychic activity on cellular and enzymatic processes, Randall suggested that it "would be of the greatest interest to discover whether the same force which can promote wound healing in mice can also induce mutations in *Drosophila* or bacterial cultures..." (p. 163). It is obvious that successful results in such experiments, hardly less far reaching in importance than the production through psi means of self-replicating molecules in a medium simulating the primordial broth (which some of you may recall was mentioned as a possibility in my previous lecture in this forum [Eisenbud, 1975]), would immediately open up staggering vistas in biology and evolution.

III

An area somewhat short of direct genic action of the psi factor that might profitably be explored would be that of psi communication not just among members of the same species, as Hardy has suggested, but among members of different species. Such a possibility was suggested some years ago by observations I made quite by chance (Eisenbud, 1966–67). The first of these, which was so seemingly odd as to immediately alert me to its possible implications, was simply the higher rate of success of a nursing cat in catching mice from a mousehole in the floor than that of a perfectly functional cheese-baited mousetrap placed there. Presumably the cheese had given off a more inviting, less alarming odor than the cat, but the mouse population kept behaving as if just the opposite were true. "Sometimes days or weeks would go by without the trap being sprung by a venturesome mouse, but the cat, once it came into the picture, for some reason—it was nursing kittens at the time—never seemed to have to wait more than a couple of hours before it would be rewarded, and this would happen several times a day. At times the cat would grow impatient and screw her eye right down to the hole as if to see why nothing much was happening, but she would then settle back a few inches and resume her wait for the mouse that sooner or later would crawl out" (p. 153 [653]).

A conceivable key to this situation was provided some months later when I noticed that a peculiar game had begun to go on between the aforementioned cat's no longer nursing kittens and a several months old shepherd-husky pup that belonged to the ranch which was the scene of the game. Again and again, one or another of the kittens would not only allow itself to be pounced upon and shaken like a rag doll by the dog, who would grasp the kitten's neck or even its entire head in its maw, but it would repeatedly invite this behavior from the dog. Each time this was accompanied by the fiercest growls on the dog's part and the most piteous meows and squeals from the kitten, who would sound as if its very life were at stake. But every time the pup, tiring of the game, would drop the kitten and settle down indifferently a few feet away, the latter, instead of scampering to safety, would merely spend a few minutes licking itself back into shape and then begin again to disport itself seductively in front of the pup. This would, in short order, have the effect of rousing the pup to pounce upon it, whereupon the (to me) alarming spectacle would begin again, once more with the most fearsome sounds issuing from the pair. I soon found that there was no point in my trying to rescue the kitten from its tormentor, since both participants in what I finally recognized as some sort of highly stylized *pas de deux* would simply move out of my reach and start all over again, sometimes one kitten spelling another for a round or two. Thus it went on for weeks. One day two of the kittens were found torn to pieces, literally limb from limb, dead but not devoured.

No one around the place could imagine how this had come about. The

166

dog's behavior, I learned, was largely an innate response called forth simply by the presence of something furry in its mouth. The puzzling thing from the beginning was not so much the dog's role, however, but the apparent need on the part of the kittens to reenact over and over again the role of prey animals about to lose the battle for survival. Something of the sort is well known among members of the same species where the loser in a fight at one point signals its submission by ceasing its defensive maneuvers and exposing itself in a way that plainly announces that it will accept a technical knockout. The victor's aggression is immediately and automatically inhibited, and no kill takes place. This dovetailing inherited species-specific behavior pattern presumably acts in the service of the preservation of the species, and also establishes the animal's position in the pecking order (which functions to the same end). But if a submission pattern of this sort were to be used with an animal of another species, it would lead only to an immediate kill (and ultimately to the genetic extinction of the trait).

Nevertheless, the seemingly ritualistic behavior of the dog and the kittens, it seemed to me, must also in some way have been the expression of built-in inherited mechanisms. The highly stylized game, played over and over again in exactly the same manner (and which I have subsequently learned was not unique in the case of the particular animals I observed) could hardly have arisen spontaneously and *de novo* but must also have called upon latent behavior patterns of ancient lineage. And perhaps what had begun as a ritual for the discharge of tension, enabling two natural enemies to live in peace, got out of hand when the dog, growing older and functioning like a bomb ticking away toward an explosion, had simply got to the point where it could no longer inhibit the powerful impulses it was repeatedly required to hold in check. The question arises whether what was invoked in this repetitive reenactment of an age-old drama may not have been the shadow of a reciprocal predator-prey duality that exists behind the scenes through nature. If so, what part might psi play in such an interplay?

Taking first simply the possibility of covert predator-prey "cooperation" (we will come to the psi aspects of the matter presently), such a notion might at first appear to be in strong contradiction to one of the chief tenets of the theory of natural selection, that the primary drive of every animal is to survive, except perhaps where its death would serve the continuance of its own species. But examples are known where members of one species become prey to those of another in highly ritualized manners, as in the case of the tarantula spider which in a most complaisant but thoroughly prescribed way allows itself to be paralyzed by the sting of the Pepsis wasp and then becomes the incubator for the wasp's larvae (Petrunkevitch, 1955). How this sort of thing can be squared with classical selection theory is not entirely clear, but a somewhat revised theory could accommodate the possibility of such "arrangements" occurring in subtle form, if needed, throughout nature. Certainly if there were a degree of flexibility whereby every

167

animal were given the option to play the game or not, such a system would possess an unsurpassable efficiency and would present the ideal paradigm for all ecological relationships.

Unfortunately, gathering examples of more subtle, less obviously ritualized predator-prey "fixes" is difficult because few eyewitness accounts of capture and kill are made (most statistics are compiled from animal carcasses and stomach contents) and those that are tend almost automatically to be "normalized"—sometimes in most procrustean fashion—to fit the classical mold. Again and again we read descriptions of "inattentive" or "lagging" or "hesitant" prey, of confused prey which zigged when they should have zagged, of prey which just made the wrong decision about when to run, where to run, how to run. Some, inexplicably—and I myself have observed this—run right toward predators, even when they have definitely sensed them (Schaller, 1972). Generally it is assumed—and there is some evidence for this (ibid.)—that it is mostly prey animals handicapped by extreme youth or age or by disease that are the vulnerable ones; but there is good evidence that this is far from always the case and that healthy prey in their prime are often taken. One conservation officer remarked that such an animal, a deer whose capture and kill he witnessed, acted plain "stupid" (Mech, 1970).

Granting the impossibility of getting inside the head of an animal at the moment of decision, one can nevertheless sometimes come across what appear to be obvious indications of predator-prey cooperation that are passed over with little or no puzzlement simply because they are being viewed through the wrong end of the theoretical binoculars. It is known, for example, that many prey which are large enough and well enough equipped to defend themselves even when dragged down (water buffalo, zebra) do not do so and give up without a struggle; and several authors have noted that horns, hooves, and tusks are used primarily in fighting among members of the same species rather than in defense against predators (Mech, 1970; Schaller, 1970). Some of this would even appear to be a kind of almost ritualized submission behavior (rather than mere "shock," as is often supposed); but for some reason no one asks how it is that such behavior (even if it should happen to be a shock response) should have been selected "in" rather than "out."

A beautiful example of the paralyzing hold of classical selection theory may be seen in descriptions of wolf predation (Mech, 1970). It is known that if moose stand their ground when attacked by wolf packs their chances of being killed are slight because the wolves almost never go in on these dangerous animals and sooner or later, tired of waiting, move off. In fact, the most effectual striking behavior in the wolf is instinctually released only by the stimulus of a fleeing moose; at the same time, moose in flight are less able to defend themselves. How is it, then, that "standing" has not been selected in and fleeing out? Would not the answer seem to be that the fleeing moose and the attacking wolf make one ecological (and evolu-

168

tional) unit, and that fleeing and chasing constitute interspecific cooperation just as effectively as the dovetailing behavior of the tarantula and the
wasp? From the conventional point of view such a duet ought to appear the
more paradoxical when it is realized that while fleeing obviously takes
more energy than standing, it is often the very animals which can least
afford such an expenditure, the old ones, that are most likely to flee. Since
these happen also to be the animals which can run neither fast nor long,
would it not seem that Nature has in this way arranged for these population
units, classically expendable from the standpoint of procreative capability,
to be expended? To the conventionally tutored eye these animals may
appear to be fleeing just as fast as they can, but from Nature's point of
view, judging from the final scores, they can only be said to be beating a
terrified advance.

Let us assume for the moment, anyhow, that the moose situation is
representative of a widespread, if subtly concealed (from ecologists, anyway), state of affairs in nature. Where would psi come into the picture?
First, it could be a major determinant of behavior at the actual moment of
encounter. "Just what makes certain moose stand their ground and others
run is unknown," writes Mech (1970). It is insufficiently appreciated to
what extent information that is conveyed and apprehended by means of psi
mediates decision of one sort or another and is not simply an inert registra-
tion in the mind of a percipient (Eisenbud, 1970, chapter 14). And since
decision, as Hardy (1965) pointed out, is necessarily a major factor in
shaping evolution—decisions about mating, about seeking new habitats,
about fighting or fleeing—any psi-mediated factor that could work in confluence with and complement normal determinants influencing behavior
might just tip the balance in one direction or another.

The second point at which psi might affect the balance of adjustment,
again by complementing normal mechanisms, would be by facilitating the
coming into each other's range of those predator-prey pairs whose ultimate
encounter would tend best to fulfill particular ecological requirements. The
prototype of this would be the way in which human individuals may be
presumed to be drawn through psi out of their normally expected paths to
consummate the fulfillment of inner needs (Eisenbud, 1963b, 1970; Stanford, 1974), including needs for punishment (Eisenbud, 1952).

How would this work? Normally, an individual animal's role in a given
ecological context is determined by a complex interplay of genetic and
psychosocial factors. It has been experimentally demonstrated (Denenberg, 1963) that variations in individual animals' alertness as well as passiv-
ity and aggressiveness in relation to other animals are conditioned by the
accidents of early development, particularly the conditions of the neonatal
and nursing period. And Wynne-Edwards (1962) has shown that animal
populations themselves tend to sort out those marginal individuals in the
pecking order who, by becoming social outcasts as it were, constitute a sort
of roving reservoir of vulnerable prey. According to classical concepts,

169

these are the individuals, along with the sick and the old, that make up the largest part of the vulnerable prey population. It would be precisely from such a reservoir that individuals (with relatively strong "death-need" predispositions, as it were) could be required for roles in psi-mediated pairings. A marginal animal might thus be drawn into position by psi to fulfill in a single act the population-limiting needs of its own species (Carr-Saunders, 1922) and the high priority survival needs (as in the case of my nursing cat) of a member of an ecologically competing species. Animals on the roam, according to this somewhat idealized paradigm, might thus be regarded as something like a fleet of radio-dispatched and radio-controlled taxicabs. As roving vehicles, they would have relative freedom to cruise and some exposure to "random" calls; but they would all the while remain subject to the requirements of their district control centers operating hierarchically in interlacing systems with mutually geared feedback mechanisms.

It should be noted, however, that psi might, if required, operate to keep prey away from potential predators, just as a psi-mediated decision on the part of a prey animal to be or not to be might go either way. Such non-random flexibility, as pointed out earlier, could be of the greatest importance in the highly complex food-chain calculus that operates in the biosphere. The mechanisms by which various populations are kept within bounds that seem imposed by Nature herself and are not allowed either to grow without limit or to die out are not wholly known (Errington, 1967). Still not entirely understood "intrinsic" compensating processes come into play long before population levels get too high or too dangerously low (just as a sensitive thermostat works long before a room gets too hot or too cold). And although predation levels do not seem to play as major a role in these processes as was at one time believed, even a slight complementation of pure chance in this area could provide the fine tuning necessary to keep things running smoothly. (All it takes, as every croupier knows, is a slight edge, like the double zero on the roulette wheel, to keep the house in business.)

In any case, and regardless of whether or not anything like psi-mediated predator-prey "fixes" play an appreciable part—or any part at all— in the balance of nature, the problem that arises in connection with whatever mechanisms do operate is that of overall control. Here ecologists become somewhat vague. By way of accounting for various feedback and buffering mechanisms, they tend implicitly or explicitly to fall back upon physiological models of homeostatis (the living organism's ability to maintain its component systems in finely balanced equilibria). But what individual organisms possess that is critically lacking in the pictures drawn by ecologists are built-in mechanisms for some sort of central control, as well as, in higher animals, more or less fail-safe nervous and hormonal means of communication between component organs and systems. Conventional informational mechanisms cannot in themselves provide this control, no matter how extensive the catalogue of their various capabilities (Wilson, 1975;

170

Wynne-Edwards, 1962) and however intricately they may seem to be woven into the manifold patterns of ecological interrelatedness, any more than the various intercommunicating bureaucracies that make up a government can govern.

IV

And this, returning now to evolution (ecology is merely evolution on the wing), is precisely the problem here too. The hope of certain biologists that new branches of mathematics or of computer science will provide the answer is as doomed as the perpetual motion machine. For mathematics, however cleverly it describes and analyzes problems of order, organization, and control, is as ineffectual as a Greek chorus when it comes to *doing* anything; and if computers were ever able to create anything like stable self-perpetuating patterns out of purely random inputs, as Waddington (1969) claims may have happened, the only plausible inference would be that the "experimenter effect" occasionally manifests itself (presumably through PK) with other fairly reliable computer hardware.

At all events, it is not simply a matter of pumping information or energy into the evolutionary system here or there in small doses by way of accounting for this or that highly improbable bit of order or organization, this pocket of anti-chance or that one; the problem is that of the overall interrelatedness of all the systems of nature—including the inanimate, when it comes to that (Eisenbud, 1956). For part solutions, like the organizing fields within which embryos manifest their "harmonious equipotential gradients" (Driesch, 1907–08; Spemann, 1933/1962) or the "autonomous centers of decision" of Polanyi (1958), which oppose the entropic push toward disorder, will not do, any more than Whyte's St. Peter at the genetic gate or any other version of Maxwell's ubiquitous demon (even that in the mind of a moose). Nor will general systems theory provide an answer that doesn't immediately beg the next higher question; for you cannot go on indefinitely in ascending hierarchies without sooner or later getting to some ultimate ground of existence whose nature has been the perennial preoccupation of philosophers and theologians and which only a handful of mystics have claimed to have glimpsed in the raw. It may be doubted that there is a patriarchal (or matriarchal) figure sitting at a celestial desk pointing to a sign saying "The buck stops here"; but it is difficult to avoid the impression that it is frequently the dread of having to confront a bogey of this sort that is responsible for the curious contortions, evasions, and hysterical blindnesses of those who, with almost religious faith, nurture their own version of the resurrection—the notion that electrons, particles, atoms, molecules, genes, organisms, and events somehow order themselves.

Sir Alister Hardy does not have a trace of doubt as to how the problem of ultimate control must find its solution. An uncompromising theist, he totally rejects the tendentious arguments of Teilhard de Chardin (1959) in this regard (as does psychologist Sir Cyril Burt [1966], who provides a penetrating glimpse of how unsimplistic informed thinking in this area *can* be), but arrives at his position through an "inner certainty" that has nothing to do with biology or logic. Although this may seem to scientists to be a sad waste of both, there it is, this inner certainty, as much a fact of nature, according to Hardy, as evolution and just as deserving of scientific attention.

It is interesting to realize, at this late date in the history of evolution and its critics, that Darwin himself was not overly disturbed by such high-level enigmas. In *The Origin of Species* (1859/1909) he took it for granted (as did Newton before him) that there was a Creator, and he more than once, when examining some remarkable bit of evolution, alluded to how infinitely superior the mind of the Creator was to the mind of man. All he was attempting to do, he asserted, was to account for the mechanism of variations and diversity, not for life itself and everything that came with it. His neo-Darwinian followers have set themselves a larger task, and some (Brooks and Shaw, 1973) have even found an extraterrestrial substitute for special creation. This would not have budged Darwin one jot. The only thing it could possibly have meant to him was that God was alive and well on some other planet too.

V

I cannot conclude without making some mention of precognition and its conceivable relation to evolution. Precognition is the process (or whatever) whereby events that have yet to happen appear capable of being apprehended apart from any possibility of rational inference and any known means of information transfer. If such a phenomen actually does occur—and there seems to be ample evidential reason to conclude that it does—would this necessarily mean that something larger and more inexorable than Waddington's creods—supercreods, perhaps—are at work guiding the entire show along a fated path? Would all seemingly related phenomena, including genetic mutations and the whole panel of behavioral responses and decisions going into the struggle for existence, then be merely so much stage direction and play acting from a script that has existed from beyond all time? Or would it still be possible to think of evolution, as did Bergson (1911), as a creative process with an indeterminate future?

You are of course aware that the basic issue here, whether or not the iron fist of necessity lies inside the velvet glove of appearance, has long been a prime philosophical puzzle even apart from the problem of precognition, and that to some—Einstein, for one (Schilpp, 1949)—this issue has enjoyed only a temporary and in fact only a pseudo-resolution in terms of the dogma of indeterminacy that currently rules quantum physics. Unfortunately, the data of precognition have not really advanced the problem beyond the point at which the Stoics confronted it since these data can not as yet be fitted into any satisfactory theoretical framework; and it may be that the problem cannot be resolved in terms of present modes of thought, that something more radical even than the major theoretical mutation called for in evolution theory will be required to get us off dead center. Meanwhile we continue to sift through what data we can gather on this strange phenomenon for clues, insights, or anything at all that might provide a chink in what now appears to be an impenetrable wall.

Curiously, the results of some experimental work on precognition in animals, though doing little to further the problem from the point of view discussed above, cast an interesting light on the factors influencing decision-making in animals and on the flexibility of this process. These experiments indicated that rodents were able, to a statistically significant degree, to avoid a future traumatic event such as electric shock or death by making a correct choice (e.g., in maze-running) from among a number of alternative possibilities (Bestall, 1962; Craig, 1973; Duval and Montredon, 1968a, 1968b; Morris, 1970). If we assume that it is the animal and not the experimenter which is responsible for such effects, we must suppose that it is utilizing a latent ability ordinarily held in check, an ability that could hardly manifest itself in such a manner in natural situations (e.g, to avoid predators and other dangers) without there soon being a rodent population explosion of such magnitude as to dwarf everything else in the biosphere. If, on the other hand, we assume that it is the experimenters who are responsible for part or all of these effects (an alternative impossible to rule out), then we must presume not only the same latent ability on the part of the rodents but also their capacity and readiness to respond to psi-mediated signals ("instructions," if you will) in essentially the manner that was postulated earlier for animals on the roam. The important point is that either way what occurred in the laboratory could only have been a temporary (quite temporary, to my mind [Eisenbud, 1963a]) suspension of the real rules of the game, the rules that apply in the field at large, as if another game entirely were being played, as indeed it was. But the very fact that this is possible reveals the leeway and the flexibility that allows whole systems in nature to adapt to each other. Such systemic rather than individual adaptation would no doubt require a certain percentage of those animals who might in the laboratory show a tendency successfully to avoid traumatic events to join the ranks of my covertly masochistic kitchen mice and the moose fleeing surely toward their capture and kill. For what is certain, whichever way the issue of predetermination is resolved (if ever it will be), is that all organisms in nature, insofar as they can exercise choice at all, must do so in accordance with overall requirements that transcend individual concerns. But if the great constants of nature have to be satisfied no matter what, if the ultimate boundary conditions (Polanyi, 1968) are as invisibly present as our persistent and multifarious background radiation, is it conceivable that this imposes on evolution a destiny and a design (homage to Alfred Russel Wallace, 1911) which the mechanics of random mutations and all kinds of psi-mediated intercommunications merely help to carry out? Conceivable perhaps, but it is unlikely that the question can ever be settled.

References

Baldwin, J. M. 1896. A new factor in evolution. *The American Naturalist* 30:354–451; 536–553.

Bergson, H. 1911. *Creative evolution.* New York: Holt.

Bertalanffy, L. 1952. *Problems of life.* New York: Wiley.

Bestall, C. M. 1962. An experiment in precognition in the laboratory mouse. *Journal of Parapsychology* 26:269 (abstract).

Brooks, P., and G. Shaw. 1973. *The origin and development of living systems.* New York: Academic Press.

Burt, C. 1966. Evolution and parapsychology. *Journal of the Society for Psychical Research* 43:391–422.

Carr-Saunders, A. M. 1922. *The population problem.* London: Oxford University Press.

Craig, J. G. 1974. Precognition in rats as a function of shock and death. In W. G. Roll, R. L. Morris, and J. D. Morris, eds., *Research in parapsychology 1973.* Metuchen, N.J.: Scarecrow Press; pp. 75–78.

Darwin, C. 1909. *The origin of species.* New York: Collier's. (Originally published in 1859).

de Chardin, P. T. 1959. *The phenomenon of man.* New York: Harper & Row.

Denenberg, V. H. 1963. Early experience and emotional development. *Scientific American* 206:138–46.

Driesch, H. 1907–1908. *The science and philosophy of the organism.* London: Adam & Charles Black. 2 vols.

Duval, P.,and E. Montredon. 1968a. ESP experiments with mice. *Journal of Parapsychology* 32:153–66.

———. 1968b. Further experiments with mice. *Journal of Parapsychology* 32:260 (abstract).

Eisenbud, J. 1952. The use of the telepathy hypothesis in psychotherapy. In G. Bychowski and L. Despert, eds., *Specialized techniques in psychotherapy.* New York: Basic Books; pp. 41–63.

———. 1956. Psi and the problem of the disconnections in science. *Journal of the American Society for Psychical Research* 50:3–26.

———. 1963a. Psi and the nature of things. *International Journal of Parapsychology* 5:245–68.

———. 1963b. Two approaches to spontaneous case material. *Journal of the American Society for Psychical Research* 57:118–35.

———. 1966–1967. Why psi? *Psychoanalytic Review* 53:147–63.

———. 1970. *Psi and psychoanalysis.* New York: Grune & Stratton.

———. 1975. The mind-matter interface. *Journal of the American Society for Psychical Research* 69:115–26.

Errington, P. L. 1967. *Of predation and life.* Ames: Iowa State University Press.

Grad, B. 1967. The "laying on of hands": implications for psychotherapy, gentling, and the placebo effect. *Journal of the American Society for Psychical Research* 61:286–305.

Hardy, A. 1965. Zoology outside the laboratory. *The Advancement of Science* 6: 221:32.

———. 1965. *The living stream: evolution and man.* New York: Harper & Row.

Koestler, A., and J. R. Smythies, eds. 1969. *Beyond reductionism: new perspectives in the life sicences.* New York: Macmillan.

Lillie, R. S. 1945. *General biology and philosophy of the organism.* Chicago: University of Chicago Press.

Luria, S. E. 1973. *Life, the unfinished experiment.* New York: Scribner's.

Mech, L. D. 1970. *The wolf: the ecology and behavior of an endangered species.* Garden City, N.Y.: Natural History Press.

Monod, J. 1971. *Chance and necessity.* New York: Knopf.

Moorhead, P. S., and M. M. Kaplan, eds. *Mathematical challenges to the neo-Darwinian interpretation of evolution.* The Wistar Institute Symposium Monograph No. 5.

Morgan, C. L. 1896. *Habit and instinct.* London: Arnold.

Morgan, T. H. 1929. Variability of eyeless. In *Contributions to the genetics of Drosophila simulans and Drosophila melanogaster.* Washington: Carnegie Institution of Washington, Publication no. 399; pp. 141–68.

Morris, R. L. 1970. Psi and animal behavior: a survey. *Journal of the American Society for Psychical Research* 64:242–61.

Petrunkevitch, A. 1965. The spider and the wasp. In *Twentieth century bestiary.* A Scientific American Book. New York: Simon & Schuster; pp. 3–8.

Polanyi, M. 1958. *Personal knowledge.* Chicago: University of Chicago Press.

———. 1968. Life's irreducible structure. *Science* 160:1308–12.

Randall, J. L. 1971. Psi phenomena and biological theory. *Journal of the Society for Psychical Research* 46:151–65.

Schaller, G. B. 1972. *The Serengetti lion: a study of predator-prey relations.* Chicago: University of Chicago Press.

Schilpp, P. A. 1949. *Albert Einstein: philosopher-scientist.* Evanston, Ill: Library of Living Philosophers.

Smith, Sr. J. 1968. Paranormal effects on enzyme activity. *Journal of Parapsychology* 32:281 (abstract).

Spemann, H. 1962. *Embryonic development and induction.* New York: Hafner. (Originally published in 1933.)

Stanford, R. G. 1974. An experimentally testable model for spontaneous psi events. I. Extrasensory events. *Journal of the American Society for Psychical Research* 68:34–57. II. Psychokinetic events. Ibid., 321–56.

Thompson, D. W. 1961. *On growth and form.* Abridged ed. Cambridge: Cambridge University Press. (Originally published in 1917.)

Thorpe, W. H. 1945. The evolutionary significance of habitat selection. *Journal of Animal Ecology* 14:67–70.

Ulam, S. M. 1967. How to formulate mathematically problems of rate of evolution. In P. S. Moorhead and M. M. Kaplan, eds., *Mathematical challenges to the neo-Darwinian interpretation of evolution.* The Wistar Institute Symposium Monograph no. 5; pp. 21–28.

Waddington, C. H. 1957. *The strategy of the genes.* London: Allen & Unwin.

———. 1961. *The nature of life.* London: Allen & Unwin.

———. 1969. The theory of evolution today. In A. Koestler and J. R. Smythies, eds., *Beyond reductionism.* New York: Macmillan; pp. 357–74.

Wallace, A. R. 1911. *The world of life: a manifestation of creative power, directive mind and ultimate purpose.* New York: Moffat, Yard.

Whyte, L. L. 1965. *Internal factors in evolution.* New York: Braziller.

Wilson, E. O. 1975. *Sociobiology: the new synthesis.* Cambridge, Mass.: Belknap Press.

Wynne-Edwards, V. C. 1962. *Animal dispersion in relation to social behavior.* New York: Hafner, 1962.

Harvey Bialy

The I Ching and the Genetic Code

Both the I Ching and the Genetic Code are transformation systems which describe both the manifestation of form and the change of form in time.

Both are *in*/formed by certain fundamental propositions (principles, laws), which follow as natural (logical, grammatical) consequences of them.

Since the systems contain elements of similar self-description, the I Ching proposes to *encompass all that is contained in heaven and earth,* and geneticists speak of the code as *universal,* we might expect each to reveal similar fundamental propositions.

It seems to me that each system maintains that the manifestation of form is the result of the interplay of two complementary forces (elementals).

The I Ching names them Yin and Yang, and speaks of their absolute penetration of the cosmos.

Molecular biologists have identified two distinct kinds of small molecules as being at the heart of our genetic system, by name, Purines and Pyrimidines.

The I Ching holds that the stability of the manifested world resides in the local perfect proportion of Yin and Yang, a proportion maintained by a third force whose description is beyond the system, and which has no name but what it is.

Modern biologists derive the laws of genetic storage and expression from the fact that Purines and Pyrimidines are so related in the DNA molecule as to occur in perfect proportions.

The basis of this precise complementarity is an electron force called hydrogen-bonding. Hydrogen is another name for the Sun. Hydrogen-bonding is the same force holding water molecules together. The nature of this force is truly beyond any of the descriptions geneticists would offer.

The *principle of complementarity* in which resides the possibility of form, is conditioned by what Heraclitus called "a constantly changing river," change without change. The snake sheds its skin, from which the word "I" in I Ching, but remains a snake. Mutation gives rise to new species whose genes are only a permutation of their newly shed skins'.

The I Ching as a specific text (system) proposed to define the ways in which Yin and Yang combine to produce a discrete number of fundamental images (forms, or as D'Arcy Thompson wrote, "diagrams of force"), and how the constant flow of one of these images to another is sufficient to account for the fact that the world experiences change without itself (its laws) changing.

The Genetic Code as a specific system proposes that there are a defined number of ways in which Purines and Pyrimidines may combine to produce a discrete set of fundamental forms, whose various arrangements are sufficient to account for all past present and future biological images.

The description of the origin and number of these primary images is curiously similar in both systems.

Modern genetics began in the early 1950's when it was generally accepted that the hereditary properties of cells resided in a particular cellular molecule called DNA (Daleth Nun Aleph = 55, the sum of 1–10, the secret number of Malkuth, the realm of the physical world).

The word genetics comes from the greek verb *gignesthai,* to be born. So that literally a genetic molecule is one which can become itself. It replicates itself as well as being capable of information transfer and storage.

The structure of DNA is precisely congruent with these two activities.

DNA is a double helix. It is composed of two molecular strands wrapped around each other in such a way as to generate a right-handed helical spiral. Each chain is composed of a "backbone" of sugar/phosphate-sugar/phosphate-etc. chemical bonds, and attached to each sugar molecule at an angle almost perpendicular to the main axis, are any one of four possible Purines or Pyrimidines. The Purines found in DNA are called adenine and guanine, and the Pyrimidines thymine and cytosine. Within any single chain the Purines and Pyrimidines are stacked one atop another as close together as their Van der Waals radii permit, a distance of 3.4 ångstroms. The complete helix makes one turn around its major axis every 34 ångstroms, or every ten bases. (See accompanying diagrams.)

Since Purines and Pyrimidines are related by a principle of complementarity, whenever a purine occurs attached to a sugar in one chain, a pyrimidine must occur at the corresponding position in the other chain. The specific hydrogen-bonding potentials of the bases allows for adenine to pair only with thymine, and for cytosine to pair only with guanine. This exact complementarity permits DNA to replicate itself, as the two chains can unwind and each serve as a template for a new complementary strand.

The information potential of DNA resides in that there are no constraints on the sequence of bases *within* any single chain. It is this "aperiodicity of the DNA crystal" which permits a genetic code. The code is a mapping rule which assigns to linear arrays of Purines and Pyrimidines the necessary information for the assembly of protein molecules by cells. By specifying the types of proteins a cell is able to synthesize, DNA carries out a hetero-catalytic function.

Proteins like DNA are large composite molecules, differing from one another as a result of the almost limitless possibilities for their twenty different smaller components, called amino acids, to be arranged. For example an average protein is composed of approximately 100 amino acids chemically bonded to each other. Since there are 20 different amino acids, there are 20^{100} different proteins of this size alone possible. This number far exceeds the number of molecules the entire universe *could* contain, if

178

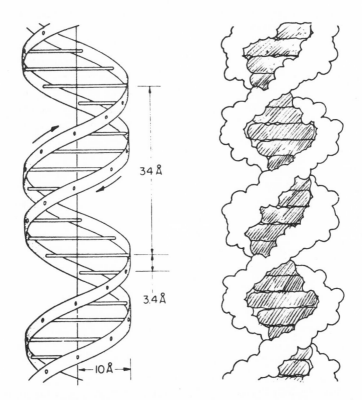

The double helix. The schematic model on the left illustrates the opposing polarities of the complementary strands and the characteristic dimensions of the B (wet) form of the molecule. The figure on the right is redrawn from the space-filling model of Feughelman et al. (1955) to illustrate the dense packing of the base pairs in the interior of the structure (shaded) and the "deep" and "narrow" grooves between the deoxyribose phosphate backbones (open).

we assume closest packing. Thus the number of possible structures is larger than any possible requirement for diversity.

The rule which relates Purines and Pyrimidines to amino acids states that along a single chain of a DNA helix, the bases are translated in *groups of three* as either one of the twenty amino acids or as punctuation signalling the beginning or end of a particular protein. (The process by which this colinearity between gene structure and protein structure is actualized is beyond the intent of this essay. The interested reader is referred to Gunther Stent's *Molecular Genetics, an Introductory Narrative,* W. H. Freeman, New York, 1970.)

There are only four Purine and Pyrimidine "letters" in this code; all possible arrangements of them in groups of three generate exactly 64 "genetic words." All biological form is a result of the interplay of these 64 elements.

Beginning with a principle of Yin and Yang complementarity, the I

Ching proceeds to define four basic subdivisions: old yang (symbolized ⚌), old yin (symbolized ⚏), new yang (⚎), and new yin (⚍). By considering all the possible arrangements of this set of four elements in groups of three, the I Ching arrives at 64 primary images. These images are called hexagrams, each being apparently composed of six lines.

Lao Tze wrote in the Tao Teh Ching *The Tao gave birth to the one, the one to the two, the two to the three, and the three gave birth to all things.* This can be read as either a description of the origin of the 64 hexagrams or the 64 codons of modern genetics.

In India the mandala of 64 squares is called Manduka, the frog, by allusion to maha-manduka, the Great Frog who supports the entire universe, and is the sign of the undifferentiated materia. As the frog is one of the clearest examples of metamorphic change, it is hard not to read a similar realization of the connection between 64 interpenetrating elements and the formal transformations of the world.

64 is also a submultiple of the fundamental cyclic number 25920 which measures the precession of equinoxes.

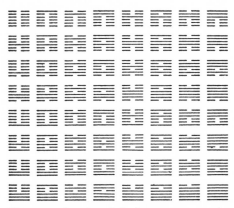

The natural order of the hexagrams.

During the history of the I Ching the hexagrams have been arranged in several different ways, of which the so-called "natural" array shown in the diagram was worked out during the Sung dynasty about 1000 years ago. The manner in which one form becomes another by a process of mutation is detailed in the I Ching on the basis of the relations implicit between these hexagrams.

The table of the Genetic Code, shown in the facing diagram, was worked out by Sir Francis Crick about 10 years ago. Similarly to students of the I Ching, geneticists have detailed the way one protein may mutate to another by studying the relationships implicit between these tabulated codons.

If each of the four basic I Ching digrams is identified with a Purine or Pyrimidine base, we can generate a one-to-one mapping between codons and hexagrams.

THE GENETIC CODE

1st↓ 2nd→	U	C	A	G	3rd↓
U	PHE	SER	TYR	CYS	U
	PHE	SER	TYR	CYS	C
	LEU	SER	Ochre	?	A
	LEU	SER	Amber	TRP	G
C	LEU	PRO	HIS	ARG	U
	LEU	PRO	HIS	ARG	C
	LEU	PRO	GLUN	ARG	A
	LEU	PRO	GLUN	ARG	G
A	ILEU	THR	ASPN	SER	U
	ILEU	THR	ASPN	SER	C
	ILEU	THR	LYS	ARG	A
	MET	THR	LYS	ARG	G
G	VAL	ALA	ASP	GLY	U
	VAL	ALA	ASP	GLY	C
	VAL	ALA	GLU	GLY	A
	VAL	ALA	GLU	GLY	G

It would seem reasonable to identify Purines with the Yang digrams on the basis of their more polarized (yang) electronic structures, and to represent the two Yin digrams by the Pyrimidine bases whose electronic configurations are more diffuse, yoni and yin-like. Further, *if and only if adenine is represented by the old yang digram,* we can draw a composite table of hexagrams and codons which preserves the natural order of the hexagrams as well as many of the generic relationships displayed by Crick's table.

The rules for determining hexagram-codon mappings are as follows:

Adenine = Old Yang

then, Guanine must equal New Yang

Thymine, or its structural RNA analog, uracil, must equal Old Yin, since T (or U) hydrogen-bonds only with A

and Cytosine then equals New Yin.

Hexagrams and codons both have direction. Hexagrams are constructed from the bottom up, and codons are translated in a particular direction. To complete the mapping it is necessary to specify that the bottom digram in a hexagram corresponds to the base in the first (left-most) position in a codon.

Using these rules the composite table shown in the diagram was generated. Several aspects of this table are of interest.

It preserves the general flow of both mandalas from a preponderance of

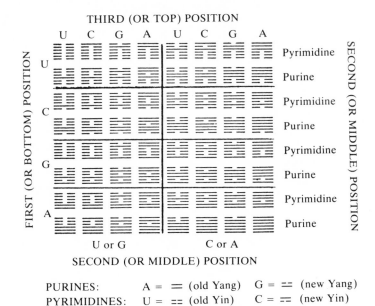

The natural order of the hexagrams and the table of the genetic code.

yin elements in the upper left corner to yang elements in the lower right.

It preserves the feature of Crick's mandala that similarly structured amino acids are grouped together.

The codon AUG which delineates the beginning of a protein chain, has for its equivalent hexagram Chieh, which literally means the "joints on a bamboo stalk," and is usually translated as Limitation.

The codon UAA which does not correspond to any amino acid and whose presence brings the process of protein chain elongation to a halt, has as its equivalent hexagram Tun, Retreat.

How much further this kind of analysis can be carried remains an open question. It is possible that a reinvestigation of the I Ching using some of the principles that appear now to be genetic might reveal unsuspected levels of meaning to hexagram relationships, or conversely might yield information pertinent to some of the unanswered questions of molecular biology, such as the origins of the code or codon degeneracy (the fact that more than one codon may represent a single amino acid).

Beyond these are the more intriguing questions about the nature of number, particularly the relationship between 3, 4 and the phenomenal world. In this respect, it is interesting that the Poincaré conjecture which would allow topological surety to propositions about the "real" world has never been proved in 3 and 4 dimensions, and we may ask along with Robert Kelly:

Are you made of numbers
or are numbers only your road
your footsteps left as you pass

Peter Redgrove

from
The Black Goddess and The Unseen Real

"The Black Goddess is so far hardly more than a word of hope whispered among the few who have served their apprenticeship to the White Goddess. She promises a new pacific bond between men and women, corresponding to a final reality of love. . . . She will lead man back to that sure instinct of love which he long ago forfeited by intellectual pride."[1]

That great Doctor of the Church, Thomas Aquinas, was in his late years converted to the worship of the Black Goddess. '. . . The long-repressed anima appeared to Thomas, in that vision, shortly before his death, in the guise of Wisdom and the bride.' She appears as a Muse, a 'feminine *pneuma* who enkindles and inspires' his work; 'the black earth is itself Wisdom,' or Wisdom is its soul which also like Ishtar, descends to the centre of earth; and she who is 'the playmate of Yaweh' 'suddenly appeared to him in personal form' with the effect of a thunderclap when 'he had taken her merely as an abstract idea.' The bride is a 'sweet-smelling *pneuma* and is thus identified with the Holy Spirit.'[2]

Even in his earlier writings, as the architect of Church orthodoxy, Thomas Aquinas advocated a science of the invisibles. He maintained that the presence of an angel could induce the *physiological* movement of humours and spirits in a way that would simultaneously present a person with a supersensible vision and enhance their intellect so that they were capable of interpreting it.

There was a passing also of invisible spirits through the medium of visible light when a man fell in love, and, when these spirits passed from the eyes of the lady and entered into the man's nature, a process could be set in motion that led to the creation of the *intelletto d'amore*: "The process would seem to involve a transformation of sexual energy, through which the love of the lady's exterior form would dissolve into love of the miraculous revelation of her soul . . .[3] The invisible thus became sensible, by the operation of spirits dependent on the physiological workings of the body.

This was the belief of the *fedeli d'amore* of thirteenth-century Italy—the 'faithful followers of love'—among whose number was Dante, and whose antecedents were said to include the Templars.[4]

What is certain is that Dante's art 'has its most direct origins in the discoveries of the troubadours writing in Southern France from the beginning of the twelfth century,' and that for these singers of the cult of love it was no mere matter of simple sexual attraction but that 'the experience of being in love totally altered their perceptions of the world . . . as they were driven to explore the essence of their sexual beings, so they experienced ever higher levels of consciousness in instantaneous but ever memorable moments of illumination . . .'[5]

It is possible to trace a whole tradition of *maithuna* (Tantric visionary sexuality) in the literature of Romance.[6] Some of it is indeed grossly erotic.[7] Guilhem Montanhagol wrote: 'A lover should on no account desire what would dishonour his lady-love.' Barbara Walker comments crisply: '. . . probably meaning an unwelcome pregnancy.'[8] Thus this kind of love is not on the ovulation side.

The love was both sensual and divine, as we have seen with the Middle-English mystics. Thus, to Guinizzelli, 'The girl he sees wearing a hat of grey squirrel fur so proudly that she leaves him trembling like a snake's chopped-off head is also the lady with the semblance of an angel.' For these Italian poets their goddess was again the Wisdom (Sapientia) of the Solomonic books: the eternally pre-existing companion of Christ—'I was daily his delight, rejoicing always before him'—and the playmate of Yaweh. The Song of Solomon was their text through the sermons of St. Bernard. They paid particular attention to the visions and dreams and, as in Dante's *Divine Comedy*, the actual initiatory power of the woman was acknowledged. 'It may be that what these poets had in common was a method of contemplation that expanded consciousness in them so that they were made open to the illumination of Sapientia . . .'[9] and this opened to them the world of imagination as perception. This method of contemplation was probably language charged with sexual illumination '. . . expressing in words not simply the ineffable experience of mystical illumination but that illumination experienced through woman, in whom divine and earthly love were united as one.'[10]

Call her Mary Lucifer—'Mary the Light-Giver'—as the Magdalene was known. She was the companion of Jesus and 'there was no grace that He refused her, nor any mark of affection that He withheld from her.'[11]

In the *Pistis Sophia*, a third-century Gnostic scripture, Mary Magdalene became the questioner of Jesus, much in the manner of the riddling of the Queen of Sheba or of the catechism of the oriental love-books between Parvati and Shiva, or between the Dark Girl and the Yellow Emperor. Again and again the Magdalene, and what Ean Begg calls the 'whore wisdom,' was associated with the establishment of cults of the Black Virgin, particularly in southern France, the Cult of Love, and the Gnostic sects. Begg says that one of the directions the Black Virgin cult points towards is '*the alternative church of Mary Magdalene*, James, Zacchaeus, Gnosticism, Cathars, Templars and alchemists.'[12]

It is as though Mary Lucifer beckons from the invisible, from the blackness, to those who can enter and return, their lives-in-the-body enhanced and nourishing the soul. For the German poet Rilke, the world must pass into its invisibility before it can be *felt*: 'Earth, do you not wish this: to arise invisibly within us? Is this not your dream, to be invisible also one day? Earth! Invisible!'[13] He also speaks of the 'vision-in-the-dark-angel.'

When discussing Rilke the literary critic Hartman echoes the parapsychologist Morris concerning the ESSP of 'Nature's untranslatable concreteness' in that it is a matter of 'non-visual bodily feelings.' If it is seen, it is 'seen with the edge of the eyes. . . . There is in the mind an instant of radiation . . . no singular percept . . .' Then the mind returns to its sleep. But 'What is the meaning of this sleep that must precede and follow such apperception?' It is black theatre, for it 'is a readiness of the body and a suspense of the will enabling total reception from the senses.' It is a girl observed, 'the beloved announced by all creation,' and at the 'crossroad of the senses' she may then return, 'made of invisible images and inaudible sounds.'[14]

Let me say why I think this presiding image of the world's hope-in-love is represented as black, and why she is feminine also. I suggest again that she is black because she is the symbol and gateway to everything we could know in the apparent blackness beyond visible sight; because she represents all those forces that surround us which are not perceived in the eyes, but which extend from the visible spectrum into unexplored modes of being, to which animals seem closer than we are, at the 'crossroad of the senses.'

Guinizzelli's experience with the lady in the grey squirrel hat shows how the initiatory lady can be, must be, a fusion of angel and animal, the Sphinx.

She is black because she is also, as Isis was with her temples of dream incubation, the goddess of the vision of the night, the dream, and goddess too of all those marvels we see by inner light when our eyes are closed. Thus the Black Virgin is sometimes referred to as Notre-dame de Lumière: Black Light.[15]

She is black also because she is the goddess of clairvoyance, clear-seeing and the second sight—and in truth of first sight as well—the lover's light of touch in bed, and the dark light of touch in the womb. She is the Goddess of Intimacy, of being 'in touch' and of that fifth window, the skin, which is black and blind until those other kinds of light come into it.

She is the Black Goddess also because she lives in the darkness men have created by their blindness. She is sometimes represented as blind or blindfolded, as Justice is, or as the Blind Shekhina who has wept her eyes out in the exile to which men have consigned her. She is also blind Salome, haunting Jung's autobiography.

Jung used to imagine a deep descent. Once, he found there an old man with a white beard, and a beautiful young girl, who was blind, and called Salome. The old man explained that he was Elijah, and they 'had a black serpent living with them which displayed an unmistakable fondness' for Jung. His comment was that Salome 'is blind because she does not see the meaning of things.'[16]

This astonishing statement in my opinion protects Jung from some of the uncomfortable scientific facts that I have attempted to uncover. Much in the same way as Tillich took the 'juice/sap' of his theologising from his fantasies of the crucified Charis, so the blind woman with the black snake (as we shall see) is an impressive vision of the oracular woman with second sight (that not depending on the eyes) at her catamenic time of prophecy. I suspect Jung knew that Elijah, the prophet, was dependent on his 'trance-maiden,' as Jung himself depended for the 'juice/sap' of his psychology on the visions of women, as we shall see the 'black magicians' do.[17]

The Black goddess: what symbol of transformation could be more appropriate than the rich darkness, the black earth of Isis the alchemist, in our world

186

where, whatever the degree of poverty, no one is ever far away in any country from the television set with its bright trivial patter, potent optical illusions or screen chattering with venal calculations? And, in a patriarchal culture, what other figure than the female mediator, the personal anima in continuum with *anima mundi*? Chipping away at Oedipal complacency, how moody she makes him with her weather changes rooted in the unconscious senses, and what a wonderful richness of connection with the real world these imply. And in a culture that has outlawed sex-without-procreation, what more transformative actuality than the initiatrix who lies with a man through the night and changes him utterly?

Modern depth psychology started with Freud's Oedipus, and stuck with him for a long time. It was thought that the Oedipus complex was the mainspring of human evolution, when it is more probably the image of disaster. Later workers in depth psychology have as an alternative pointed to the truly evolutionary figure of the Black Goddess. Ean Begg is one of this important group.

Begg confirms that Jung himself distinguished two poles in the feminine archetype: the Virgin and the Whore. In Christian mythology the Virgin is assumed bodily and crowned by the Sun. Thus 'the Eva cycle is fulfilled.' But 'the Magdalene is still the lost sheep and still, as the Black Virgin, the secret, dark wisdom of the serpent, sells herself to all who desire her.' Thus, the ovulation, 'Eva,' is differentiated from the 'black sheep' or black serpent of the menstrual pole of the cycle.[18]

For Begg, the Black Virgin 'plays the leading role in the mysteries of death, rebirth and the underworld.' In well over 200 famous Western European shrines of the Virgin, her image is black. She is the 'shadow aspect of the Madonna' relating to heretical knowledge. Blindness and its cure are a province of Sicilian Persephone, a pagan Black Virgin. Candlemas (2 February) is important to the Black Madonna (as it is to the witches). At Ephesus she may have been a black stone, like the Ka'aba, and a famous statue of Cybele had a black stone for a head.[19] He says: 'Black is the colour of the unknown, the unconscious, and it is there that we must seek whatever it was that was repressed and lost. . . .'

Lilith is described with her Sphinx-like, part animal nature, called Lamia in the Vulgate, as the 'image of the fallen, expelled feminine principle that turns negative and wreaks revenge on mothers and their children' (because non-ovulatory). Yet she 'is a ladder on which one can ascend to the rungs of prophecy,' just as 'the Sphinx is well known for her perilous riddles . . . yet is hymned as the wise virgin. . . .[20] Only in India has her cult persisted unbroken through the centuries of Kali-Lalita, the dark flame.[21] However, in the nineteenth century Michel Vintras, under the Black Virgin's auspices at Sion-Vaudemont, preached again Joachim's prophecy of the advent of the age of the Holy Spirit and a redemption brought about by the Virgin mediatrix and her priestesses, in which the sexual act would be the high sacrament, restoring the original androgyny.[22] Could this be the wonderfully perfumed feminine *pneuma* or Muse known to Aquinas 'who kindles and inspires' and makes a one body out of the separate beings of her worshippers? Certainly the wonderful Gnostic hymn of the Black

Goddess speaking as Prunikos (the 'lewd') quoted by Begg begins to suggest this, and the experience of coming closer to the invisible and actual creatrix:

For I am the first and the last.
I am the honoured and the scorned one.
I am the whore and the holy one . . .
I am the one whom they call Life
and you have called Death.
I am the knowledge of my enquiry,
and the finding of those who seek after me . . .
I am the substance and the one who has no substance.
What is inside you is what is outside of you
and the one who fashions you on the outside
is the one who shaped the inside of you.
And what you see outside of you, you see inside of you;
It is visible and it is your garment.[23]

End Notes

[1]Graves (1965), p. 164.

[2]Von Franz (1966), pp. 428, 159, 300, 368, 242, 192, 379. Arguments for authorship, pp. 407-31. *Aurora Consurgens* draws heavily both on The Song of Solomon and alchemical literature.

[3]Anderson (1980), p. 110.

[4]Ibid., pp. 84-5.

[5]Ibid., p. 92. The whole question of visionary sexual love is treated with great sympathy and scholarship in this book.

[6]Walker (1983), pp. 859-64.

[7]Briffault (1927), vol. iii, pp. 477-83.

[8]Walker (1983), p. 862.

[9]Anderson (1980), pp. 112, 115.

[10]Ibid., p. 116.

[11]Walker (1983), p. 613.

[12]Begg (1985), p. 145 (my italics).

[13]'9th Duino Elegy'—author's version.

[14]Hartman (1966), pp. 86-9. The whole book in effect studies the struggle with nonvisual perception of Wordsworth, Hopkins, Rilke and Valéry.

[15]Begg (1985), p. 14.

[16]Jung (1963), pp. 174-5.

[17]As, for example, in his first truly Jungian book (Jung 1956) and Jung (1976).

[18]Begg (1984), p. 69.

[19]Begg (1981).

[20]Begg (1982).

[21]Begg (1984), p. 80.

[22]Begg (1985), p. 12. This book is a thesaurus of further information. Another excellent source   is Pope (1977).

[23]Begg (1984), pp. 73-4.

Richard Grossinger

from

The Night Sky

The early scientists did not give up the divine sky all at once, but it came to resemble a mind, a puzzle, a cryptogram, more than a myth. Neither Kepler nor Newton foresaw the implications of the modern linear sky they helped to create. For both of them, the sky remained an otherworldly mystery and a reflection of a more perfect geometry beyond it. Motion and gravity were visible forms of invisible forces. Still, they had dislodged the spiritual underpinning of heavenly movement; they had reduced the cosmic basis to numbers and geometries. Gradually, even the riddle and the mind of God disappeared, even though, well into the twentieth century, astronomy books continue to discuss, almost nostalgically, the place where God might fit into the eternal collection of stars and galaxies.

The City of the Sun was mapped by the revivalist hermetic movement of the sixteenth century but was more fully conceived by the science and astral magic of the following century. Tommaso Campanella, the Italian philosopher, was the transitional figure. He wrote the book *Città del Sole*. If the correct stellar influences could be drawn into the habitat of man by the proper talismanic figures and perfect circles, the celestial order would begin to shine in the houses and streets. The city might itself light automatically by divine sympathy. Angelic light would be drawn numerologically into its lanterns. In such a place, there would be no criminals; laws could not be disobeyed.[1] Fantastic as this may sound, it stands directly prior to Newton in the tradition that gave us electricity. Electricity would have satisfied Campanella too; it was stellar and geometric enough. But he would have been appalled to know that natural forces did not guarantee universal justice, plenty, and eternal brotherhood on Earth. His goal was to rule human society not by the sympathetic and synchronous magic of the heavens, as in astrology and the occult sciences, but by the mathematical and structural laws of the heavens applied to human society. Where else would justice and harmony reside but in the night sky? Where else could we seek the end to the discord of nations and the slaughter of man and beast?

By now we have grounded our stellar formulas, and we have tried parliaments, democracies, and capitalism. The industrial and socialist states of the modern world derive from this vision. And if we have not found what we were looking for, we have certainly learned the contents of that particular night sky.

The early hermetics and Rosicrucians, however, saw only the initial benign face of science. Hermes was an ancient Christ to them, a healer and a wise king. He was also the original star magus. If the great puzzle of motion in the astrum could be solved through mathematics, that same mathematics could show the way for troubled and unjust society. The old wars may have been Martian or Jovian, as man sought astrological explanation and legitimacy. The new revolutions, in the eighteenth century, were specific attempts to drive the lineage of kings from their thrones in the heavens down onto Earth, where scientific and rational man, common terrestrial humanity, could transpose the actual order of the stars. This is not the way history or the chronicles of the times describe it, but it is a possible way to understand the simultaneous evolution of astronomy, which describes the background against which man acts, and his moral order and society. A couple of centuries later, the task would be given to the proletariat, and Marxism would replace stellar law.

After the European revolutions against monarchy, with science providing a thousand promising paths to utopia, these ideas were secularized in the writings of the eighteenth-century *philosophes* and were embodied, in fact, in the Constitution of the United States. The idealism of America is, to a large degree, the idealism of the hermetic enlightenment, containing its belief in symmetry, the balance of power, and the harmony of the parts: a judicial, legislative, and executive system that mirrors the astral and elemental balance of forces. Thomas Jefferson was unintentionally a proxy Rosicrucian sage. We have long ago departed from the idealism, but it remains the clandestine optimistic image in American society. The pyramid on our dollar bill recalls its quasi-Egyptian origin.

The historian Carl Becker captures what this process meant to the eighteenth century, and what the United States inherited:

> The new heaven had to be located somewhere within the confines of the early life, since it was an article of philosophical faith that the end of life is life itself, the perfected temporal life of man; and in the future, since the temporal life was not yet perfected. But if the celestial heaven was to be dismantled in order to be rebuilt on earth, it seemed that the salvation of mankind must be attained, not by some outside, miraculous, catastrophic agency . . . but by man himself, by the progressive improvement made by the efforts of successive generations of men. . . . Posterity would complete what the past and the present had begun.[2]

The eighteenth century was no longer involved with astral magic, but it was far more aware than we are of the consequences of astronomical theory on society and vice versa. Enlightened government was a transposition of "the regular and constant order of facts by which God rules the universe."[3] Man had inherited God's logic, so he could be like God. Furthermore, he would *have* to be like God, for he was subject to the same universal law. And man had looked through a telescope into the workings of the upper spheres, the operations by which creation was held together. Gravity, light, and molecular structure had shown how God works. If He could keep order in His kingdom, containing such enormous objects and vast realms of space, surely man could derive regional laws from the cosmic laws and create a workable society.

One is uncomfortable thinking about nuclear war; yet the stars are nuclear war

190

writ large—enormous fires whose death throes will destroy planets and whose ultimate compacting (if true as proposed) will mark the end of the material universe. People who carry skulls and dress in death costumes throwing ashes to indicate the consequences of humankind tangling with this energy are enacting, on the one hand, a profound truth about something that has gone wrong in our time (the sloppy use of crude stellar energy in short-term schemes), and, on the other hand, a satire of what is shown in space: death of suns and stars too, death of the universe, which has been offered in place of religion, in place of internal process, and in place of life methodology. Our own age is threatened by a holocaust of man's own making (unless there be accomplice wizards and demons or extraterrestrial intelligences behind man himself), and it is no accident that scientific theology of this age proposes a cataclysm that will obliterate everything and what everything is—things which were ostensibly once brought into being by just such a cataclysm. We have hardly been less arbitrary and cruel to each other.

The "starring of the Earth" is now complete (if we may call it that by parallel with Charles Reich's 1960s fantasy of the "greening of America"). The explosion of nuclear weapons, imitating the Sun's own fueling process, is finally the epitome of relocating stellar law on Earth. The locomotives and early automobiles share something with Kepler's vision of the orbit of Mars and Newton's mathematicization of the gravitational force. Man thought he saw a retrievable being in the sky, but when he captured it, it was an unknown intruder and the sky became incidental. In fact, the sky, in the sense of original forces of physics, is everywhere, and it is no longer necessary to have reference to the actual radiance. The preference for social programs instead of the space program is a symptom of this dislodgement. Some want more bombs, others want more welfare checks, but they don't want the sky unless it serves them directly, either as a weapon or a controlled weather system. Our societies pretend to sit by themselves on their own terms, though the same universal laws, whatever they are and however we interpret them, hold everywhere.

Looking down on the Earth from space, Michael Collins understood our dilemma. We are like ants, digging up trifles from under the surface, oil and coal, as if they were limitless and as if this behavior were enlightened or even sane.[4] The only future that man can have at this rate must set imaginarily in future worlds of outer space. In terms of the Earth, man has failed to grasp in any economically or politically viable way that it is a planet, a single planet. There are no others; to imagine them does not create them.

Meanwhile, science has given us another sky with the seeds of a new ecological morality. The fossil fuels are solar energy, altered by photosynthesis and aeonic chemical activity. The winds are also solar, or gravitational, in their origin. The tides are lunar gravitational energy. Life is stellar chemistry. All the rivers flow into all the seas, and all the clouds arise from the whole and stand against it atmospherically. The lightning and the radiation of the ionosphere are aspects of a single field. It is one boundaryless chemical droplet, steaming from its seas and lapping up into ice, with clouds strung through the invisible winds. "Brown-red is the color," wrote the poet Charles Olson, "of the brilliance of earth."[5]

This was the first gift of Whole Earth consciousness. We were allowed to see a unity directly, and it was a unity expressed throughout mankind: in other ways in the writings of the alchemists and Taoists, in Zuni creation myths and the *I Ching*. Nature is a one, a harmony of diverse elements, and it acts as a one: the clouds, the Arctic ice, the open seas, the Sun penetrating the whole thing, making its radiance in the guts and giving it a blue aura that separates it from the surrounding space as a fine engraving is different from the unmarked jade around it. If it were not for our fearful greed and fatal existential doubt, we could almost come home in this century.

Solar energy is atomic energy too—not the direct explosion in imitation of the star core but its medicinal by-product passing through space. We can call it medicinal without fear of metaphor or sentimentality because the process of photosynthesis is the protean medicinal process. It weaves the strands that become the self-healing replicating cells. It creates the flesh and blood of the nuclear scientists and engineers and the antinuclear demonstrators counterposed in the atomic sunlight. The problem of the sources of matter and energy is a far more complex one than the pros and cons of any politicization reveal. We are the products of explosions, we contain explosions, and we keep ourselves going with a tinder box.

To accept solar energy and reject atomic energy may seem a contradiction, but it is a practical strategy. It also relives an ancient mythology. Solar energy is what the universe gives us of itself at this distance: Take this and you will be enlightened, take this and you will be healed. And we have not been wrong yet. We have waited to be born, and the seas have filled with life. We have waited while life crawled onto the land and established itself, and we understood that we were born already, and then we came more fully into being and built our farms and manors, our astronomical observatories and our cities. In these we understood the Sun again, the measure of our place in the cosmos—as simple as units on a sundial, the fields of barley and bulgar in the Near East, the vast rainbow corn of the New World. Our solar society existed for millennia. It was a society of flowers, grains, fish pools, tonics, mirrors, and delicate parchment. All of this came from the stark abyss of fiery hydrogen gases a mere stone's throw away. Gravity covered it, and light dispersed through the sky into colors which formed eyes to see them. It couldn't have been a better universe. It couldn't have happened to a better universe. It said: wait and I will happen. And it did.

The new atomic universe of radio astronomy and particle physics is a terrifying one, and we have become its dull-witted targets. We are blind to the particles we are meant to avoid, radioactivity and decayed nuclear matter, and we cannot see, even with our finest telescopes, the chaos and violence that is destroying the cosmos. Its warnings and prophecies are all about us, yet we are somehow spared and allowed to go on living in what is essentially a Greek city.

The two terms of the paradox must go together: death by too much energy, panic from too little energy—panic and starvation.

The physicists have given us nothing. They have failed us. The very sound of radio noise in the sky is the crackle of our own anxiety, and it is also the crackle of our present cosmological insufficiency. The great violence we perceive in space may be more than our own destructiveness; it may be the suppression of our creative abilities to harvest inner space, a perception that the inner spaces are in turmoil and we are cut off. But what if we are not? How dread the responsibility then to make a decent world and recover our birthright.

We stand before an incredible task. It would be something for even a planet of supermen who could fly into space. We must, if we too are to survive, avert the destruction of the universe. We must reverse the Big Bang. Which is to say, we must prevent the destruction of our own planet and its systems of meaning. We must pass through the Big Bang, even as we must pass through existentialism, Marxism, capitalism, materialism, and all the other tricks of the atomic age, and we must make a new universe, something like the Ionian and Hindu ones but without exactly those features that lead inevitably and rightly back to the present condition. The darkness is not something that we can go back on. Its riddle itself is our destiny.

End Notes

(The Night Sky, Chapter 23, Star Myth)

[1]Frances A. Yates, *Giordano Bruno and the Hermetic Tradition* (Chicago: University of Chicago Press, 1964), pp. 367-370.

[2]Carl L. Becker, *The Heavenly City of the Eighteenth-Century Philosopher* (New Haven: Yale University Press, 1932), p. 129.

[3]Ibid., p. 45.

[4]Isaac Bashevis Singer, *The Family Moskat*, translated from the Yiddish by A. H. Gross (New York: Knopf, 1950), p. 594.

[5]Charles Olson, *The Maximus Poems. Volume Three* (New York: Grossman, 1975), p. 39.

Stage and Meadow
from Cosmic Superimposition

The basic interest in the subject of this publication is human and not primarily astrophysical. *In what manner is man rooted in nature?* is the question around which the theme revolves. It is doubtless the orgone energy function in man's reasoning that touches on reality.

The character structure of man, the frozen history of the past four to six thousand years of human society, will determine man's fate and conditions in the near future. Looking forward through a dense fog, which has obscured man's view for several decades now, the author has tried to draw the ultimate consequences from what he has learned about human functioning over a period of more than thirty years of intimate knowledge of the characterological backstage of the public scene. Very little of the actual drama of present-day social struggles will appear in these pages, however. The author did not intend to study the impact of the backstage events upon the performance of the public stage. On the contrary, he has opened the door that leads from the backstage of the theater to the spacious fields and meadows surrounding the theater of present-day human affairs. Observed from these meadows, under glittering stars in endless heavens, the show on the stage appears strange. Somehow, the endless heavens on silent nights do not seem in any sort of accord with the show inside the theater or with the subject of the performance. All that belongs to the show seems far off, unreal, and very much out of place if seen from *outside* the theater building.

Why does man present gay or tragic or pornographic love stories on the stage, with people crowding into the auditorium to laugh or cry or to shudder with lust, while deep in the woods that surround the meadows, policemen are busy disturbing lovers in silent, quivering embrace? It does not seem to make good sense.

This is only one small, insignificant example of the great discrepancy and the varied nonsensicalities in man's existence. We shall not delve into any of these social, psychological, biological or political issues, which have been thoroughly elaborated by the author in previous writings. The social problem does not seem to yield to any kind of inquiry within the sphere of man's thought and actions during the past few thousand years. Let us therefore try to look at it from outside.

The impetus to the present study came from some disturbing experiences in the Orgonomic Infant Research Center, which was founded by the author for the purpose of studying nature in the newborn infant. Orgonomic research had broken down completely the boundaries between the *bioenergetic* and *astrophysical* realms, heretofore kept strictly delineated by mechanistic natural science and transgressed only in mystical experiences, in a factually useless way. The newborn infant appears as an energy system that brings some definite cosmic laws of functioning into man's realm of operation, i.e., to remain with our analogy, with the infant, definite cosmic functions pass through the door that leads from the meadow and the open fields into the theater building and onto the stage of human drama.

In this respect, the newborn infant is comparable to the experience one often has when working with orgonotic pulses on the Geiger counter or on the oscillograph. One can easily switch over from pulses in the living organism to the same type of pulses in the atmosphere. One operates in a practical manner with the *common functioning principle,* the CFP, of man and cosmos. There is no longer any barrier between a human organism and its cosmic environment, which, of necessity, is and always has been its origin. One forgets the show on the stage and concentrates on this amazingly practicable identity of living and non-living functions.

On the human stage, it is forbidden by law under punishment of fine or imprisonment "or both" to show or even discuss the embrace between two children of the opposite sex at the age of three or five. Somewhere in the audience sits a human being, broken in his emotional security, full of perverse longings and hatred against what he has lost or never known, who is ready to run to the district attorney with the accusation that children are being misused sexually and that public morals are being undermined. Outside on the meadow, however, the genital embrace of two children is a source of beauty and wonder. What drives two organisms together with such force? No procreation is involved as yet, and no regard for the family. Somehow this drive to unite with another organism comes with the newborn when it passes from the meadow onto the stage. There it is immediately squelched and smolders under cover, developing smoke and fog.

Inside, on the stage, the embrace between two children or two adolescents or two grownups would appear dirty, something totally unbearable to look upon.

Outside, under the glimmering stars, no such reaction to the sight of the embrace of two organisms would ever occur in sane minds. We do not shudder at the sight of two toads or fish or animals of other kinds in embrace. We may be awed by it, shaken emotionally, but we do not have any dirty or moralistic sentiments. This is how nature works, and somehow the embrace fits the scene of silent nights and broad meadows with infinity above. The intellectual cynic and the smutty barroom hero, of course, belong on the stage and not in the meadow, where they would certainly disturb the harmony and not fit into the picture. But we would refuse to believe that a meditating Indian sage would object to the sight or not fit in.

Somehow, the deeply searching human mind has never failed to find itself in the meadows of nature, outside the theater of human stage shows, be it on high mountains or beside blue lakes. Somehow, the harmony in natural functioning belonged to the sage. It does not matter here whether or not human meditation has ever succeeded in lifting the veil. It has at least tried to do so and always outside the realm of human stage performances, be it a theater, a political gathering or a religious ceremony. When Christ found himself in trouble, he went to meditate completely alone on a meadow or a hill, in silent spaces. And again, something important, though inscrutable, was brought back from the meadow or the mountain onto the human stage.

Every single religious movement in the history of man has tried to bring the message of the emotional depth from the meadow onto the stage inside, in vain.

Tolerance, goodness, patience, brotherhood, love and peace are, as elements of this mood under glittering stars, contained in every religious creed; but the moment they were brought to the inside of the theater and onto the stage, they became a farce and a sham. Why?

Astronomy has always been in close touch with this same mood. Kepler brought the idea of a living force, the *vis animalis,* that governs the heavens as it governs the living organism right onto the stage. It did not survive.

The constellations of the stars in the heavens in ancient times were represented, most fancifully, by different living creatures—the scorpion and the bear, Andromeda and Hercules and Pisces, etc. Thus, man knew that somehow he came from the heavens into which, in nearly every religion, he believed he would return after death on earth.

For ages, man has projected his own image onto the heavens in the shape of different gods in human form, again showing that he believed himself to be somehow rooted in the heavens.

In the belief of the return of the soul, of reincarnation (and the believers have not been simple fools, as the dried-up creatures on the political stage want us to believe), man has somehow searched for a reality in which to root himself in the vastnesses of the universe. So far, in vain!

In recent times, more and more human thinking has come to assume that the idea of a universal natural law and the idea of "God" are pointing to one and the same reality.

Abstract mathematics, from the Pythagoreans to the modern relativists, has somehow assumed that the human power of reasoning is closely related to cosmic functions. True, no concrete links between reason and universe became evident. Still, the close connection was taken for granted. Mere reasoning seemed to have corroborated such a close interrelation between "mind" and "universe." However, it is not readily comprehensible what these links are. Orgonomy has contributed some major insights into this riddle by disclosing the transitions from reasoning to emotions, from emotions to instincts, from instincts to bio-energetic functions, and from bio-energetic functions to physical orgone energy functions.

Thus, the impelling force to search and the religious belief meet somewhere in the vast spaces. But both reasoning and belief instantly distort the clarity of the meadow experience when they transfer it onto the human stage. WHY? Is it because man is a different being on the meadow from what he is on the stage? Probably, but the answer is not good enough.

Now, the boundaries separating religious belief and pure reasoning have been crossed, or rather wiped away by orgone research. It was shown in *Ether, God and Devil* that both reason and belief are rooted in the orgonotic, bio-energetic functioning of man. They are both rooted in one and the same functional realm.

Thus, it appears that all the events on the stage are somehow rooted in events on the meadow. But the common root is obfuscated by definite changes that occur during the passage through the door leading from the vastnesses of nature to the narrowness of the stage. Outside, everything seems to be ONE. Inside, the stage proper is cleanly separated from the auditorium. Outside, you can appear as you are. Inside, you have to disguise your true appearance by a false beard, or a false pose or a make-believe expression. Outside, two children in deep embrace would not astonish or shock anyone. Inside, it would immediately invoke police action. Outside, a child is a child, an infant is an infant, and a mother is a mother, no matter whether in the form of a deer, or a bear, or a human being. Inside, an infant is *not* a infant if its mother cannot show a marriage certificate. Outside, to know the stars is to know God, and to meditate about God is to meditate about the heavens. Inside, somehow, if you believe in God, you do not understand or you refuse to understand the stars. Outside, if you search in the heavens, you refuse, and rightly so, to believe in the sinfulness of the natural embrace. Outside, you feel your blood surging and you do not doubt that something is moving in you, a thing you call your emotion, with its location undoubtedly in the middle of your body and close to your heart. Inside, you do not live with your total organism, but only with your brain; and not only is it forbidden to study emotions, more, you are accused of being an adherent of phrenology and mysticism if you experience emotions in the same way inside as you do outside. Outside, there is such a thing as the movement and quivering of everything, from the atmosphere to your nerves; inside, there is only empty space and atoms dissolved into an endless row of "particles."

Let us stop now. It is enough to have shown the great discrepancy.

We are now moving into the open spaces to find, if possible, what the newborn infant brings with it onto the human stage. This study will, among other things, deal with hurricanes, the shape of the galaxies, and the "ring" of the aurora borealis. This will astonish many a reader. What, he will inevitably ask, has a well-known, distinguished psychiatrist to do with hurricanes, galaxies, and the aurora borealis? Is not this proof enough of the rumor that he went "off the beam" some years ago, after having reached a high degree of distinction in the field of psychiatry? It is not the writer who went "off the beam," but the reader who thinks that way. He has forgotten his origin and refuses to be disturbed in the enjoyment of the stage show make-believe.

He has refused to leave the theater and to follow us through the door onto the vast meadow whence all being stems. He has not realized that a newborn infant cannot possibly be understood from the viewpoint of a culture into which it is being born. This is its future. It can only be understood from where it came, i.e., from OUTSIDE the stage.

Hurricanes, galaxies and the aurora borealis come into the view of a human being who deals with the mentally sick and with newborn infants if he follows consistently the red thread of inquiry and reasoning that leads outward from unhampered observation of man's behavior toward his origin in the cosmic realm of functioning. Those who wish to stay inside and refuse to move out are, of course, entitled to do so. But they are not entitled to pass judgment on the experience of others who do not believe in the rationality of the stage show, who refuse to accept the dogma that what man displays inside the narrow space on the stage is his true being and his true nature. Those who remain sitting in the tight little place have no right whatsoever to judge what the wanderer on the outside experiences, sees, smells, lives through. No dweller on 32nd Street who never left New York would dare pass judgment on a report from an explorer of the North Pole. Yet, without ever having cared even to peep outside through the keyhole of the door, he usurps the right to pass judgment on the experiences of orgonomy, which operates far outside his narrow, tight, little stage. Let him be modest and confine himself to his own little world. We do not permit him to have opinions, and with a show of authority to boot, about things he never dreamed of approaching. He may be an authority on the stage of the theater, or a well-trained critic of the play, or he may be an actor playing the role of a professor of biology or astronomy. But in all these cases he is within the theater building. And unless he actually steps outside onto the meadow and looks around himself, seeing what is to be seen there in the open spaces, he had better be quiet and remain sitting comfortably where he is. Nobody will blame him. Outside, however, he is no authority whatsoever. There are no false beards outside, only living beings searching and wondering about where they came from and why they are there. We shall be glad to take his hand and lead him out into the night, where we have learned first to see and to feel what we intend to measure. We shall be happy to do so. But first let him remove his false beard of dignity. Let him be a man first.

Finally, it should be clearly stated that the seeming immodesty of the scope of this investigation is a quality of the function "cosmic superimposition" and not of the investigator. We are dealing with cosmic dimensions to be measured in "light years," not in seconds.

Michael McClure

from
Wolf Net

Being is the creature's contact with its surroundings and the accumulation of instinct and experience-information. An animal's contact with environment is obviously physical. Storage and circulation of information is material (atomic, molecular, chemical). More and more light is shed on the nature of the storage as each decade passes.

In the religion of *being* the universe is the Messiah. For the creature to know itself it must touch physically, or physically reconstellate information. Without touch, sight, taste, smell, affective perception, memory, and imagination there can be no body image. If there is no body there is no being. All life is sensate and sensitive. Life is aware of itself by the abrasion of the so-called inorganic world, or by other creatures in the organic world. But it would be a mechanistic error to allow only the types of matter that we are aware of to represent the possibilities of matter.

There may be physical constellations of a kind that we do not yet perceive. These might be true post-technological bodies of knowledge and awareness that go far beyond the dreams of simplistic astrology. We must remember that we have a given number of senses to perceive the outward universe—and yet we can easily imagine, or intuit, that the universe is infinite both dimensionally and as a field for undreamed senses.

A ribosome in a liver cell in a salmon might relate to a field of energies or a "position" within a quasar or in a distant sun. There might be interlocked and predisposed relationships of these, and other constructs. That is speculation and any knowledge of it presumably comes in the distant future or in the perceptions of a visionary. If the universe is a single flow, vibration, or aura, it seems highly likely that such interrelationships exist. And the universe IS indeed an aura of trillionically multiplex interrelations. And it is primarily comprised of natures of matter that we do not, certainly not consciously, contact. We cannot perceive an anti-matter universe—yet everything that we perceive as real might be an empty pinprick of nothingness within a nirvana of anti-matter beyond comprehension.

Nineteenth and twentieth century science tend to deny that creatures can touch each other without putting paw to antler, or hand to another body or hand. It must not be considered that physical touch is solely as gross a thing as it is construed to be by formulaic scientists. The animal body undoubtedly gives off energies, and may have fields, of which we are not yet aware.

Probably we live within such auric fields, in addition to the obvious ones of odor and electricity. When they are discovered they will be considered physical.

All life is a single unitary surge, a single giant organism—even a single spectacular protein molecule. In the four billion years life has grown on this planet it is not possible to imagine (in view of its whirlwind energy and delicate complexity) that there have not developed interacting fields, forces, auras, within the behemoth topology of it. If life could be seen as a structure, not against a background of time, but all at once as a free-standing sculpture, the sight would be illuminating and staggering. We would then form new concepts of interrelations of life that we do not now have.

As a creature presses itself against its physical environment, known and unknown, conscious and unconscious, it discovers the contours of its body. In growth, death, injury, expansion, contraction, movement, perception, etc., it discovers and forms itself from the genetic possibilities that it contains. It fills out a general pattern and becomes an individual in the precise and unique blow-up of the generalized possible construct.

Intellectual concepts that society has imagined to be the test of the creature are not the test of being. Being is the body of acts, gestures, fears, loves, hungers, that are manifested against the field background of the universe.

If proportion, comparison, measurement, and statistics are put aside, and the universe is envisioned as a vibrational timeless and time free sculpture—then any part of the structure is of equal importance. The surface of the earth means no more, *and no less,* than a hundred thousand spiral galaxies. Mozart and a wolf are no less important than a star—all is part of a giant constellative configuration. The configuration does NOT match our traditional cultural concepts of it. The model proposed to us by history and culture is too removed from an overview to be of service.

Man's societal intellectual processes have made a graph, a statistical chart, from views that are biologically irrelevant. An overview is not possible when the accumulation of insights are programmed through a non-biological structure.

The universe is the Messiah because it is the possibilities of our being. We are that Messiah, yet we brush, hurl, and gently touch our beings against it to experience it. Our experience of the universe is also the universe perceiving itself. One point of perception is no less subjectively relevant than another—all are part of a whole. Subjectivity and objectivity resolve themselves as meaningless scratches on a mechanical graph.

For questing creatures of our type the necessity of a frontier, psychic or physical, is a constancy. The psychic frontier is not satisfying in itself. We are part of a surge destined to expand. To conceive of the flow as a culture of bacteria on a plate of agar is negative, cynical, and a defiance of what it means to be a creature. It is a human view and not an animal view. On the brilliance to be among the progenitors of poison gas and the H-bomb as well as moonflight and OP art.

The more brilliant the contribution, the greater is the addition to the culture that encircles and snares man. But the achievements of outstanding individuals are the achievements of outstanding animals. The finest animal achievements are vigor, and the marshalling of the selves of the self into the pursuit of an extraordinary goal.

The unified, and unifying culture structure has twisted all achievements, plundering the surface of the earth that life partakes of and rises from. The living soil is turned to explosives to be dropped on another race on another continent. Fossil fuels are sought after and combusted, polluting the atmosphere that is one of the progenitors and necessities of life. Major plant life, necessary to the carbon dioxide/oxygen cycle, is ruthlessly devastated to create multitudes of useless unappetizing objects for amusement and disposal. Waste is a pleasure natural to man as an animal—it is exploited by the culture. Sexual pleasure has been dampened so that architecture may be accomplished. Simultaneously sexuality is encouraged, exalted, and great attention given to erotism in the social dream-images of the media. This intensifies horizontal stresses in personality and culture.

The wild animal populations (those that survived or came into being after the glacier-thermal changes) have been eaten, or destroyed for pleasure or conquest of land. Forests are demolished. Domesticated animals overgraze the land. Deforested areas are biocided where the grazing has taken place. The madness increases as technological propensity for madness increases—and as the earth's surface becomes less and less capable of sustaining strife and overpopulation. The game seems to be up. Therefore, unless it is part of a joke, that all who can think clearly have decided to see through, it is time to change the game.

The game has been, for thousands of years, that man is not an animal. Man's desire to be special, in view of the cruelty he reads into nature, is not surprising. At fault is the idea that he is NOT an animal! He does not address himself to nature in a unique way—he utilizes, he exploits, moves, explores, lives, dies, gives birth, expands, grows. But he has been over-successful and must review his successes. There are genetic patterns within the body and the species. There are patterns within the surge of the whole life flow. Some of these animal patterns limit success. Some limit it *finally* for types or species.

For Cro Magnon man life was extremely pleasurable much of the time. His complex consciousness of self was rewarding. The relationship of himself to his group members, family, beloveds, enemies, and environment was satisfying for moments. These moments fed his energies in a way that we cannot imagine today. Being a relatively rare animal, surrounded by easily obtainable foodstuffs and common dangers, he appreciated fully the lives and deaths of his friends and relatives. The band was too small to other hand, to imagine that creatures of this planet are destined to survive, continue expanding, and will ultimately triumph no matter what the impediment is unrealistic. The surge of living material that we are part of is a particle of the larger structure that we cannot comprehend. Imagining our humanistic longings to be representative of that structure is a dubious stance.

We CAN imagine ourselves to be the universe experiencing itself—and the universe as the field and background (the meat) for the experience and self-experience. If we realize that the relative importance of occurrence to occurrence is a judgment made by the humanistic tradition and not an insight into the nature of the universe—then we are free to feel biologically that each point of perception is of importance.

Each life is a tentacle, or finger, or extrusion of Messiah or Tathagata experiencing self and the universe through entrances of perception, movement, and contact. But to give it human nature, any more than to attribute the nature of a sea cucumber to the Messiah is beyond reason. We are not more alive than a protozoan—we are more complex. We are multiple trillions of cells, a miniature universe of molecules, rather than stars. As we are clusters of cells in a multiplex structure, we are also not a SELF or an INTELLIGENCE. We are congresses of SELVES and of INTELLIGENCES. When the congress agrees we please ourselves.

We may speak of the universe because we are part of it. We partake of it and it partakes of us and we shape ourself against it. When we decided to become human and not animal we invented measurement and statistic and proportion to shield us from our natures. These are man's most fantastic inventions and the root for all technological and civilizational construction. The question is whether to keep the inventions and hope to supersede them by recognizing our creature being, or whether we are in the process of extinguishing ourselves in honor of the discoveries.

Man is greatly concerned with his individual survival. He is aware of the preciousness and uniqueness of his individuality. This awareness created an arrogance which demands that he see *himself* enshrined as he originally pedestalled his gods. It became his nature to be a carnivore and perhaps a killer. After he enshrined himself, man began to regret his nature and to deny it. Man is in a time of swift change—the gene pool allows new possible types and consequently new possible perceptions. Intellectivity is enshrined and given lip service while the masses move to old dances of death which almost generationally change the names on the banners above the melée.

The machine is now the executor of the death writ. The machine began with measurement, with proportion, and with statistic. Michelangelo, the Greek sculptor Phidias, the forgotten Aztec architects, Pythagoras, and Euclid are among the grandfathers many-times-removed of computers that plan the war and direct young men involved. It is part of their cultural unnerve him with social stress. His life fit into a social pattern in which he took an obvious biological position in relationship to other members of the group. As he grew older, his role shifted enough to be novel or pleasurable yet kept a stability that was gratifying. The dominant protected the weak whenever it was practical. Or possibly there was more idealism than that. The biologically capable individual had a chance to explore his potentialities within the social structure.

Apparently sympathetic hunting magic existed as a ritual for the Cro Magnon. Neanderthal relics still exist—earth altars over which an animal skin was stretched. (It is interesting that the earliest altars were representations of animals. It is only later that man placed his own image upon the altar so that he might see himself exalted.) It is wrong to view this rite of hunting magic as anything approximating religion. There are inherent animal rituals; a father makes faces at his child; children hide and jump out at each other; a grown man sneaks up on his wife and scares and kisses her— as a wolf does with his bitch. These are natural animal games and rites. They fulfill a shape of training, or act out internalized desires and energies. The rites fill out natural longings, or are concomitant with rearrangements of perceptions and activities that stimulate a ludic sense. It is only speculation that these Paleolithic altars, punctured with spearholes, and the wall paintings are sympathetic magic. It is as conceivable that they were a game performed in moments of leisure—or to recall pleasures of the hunt. The modern religious view is *religiomorphic*. It wishes to attribute religion (developing religion) where such a thing may not have existed.

It is as likely that Cro Magnon WAS a religious being, did conceive of himself and the universe about him as a reality, a dream, a structure he partook in. Keats, the English poet, and a wolf, have no need for institutionalized religion. They seem fully pleased to perceive external and personal being. Atheistic Keats said that life is a vale of soul-making.

The mystic Meister Eckhart held that *belief in God might debilitate the religious experience.* To know God, his shape, form, color, size, attributes, temperament narrows perceptions. It inhibits clear sight by making rigid structures upon which experience must be hung, or a graph against which all things *must* be seen.

Biological experience is religious in itself if it can be felt within the world-field in which each creature evolved. But when the endocrine system is exhausted by stress of overpopulation and technology, a brainwashing takes place. The body releases urine, salts—loses its chemical balance. Life stances and intellectual and intellective positions are reversed in reaction to the slide of circumstances. We are unable to feel clearly. The individual creature is cut adrift from the surge of which he is a part. He cannot partake in the unique and universal vision.

THE BODY IS A FAIRYLAND—or more correctly, is congeries of FAIRYLANDS and ELFLANDS. The invention of the electron microscope has made possible viewing of the micro-detail of cellular infrastructure, and Xray diffraction techniques have enabled men-creatures to view the molecular structure of parts of the cell. With mild enlargement (sixty magnifications) of the surface of the tongue, the tastebuds can be seen as a garden of individual beings serving to taste and to guide the macro-being. A skin pore magnified several thousands of times is seen as a naturally irregular meat cave not a smooth glabrous mimic of a machine. The pores are inhabited by bacteria natural to the ecology of the skin.

Under electron magnification the sleek (to the tongue) surface of the teeth is seen to be a multiplicity of fairy caverns. The structure of bone is an airy pixie lattice resembling the most fantastic constructions of calcareous sea creatures. The surface of the hand resembles an arid deltic plain. The hair is a forest. Under further magnification the surface of the hair is scaled and overlapped protein bark. The saucer-shaped red cell can be seen as an entity—trillions of them can be seen in the activity of carrying oxygen and returning with CO_2. The phagocytes can be seen as lovely shapefully shapechanging creatures extruding themselves to ingest harmful bacteria. Under intense magnification of the electron instrument the coiled genes of bacteria are visible. It can be presumed that Science is as erroneous in many of its assumptions as is any religion, but no religion is needed in an expanded view of the BEING of life. We can see more and more of the Messiah as we press ourselves against, as we are part of, and as we intuit with extensions of ourselves new interior landscapes. Intellectivity has a groundwork, shaky or not, for further and further imagination.

The radiotelescopes, and sensory devices placed, and to be placed, on satellites tell us undreamed information about macro-objectivity. We discover that the stars seem to be present in galaxies in a ratio equivalent to the density of molecules in a thin gas. Contrariwise the billions of galaxies appear to be related to each other in a density comparable to molecules in a liquid.

It is as ridiculous to buy the bag of molecules, electrons, protons, atoms, etc., as it would be to hold firm belief in the diagrams and symbols of the Gnostic philosophers. Yet as all open systems seem to work for a vantage, the sensory devices of the new sciences give groundwork for greater and greater imagination. It can be hoped that if mammal-man allows the expansion of new sensory sciences, that the sciences will supersede themselves and become a new, real, truer, alchemy. If man looks to these sciences as a mammal, and as one cousin in a life surge, and if he sees himself as a representation of a high degree of complexity in a universe that is a being-and-messiah experiencing himself, he will find that his most biologically idealistic concepts are true and that they will expand themselves in a systemless system. Perhaps finally he will discover many of the possibilities latent within BEING and within his being.

These new discoveries of science are useless and meaningless in the intellective life of societal-existential man. He feels neither the immediate pleasures that he is open to, for the most pleasurable are forbidden, nor does he feel the new sensory expansion. This is because his training is anti-biological. Rather than awareness that he is spiritually proportionless, as is any extrusion, or facet, or scintilla of being, MAN is aware of his immediately possible extinction. The net of chemical-biological-atomic weaponry constantly surrounds man. The bombers fly to Asia or elsewhere like metal pollen from a machine society.

Some of the most intelligent adopt the viewpoint that man is like a culture of bacteria. They draw attention to the resemblance of city spires and topology to bacterial colonies. Given limited nutriments the bacteria expand till they poison themselves with their wastes. The colony becomes extinct. It is probably true that men in the mass of society are as mindless, and meaningful, or meaningless, as a single bacterium extinguishing itself. BUT it is not a manifest destiny of a mammal to be like bacteria. It is even conceivable that we, or our genus, (as the butterflies are the fruiting body of their egg-caterpillar-flying plasm) are the sporing body of this planet—the tinkertoy rocketry of aerospace programs might be proto-spores in the evolution.

It does not seem likely that either man, or the planet will travel far in metal capsules. But if the finest sensory perceptions of science are enabled to alchemize themselves into a new condition, unimaginable travels might be at hand. It is possible that gene pools in places of the future or past might create new and beatific frontiers of the now defeated Pleistocene. Men and men-mammal creatures of unimaginable types may spread the complexity of the surface of the planet—or meet with other such bodies elsewhere. Constant latent possibilities may blossom in inconceivable ways. There is no need that such expansion be either Faustian or Humanistic. Man need not project his features upon the being of the universe. Or even divide life from non-life in the spectrum. We do not know what *biological* is or might be or become. That man is blinding himself to being, and *to* his being, is a cruelty, and a torture that he feels with each breath. The torture has come to be a field background. One can learn to live with the sound of jackhammers on the street and eventually consciously forget the pain. But one is not likely to have high creature morale in such real anguish.

Man is in pain—the pain of pollution—and in pain of sensory and spiritual blindnesses. There is no finer thing than to be a mammal, or a living, complex, sensory creature of meat and blood, and protein, and muscle. But the macro-organism (human) is self-hypnotized by the perversions of a few of his natural desires.

Society is as demoralized as the individuals, who become mindless, within the structure. And there is no solution. Solutions may only be worked and hoped for—BUT the solutions will not come from either mass-society or from a single individual or from a *few* individuals.

The mammal creature man certainly will not continue long without a high degree of morale and a surrender of perverse and decadent blinders.

In view of the new sensory expansions it is a very normal idea that LIFE IS SPIRIT, that life is not separable from matter (except arbitrarily) and that conceivably ALL THE MESSIAH is spirit—all is matter. And we know very little about MATTER—and it would be better to be plural and say "MATTERS"! A mammal, a wolf, or a man-mammal is an evident material creature unless one is wholly solipsistic. The creature is examined and it is found to be comprised of organs, tissues, bones, fluids. These parts are composed of cells, or in the case of fluids are the products of cells.

When cell interiors are examined under new sensory devices, and with new methods of examination, it is found that the cells are topologically complex structures. They are functioning and in motion. They are neither liquid nor crystal but have the properties of both and perform activities that we attribute to living material. The organelles and the ultramicroscopic surfaces are also sometimes in motion either actually "morphologically" or chemically. Some of these reproduce, create new substances by chemical combination, or transmit codes for such activity. Meat is the only known anti-entropic system. We can move further to the level of the gene within the nucleus of the cell and find the gene is an extremely long molecule comprised of thousands of sub-molecules. The threadlike molecule is a double molecule—it mirrors itself—being two threads. This double-thread molecule which is of extraordinary length and thin-ness compared to other natural molecules has compressed, or encapsuled, or shaped itself into a compact bundle. It is seen that these genetic molecules (which are the memory of the meat plasm) are comprised of atoms of perfectly normal and abundant elements found on the surface of the earth.

It is apparent that these atoms come from the earth. We are sure that there was once no life and there has come into being more and more life over billionic years. This atoms in living structures derive directly from the surface of the planet. The planet surface becomes more and more complexly arranged by changing to life. The energy trapped in the complex structures is the energy of the sun's rays as they touch the living and becoming-living surface of the earth. The trapped energy begins in simple plants and is passed up a food chain. (We are told that certain atoms in the earth, in the cells of life, are of elements that were forged billions of years ago in stars existent before this galaxy was shaped.) All of the atoms and molecules in the cell, and in the creature, and in the structure and being of the creature are ordinary, normal parts of the planetary surface and its being. There is no clear demarcation of where these complex acid molecules cease being inert and come to be what we call life. It is clear, that under certain circumstances the self-formation of these life molecules is a natural phenomenon. The only argument is whether it is a rare or common occurrence. The point however is that it occurred. (I have heard that the great Russian scientist Oparin believes there may be trigger mechanisms that drift through space and land on planetary surfaces and bring the organic into being. Perhaps somewhere on some other surface, though chances might be quintillionically against it, there are moas, glyptodons, Carolina parakeets, passenger pigeons, herds of bison—or similar creatures.)

The earth and sun are part of the total and visible galaxy we inhabit. They are inter-related by processes that we have not settled yet in our perceptions. A simple verbal equation can be derived: CREATURE/ CELL / CELL INTERIOR / GENE / PLANET SURFACE / PLANET / SUN AND SOLAR SYSTEM / GALAXY / UNIVERSE / UNIVERSES. It is a single being. It is impossible to imagine that this being is bound by the few rules that our meat bodies experience as time, space, objective reality. It could also be assumed that we view only the *matter* origin of our bodies and that there are other matters and relationships that extend in unknown manners from the apparent physical beings and invisibly (to us) link with the totality.

It may be seen that sperms dance with the egg within a fluid, spinning the egg with their tails till a single sperm capsule attaches itself to the surface of the egg and extrudes its halved gene material into the halved gene material of the egg and a unique confluence of events takes place—a creature is united in its first being. With the specific genetic information is created a wolf, a Mozart, a mouse, or a penguin, from the vast but somewhat defined propensities of the single living plasmic expanding being. The creature moves on the surface frontier of the planet earth, looks out into being and the universe and says, "MEAT IS SPIRIT. I feel it. I am it. I touch it. I see it. I perceive with the senses I am given in the possibility of the surge. I constellate and reconstellate the information I am given. I move. I am. I be. I may even envision the whirling gyre of millionic stars that vaguely resembles the helix directing my cells."

It is conceivable that the most colossal example of vanity that can be found in history is held by the peoples of contemporary North America. We have been immaculately propagandized to unexcelled heights of delirium. The Puritans landed on this continent bringing with them the concept of their divine destiny to fulfill God's Providence and enact his will on this most nearly virgin continent. Europe and Asia had already been eaten up, overpopulated, and then blighted by plague. The new fisheries off the coast of this continent fed the populations of Europe. The potato, corn, beans, the peanut, and the other cultivated plants of this new continent were sent back to Europe as a new source of foodstuffs to grow in the depleted soils. The soils of North America were nearly untouched—broadcast agriculture was introduced—the plow entered. Rice, rum, gold, cotton, and furs were pumped into the old continent. The Indian, representative of another relationship to nature, was easy prey for the newcomers. Fossil fuels, metals, forest, wild meat, existed in unbelievable abundance—

in a flow and depth inconceivable to the European. Today one can not imagine the fertility and luxuriance of the Great Plains, the South-eastern forests, the oak forests, and the rain forests of the West. A single fir forest stretched from Monterey Bay to Vancouver. Newly introduced domesticated oats grew six feet high at the forest edge. Glimmerings of the *surface* wealth of the continent can be obtained from the journals of Audubon, and the writings of William Bartram. Hundreds of thousands of wild birds flew with a roar of wings from lakes at the sound of a rifle shot. It is possible to go to modern bird preserves that give the faintest hint of the remaining Pleistocene that existed upon the arrival of the Europeans.

In addition to the untouched physical wealth of the continent was another wealth. THE WEALTH OF SPACE IS FRONTIER. Space for MOVEMENT, and for EXPLORATION, as well as for EXPLOITATION, seemed to open forever into the West. A systemless system for human acquisition of territory and space and wealth seemed to be present. THERE CAN BE NO DOUBT OF THE PSYCHIC EBULLIENCE AND GIFT OF NEW MORALE THAT ACCOMPANIES SUCH A FORTUNATE POSSIBILITY. There is no doubt that Whitman's joy and euphoria represented the spirit of the times. We have become Pinocchios growing asses' ears in our exploitation.

Utilizing the incredible wealth, the U.S. became the ultimate technological social centrality. We depleted the riches and turned the metals into structures that will have to be reclaimed and recycled. Spaces will have to be opened to recover the possibilities of territorial sanity. But the space is not there. The cousinship of living creatures will have to be acknowledged or we will find that we are alone on the earth with no other living creatures but domesticated ones and their parasites. We automate and (theoretically) increase the lifespan of individuals. We find there is joblessness and demoralization. We are aware that there is sufficient wealth of goods and time for all men (in the U.S.) but the sufficiency is temporal—and limited. Soon we will be in worse shape than the nations of Europe at the time of the discovery of the New World.

Never has there been a greater urgency for work, or a greater necessity for human labor, and the exploration of new life-styles. Because of the unified one-world, but self-competitive and self-divisive, culture it is impossible to outline the new works that are necessary for man to preserve himself and his fellow beings in the surge.

It is clearly true that man in the group is as mindless, or almost as mindless, as the inert matter from which his protein derives. The masses of men in the structure cancel out the creativity that the individual, or constructs of individuals, might bring about. Society mimics the machines that it produces. More and more LESS AND LESS is man, as a group, aware of his biological and mammal being. The young are presented with false goals and morals in their most developmental periods. They cannot see through the glut of manufactured objects, ideas, and concepts. Yet, the whole of the planet must be replanted, and reseeded with life. The population, while it is swiftly and gently brought to a biologically bearable density, might be employed in necessary bio-positive tasks. This possibility is almost an AGONY because of the apparent impossibility of men conjoining themselves in a new confluence. Man must re-view himself to find the possibility.

Travelling on a small ship to the Farallon Islands near the San Francisco coast, I spoke with a virologist who had just returned from Australia. He had studied plagues and the introduction of plagues into the dense rabbit populations. He was travelling to the Farallons to study a rabbit type there. A lighthouse keeper's son had a pair of rabbits that escaped on the island. The rabbits and the progeny devastated the island of every blade of plant-life. The island was left bare rock, without any vestige of higher plantlife. The virologist contended that the rabbits—still populous on the island— ate the dessicated corpses of gulls and seabirds. His opinion was that only one specific blood type of rabbit had the capability of surviving in this nutrimental condition.

I wandered on the island—seeing a rabbit and traces of rabbits—but not a blade of grass or a bush. The island is rocky, craggy, like a miniature, bare, eroding crest of the Alps. After climbing the tiny peak, I descended to the beach. The beach was scattered with boulderlike rocks. Mounting one of the rocks I found myself looking down onto a basking herd of sea lions. The closest of them was no more than thirty feet away. They were drowsing and lolling in the sun. Seeing something comic in the scene I raised my hand and began speaking to the sea lions as if I were delivering a sermon to them. The asonished sea lions resting on the rocks dived into the ocean. The ones in the ocean swung about to see me. They instantly began a chorus of *YOWPS,* and huge angered MEAT CRIES dense in volume and range. I continued my lecture and they continued their amazingly loud yowping. Perhaps thirty or forty of the animals were yowping at one time. They were FURIOUS, ENRAGED, ASTONISHED. Their voices were driven by hundreds of pounds of meat force and energy. I was frightened and wondered if they might change about, clamber out, and pursue me. They remained in the water cursing me in a clear ancient language with little doubt about their meaning.

AND THEN I knew that not only were the monster shapes of meat enraged, they were PLEASED. THEY WERE SMILING AS WELL AS ENRAGED! They were overjoyed to be stimulated to anger by a novel—and clearly harmless—intruder. Undoubtedly they enjoyed my astonishment and fear as well as the physical pleasure of their rage. Perhaps they relished my physical reaction to their blitzkrieg of sound. They began to yowp not only at me but to each other.

My ears could not take it any longer and I began walking up the beach. I walked halfway around the island. Five assorted members of the tribe followed me in the waves as I walked. They watched, yowped, taunted, encouraged, scolded, and enjoyed me to the fullest. I have not been in finer or wittier company.

Can the human type know more mammal experience, universe perception, and possibilities of joy or of the cherubic? The music of the body is as lovely as Mozart. Hail Saint Rimbaud. Hail Saint Jesus. Hail Saint Raphael! Hail Mohammed Ali! Hail Sainted painters of the Sung Dynasty! Hail Saint Sir Francis Crick! Give me your gift, but do NOT *intercede* for me with a messiah that YOU visualize. Within me is the UNIVERSE—and outside it is there. We are extrusions, facets, auras, in the dial of a vibratory flowing surge of infinite possibilities.

I AM A MAN AND I AM A MAMMAL!

—I

KNOW

I AM.

WHEN A MAN DOES NOT ADMIT HE IS AN ANIMAL, he is less than an animal. Not more but less.

At first glance it seems apparent that attempts to return to hunting and gathering or "primitive" agricultural styles are foredoomed. In late Pleistocene, the interglacial periods presented abundance to the hunter and gatherer and the sparsity of population caused no untenable pressure on the mammal herds or the lush lands of edible grasses.

England, within recent times, was connected by marshes to the mainland of Europe. As the Channel rose it was left standing as a beauteous near virgin outgrowth of forested and game populated rock—like a stone in a clear pool covered with lovely moss. Greece, China, North Africa, as well as England and Europe have been deforested for the building of warships, homes, firewood, and agriculture. Overgrazing has extinguished the natural arability of the land in the most desirable sites. There are few places where either hunting and gathering or simple agriculture will suffice for a desirable life style. It is quite clear that often in earlier times men lived amidst another type of natural abundance. —Not a golden age—but an abundance.

Society as it continues acceleration of the planetary technology will eradicate man. Yet the lives of the billions of men and women are, in almost all cases, absolutely dependent upon the techno-economy to provide them with the necessities of life. The people of the metropoles and megametropoles would starve and die of thirst without the requisites that are piped, trucked, and flown to them. The populace would die as swiftly, or nearly so, in the countryside. Contemporary agriculture is a technology and with its sudden collapse would come the end of nearly all human life.

(Soil in most modern countries is only arable because of artificial fertilizers and soil treatments.) It is doubtful that the sanity of those who would be able to survive the sudden end of technology could be maintained. (Sanity is meant to be a biological term—for it is not likely that the normal man today is sane.) The death of billions would bring madness for the survivors who are trained to think and feel humanistically and socially—and surely there would be epidemics eliminating accidental survivors.

It is a razor thin edge for the drama of survival to take place upon. Society and the unitary culture has developed planarly and interlocked itself into a rigid structure. The Soka Gakkai Buddhists are subject to the same pressure lines and stresses as Wallace's American Party. Thiose directed by the Whitehouse, the Pentagon, the Papacy, the Politburo, or Peking are all conjoined. Only with great will can existing generations throw down the evangelisms and have mutual survival. Only those alive now can prepare a forthcoming generation for perception of the total situation.

Preparation for battle between political frontier is a comedy developed beyond the reasonable bounds of humor—it is a psychosis.

What technologies must be maintained to keep alive in acceptable lifestyle the mass of the world's outmoded humanistic population?

What steps must be taken to maintain the MORALE of the human species?

The progressive demoralization concomitant with socialization is already devastating. Any individual who has been on this planet for thirty years is able to comment on the change of biologic morale.

The wastefulness of space exploration programs is even more staggering than the thought of the human being, in the given world state, returning to hunting. The hairy rhino, the bison, the passenger pigeon, the giant deer are not there to be feasted on. Nor can the planet support background radiation (not to mention fall-out), thermal pollution, and possibly even oxygen deprivation, and the rapidly appearing dead-ends accompanying what is called progress.

It does not seem reasonable to retreat from the possibility of space exploration—or to carry it on. Space exploration may be the natural gesture of the surface of this earth—to spore and expand in a systemless system. Further, it is highly unlikely that man can live in any satisfaction solely in the new cult of inner space. Man is a creature and desires as all creatures FRONTIER. Frontier must be accompanied by inner exploration. But inner space will not substitute for frontier. The substitution of one for another, or the eradication of either, is a facet of madness. The dangers of technology must be DISMANTLED and the positive necessary aspects made noncompetitive. There is a question that WE cannot easily answer. What elements of the technology, art, science, of this here and now society will be of use to our progeny?

We can begin to conjecture which elements are destructive to the survival of our children, and children's children. ONLY AS THOSE CONCERNED IN REVOLT MAKE REASONED, AND REASONABLE, PRO-BIOLOGIC EXAMPLES AND ACTIVITIES CAN LEADERSHIP BE TURNED OVER TO THE MOST VITAL INTELLIGENCES OF

THE NEW GENERATIONS. Youth must cease to be a caste. The old must make reasons to be honored for their labor and examples.

There must be constant work among all generations for the achievement of eco-biological transfer. The lumpen men are propagandized and indoctrinated to a grim degree. Only a revolt, on the part of each person able to do so, will begin to shape the change. The necessary activities in personal revolts may not bring societal rewards and probably most often will not do so.

The reward of life is BEING, is motility, and is action—both interior and on the frontier.

THERE IS NOT A UTOPIA AT HAND. There will not be golden towers of progress, nor will there be an angelic or seraphic nostalgic new society of the innocent Paleolithic or Neolithic. There is not a Messiah because *being* is messiah. There is not a SOLUTION because there must be many solutions. Solutions are, at best, temporary.

The inactivity and dullness of the bliss of conjectured utopias are pathetic in light of the world situation. Drugs, yoga, politics, trance-dancing, or religion will not save one's cell tissue from the immediately apparent fate. Religion and politics are both inner frontiers taking place on the topology of the giant cell of technological society. A man must have space and action for the motions of his real body, and the accrued constellation of perceptions, if he is to exist as a mammal rather than as a ghost or stupefied creature. What must be made is the most reasonable and meat-real confluences that can be conceived. Definite, clear, choices must be made by those who prepare themselves to see the nature of the choices.

Much of what has occurred a priori from this given (now) vantage appears to be natural biological error. Evangelisms and quests for utopias have brought immense grief. The universe is living. We are a part of it. It does not alter itself for our imagined human pleasures. We are the universe manifesting and experiencing itself. We have bee propagandized otherwise. THIS IS A NATURAL STATE. THERE ARE OTHER NATURAL STATES. This natural state is drawing to a close. The selves of the human self are constricted in natural displeasing ways. The exterior world is a reflection as much as a cause of this condition. It is possible to begin the alterations of the conditions.

The administration of this geo-political "sector" (to quote administrative jargon), invites personal action in the "Environmental Crisis." But the evangelistic progress-oriented unit cannot escape from its interlocking business/war/technology, or do more than minutely shift the checks and balances. It is possible that this call to personal action is a piece of LUCK. Revolutions have become sentimentality. Only personal meat-biological revolt will obtain the necessary views and actions. It is barely possible that the incapacity of the political administrative structure will enrage individuals and challenge their intellective and physical capacities—perhaps this will contribute to a greater change than a revolution.

Charles Olson

Enyalion

                    rages
                    strain
                Dog of Tartarus
                Guards of Tartarus
            Finks of the Bosses. War Makers

                    Not Enyalion. Enyalion
        has lost his Hand, Enyalion
        is beautiful, Enyalion
        has shown himself, the High King
        a War Chief, he has Equites
        to do that

                    Enyalion
        is possibility, all men
        are the glories of Hera by possibility, Enyalion
        goes to war differently
        than his equites, different
        than they do, he goes to war with a picture

                far far out into Eternity   Enyalion,
        the law of possibility, Enyalion

        the beautiful one, Enyalion

        who takes off his clothes

        wherever he is found,

        on a hill,

        in front of his troops,

        in the face of the men of the other side, at the command

        of any woman who goes by,

        and sees him there, and sends her maid, to ask,

        if he will show himself,

        if the beauty, of which he is reported to have,

        is true

        he goes to war with a picture

                                    she goes off

in the direction of her business

        over the city   over the earth   –   the earth

is the mundus brown-red is the color

                                    of the brilliance

                                    of earth

he goes to war with a picture in his mind
that the shining of his body

            and of the chariot
            and of his horses
            and of his own equites
        everyone in the nation of which he is the High King

he turns back

into the battle

                        Enyalion

is the god of war   the color

of the god of war   is beauty

                        Enyalion

is in the service of the law of the proportions

of his own body   Enyalion

                        but the city

is only the beginning of the earth   the earth

is the world · brown-red is the color of mud,

                                    the earth

shines

shines

        but beyond the earth

           far off Stage Fort Park

    far away from the rules of sea-faring far far from Gloucester

far by the rule of Ousoos   far where you carry

the color, Bulgar

         far where Enyalion

      quietly re-enters his Chariot   far

by the rule of its parts

           by the law of the proportion

               of its parts

over the World   over the City   over Man

Jacques Vallee

from
Dimensions

The Landing at Eagle River

It was an unusual day in 1961 for the Food and Drug Laboratory of the U.S. Department of Health, Education and Welfare, when the Air Force requested an analysis of a piece of wheat cake that had been cooked . . . aboard a flying saucer! The human being who had obtained the cake was Joe Simonton, a sixty-year-old chicken farmer who lived alone in a small house in the vicinity of Eagle River, Wisconsin. He was given three cakes, ate one of them, and thought it "tasted like cardboard." The Air Force put it more scientifically:

> The cake was composed of hydrogenated fat, starch, buckwheat hulls, soya bean hulls, wheat bran. Bacteria and radiation readings were normal for this material. Chemical, infrared and other destructive type tests were run on this material. The Food and Drug Laboratory of the U.S. Department of Health, Education and Welfare concluded that the material was an ordinary pancake of terrestrial origin.

Where did it come from? The reader will have to decide for himself what he chooses to believe after reading this chapter. It includes the Eagle River incident because this is a firsthand account, given by a man of absolute sincerity. Speaking for the U.S. Air Force, Dr. J. Allen Hynek, who investigated the case along with Major Robert Friend and an officer from Sawyer Air Force Base, stated: "There is no question that Mr. Simonton felt that his contact had been a real experience."

The time was approximately 11:00 A.M. on April 18, 1961, when Joe Simonton was attracted outside by a peculiar noise similar to "knobby tires on a wet pavement." Stepping into his yard, he faced a silvery saucer-shaped object, "brighter than chrome," which appeared to be hovering close to the ground without actually touching it. The object was about twelve feet high and thirty feet in diameter. A hatch opened about five feet from the ground, and Simonton saw three men inside the machine. One was dressed in a black two-piece suit. The occupants were about five feet tall. Smooth-shaven, they appeared to "resemble Italians." They had dark hair and skin and wore outfits with turtleneck tops and knit helmets.

One of the men held up a jug apparently made of the same material as the saucer. His motioning to Joe Simonton seemed to indicate that he needed water. Simonton took the jug, went inside the house, and filled it. As he returned, he saw that one of the men inside the saucer was "frying food on a flameless grill of some sort." The interior of the ship was black, "the color of wrought iron." Simonton saw several instrument panels and heard a slow whining sound, similar to the hum of a generator. When he made a motion indicating he was interested in the food one of the men, who was also dressed in black but with a narrow red trim along the trousers, handed him three cookies, about three inches in diameter and perforated with small holes.

The whole affair lasted about five minutes. Finally, the man closest to the witness attached a kind of belt to a hook in his clothing and closed the hatch in such a way that Simonton could scarcely detect its outline. Then the object rose about twenty feet from the ground before taking off straight south, causing a blast of air that bent some nearby pine trees.

Along the edge of the saucer, the witness recalls, were exhaust pipes six or seven inches in diameter. The hatch was about six feet high and thirty inches wide, and, although the object has always been described as a saucer, its actual shape was that of two inverted bowls.

When two deputies sent by Sheriff Schroeder, who had known Simonton for fourteen years, arrived on the scene, they could not find any corroborative evidence. The sheriff stated that the witness obviously believed the truth of what he was saying and talked very sensibly about the incident.

Food From Fairyland

The Eagle River case has never been solved. The Air Force believes that Joe Simonton, who lived alone, had a sudden dream while he was awake and inserted his dream into the continuum of events around him of which he was conscious. I understand several psychologists in Dayton, Ohio, are quite satisfied with this explanation. So were most serious amateur ufologists of the time. Alas! Ufology, like psychology, has become such a narrow field of specialization that the experts have no time for general culture. They are so busy rationalizing the dreams of other people that they themselves do not dream anymore, nor do they read fairy tales. If they did, they would perhaps take a much closer look at Joe Simonton and his pancakes. They would know about the Gentry and the food from fairyland.

In 1909, an American researcher named Walter Evans-Wentz, who wrote a thesis on Celtic traditions in Brittany, devoted much time to the gathering of folk tales about supernatural beings, their habits, their contacts with men, and their food. In his book *The Fairy-Faith in Celtic Countries*, for example, he gives the story of Pat Feeney, an Irishman of whom we know only that "he was well-off before the hard times," meaning perhaps the famine of 1846-1847. One day a little woman came to his house and asked for some oatmeal:

> Paddy had so little that he was ashamed to offer it, so he offered her some potatoes instead, but she wanted oatmeal, and then he gave her all he had. She told him to place it back in the bin till she should return for it. This he did, and the next morning the bin was overflowing with oatmeal. The woman was one of the Gentry.

It is unfortunate that Paddy did not save this valuable evidence for the benefit of the U.S. Department of Health, Education and Welfare's Food and Drug Lab. Perhaps the lab would have explained this miracle of the multiplication of the oatmeal, along with other peculiar properties of fairy food; for it is well known in Ireland that if you are taken away by the Gentry, you must never taste food in their palace. Otherwise, you never come back; you become one of them.

It is interesting that the analysis performed for the Air Force did not mention the presence of salt in the pancakes given to Simonton. Indeed, Evans-Wentz was told by an Irishman who was quite familiar with the Gentry that "they never taste anything salt, but eat fresh meat and drink pure water." Pure water is what the saucer men took from Simonton.

The question of food is one of the points most frequently treated in the traditional literature of the Celtic legends, *along with the documented stories of babies kidnapped by the elves* and of the terrestrial animals they hunt and take away. Before we study this abundant material, however, we should supply some background information about the mysterious folks the Irish call the Gentry and the Scots call the Good People (*Sleagh Maith*): "The Gentry are a fine large race who live out on the sea and in the mountains, and they are all very good neighbors. The bad ones are not the Gentry at all, they are the fallen angels and they live in the woods and the sea," says one of Evans-Wentz's informers.

Patrick Water gives this description of one of the beings:

> A crowd of boys out in the fields one day saw a fairy-man with a red cap. Except for his height he was like any other man. He was about three and a half feet tall. The boys surrounded him, but he made such a sputtering talk they let him go. And he disappeared as he walked away in the direction of the old fort.

There were few places where one could still see such creatures, even in Great Britain or France, after 1850. All the storytellers, all the popular almanacs, agree that as civilization advanced the little folks became increasingly shy. A few untouched places recommended by Evans-Wentz, however, are the Yosemite Valley in California and the Ben Bulben country and Ross Point in County Sligo, Ireland. Dublin seers are known to have made many trips to Ben Bulben, a famous mountain honeycombed with curious grottoes. At the very foot of the mountain, "as the heavy white fog banks hung over Ben Bulben and its neighbors," Evans-Wentz was told, the following incident occurred:

> When I was a young man I often used to go out in the mountains over there to fish for trout or to hunt. And it was in January on a cold, dry day while carrying my gun that I and a friend with me as we were walking around Ben Bulben saw one of the Gentry for the first time. . . . This one was dressed in blue with a headdress adorned with what seemed to be frills. When he came upon us, he said to me in a sweet and silvery voice, "The seldom you come to this mountain the better, Mister, a young lady here wants to take you away."

Then he told us not to fire our guns, because the Gentry dislike being disturbed by the noise. And he seemed to be like a soldier of the Gentry on guard. As we were leaving the mountain, he told us not to look back and we didn't.

Evans-Wentz then asked for a description of the Gentry, and was told the following:

The folk are the grandest I have ever seen. They are far superior to us and that is why they call themselves the Gentry. They are not a working-class, but a military-aristocratic class, tall and noble-appearing. They are a distinct race between our race and that of spirits, as they have told me. Their qualifications are tremendous: "We could cut off half the human race, but would not," they said, "for we are expecting salvation." *And I knew a man three or four years ago whom they struck down with paralysis.* Their sight is so penetrating that I think they could see through the earth. They have a silvery voice, quick and sweet.

The Gentry live inside the mountains in beautiful castles, and there are a good many branches of them in other countries, and especially in Ireland. Some live in the Wicklow Mountains near Dublin. Like armies they have their stations and move from one to another. My guide and informer said to me once, "I command a regiment."

They travel greatly, and they can appear in Paris, Marseilles, Naples, Genoa, Turin or Dublin, like ordinary people, and even in crowds. They love especially Spain, Southern France, and the South of Europe.

The Gentry take a great interest in the affairs of men and they always stand for justice and right. Sometimes they fight among themselves. *They take young and intelligent people who are interesting. They take the whole body and soul, transmuting the body to a body like their own.*

I asked them once if they ever died and they said, No; "we are always kept young." Once they take you and you taste food in their palace you cannot come back. They never taste anything salt, but eat fresh meat and drink pure water. They marry and have children. And one of them could marry a good and pure mortal.

They are able to appear in different forms. One once appeared to me and seemed only four feet high, and stoutly built. He said, "I am bigger than I appear to you now. We can make the old young, the big small, the small big."

The cakes given to Joe Simonton were composed of, among other things, buckwheat hulls. And buckwheat is closely associated with legends of Brittany, one of the most conservative Celtic areas. In that region of France, belief in fairies (*fees*) is still wide-spread, although Evans-Wentz and Paul Sebillot had great difficulty, about 1900, finding Bretons who said that they had seen *fees*. One of the peculiarities of Breton traditional legend is the association of the *fees* or *korrigans* with a race of beings named *fions*.

*   *   *

Whether the creatures come down in flying saucers or musical baskets, whether they come out of the sea or the rock, is irrelevant. What *is* relevant is what they say and do: the trace each leaves in the human witness who is the only tangible vehicle of the story. This behavior presents us with a sample of situations and human reactions that trigger our interest, our concern, our laughter. Joe Simonton's pancake story is cute; the tales of fairy food are intriguing but difficult to trace; the rings and the nests are real, but the feeling they inspire is more romantic than scientific. Then there is the strange beings' peculiarly insistent desire to get hold of terrestrial flora and fauna. The stories quoted in this connection verge on the ludicrous. But to pursue the investigation further leads to horror. This is a facet of the phenomenon we can no longer ignore.

Perhaps I have succeeded in evoking a new awareness of a parallel between the rumors of today and the beliefs held by our ancestors, beliefs of stupendous fights with mysterious supermen, of rings where magic lingered, of dwarfish races haunting the land. In this chapter, I have limited the argument to the mere juxtaposition of modern and older beliefs. The faint suspicion of a giant mystery, much larger than our current preoccupation with life on other planets, much deeper than mere reports of zigzagging lights—perhaps we should try to understand what these tales, these myths, these legends are doing to us. What images are they designed to convey? What hidden needs are they fulfilling? If this is a fabrication, why should it be so absurd? Are there precedents in history? Could imagination be a stronger force, to shape the actions of men, than its expression in dogma, in political structures, in established churches, in armies? If so, could this force be used? Is it being used? Is there a science of deception at work here on a grand scale, or could the human mind generate its own phantoms, in a formidable, collective creation mythology?

"Man's imagination, like every known power, works by fixed laws." These words by Hartland, written in 1891, offer a clue. Yes, there is a deep undercurrent to be discovered and mapped behind these seemingly absurd stories. Emerging sections of the underlying pattern have been discovered and mapped in ages past by long-dead scholars. Today we have the unique opportunity to witness the reappearance of this current, out in the open—colored, naturally, with our new human biases, our preoccupation with science, our longing for the promised land of other planets.

A new mythology was needed to bridge the stupendous gap beyond the meaningless present. *They are providing it.* But who are *they*? Real beings, or the ghosts of our own dreams? They spoke to us "in smooth English." They did not speak to our scientists; they did not send sophisticated signals in uniquely decipherable codes as any well-behaved alien should before daring to penetrate our solar system. No, they picked Gary Wilcox instead. And Joe Simonton. And Maurice Masse. What did they say? That they were from Mars. That they were our neighbors. And, above all, that they were superior to us, that we must obey them. That they were good. Go to Valensole and ask Masse. He will tell you, perhaps, as he told me, how puzzled he was when suddenly, without warning, he felt inside himself a warm, comfortable feeling—how *good* they were, our good neighbors. The Good People. They took a great interest in the affairs of men, and they always stood for justice and right. They could appear in different forms.

With them Joe Simonton exchanged food. So, in times gone by, did Irishmen, who talked to similar beings. In those days, too, they were called the

Good People and, in Scotland, the Good Neighbors, the *Sleagh Maith*. What did they say, then?

"We are far superior to you." "We could cut off half the human race."

It does begin to make sense. These were the facts we have missed, without which we could never piece the UFO jigsaw together. Priests and scholars left books about the legends of their time concerning these beings. These books had to be found, collected, and studied. Together, these stories presented a coherent picture of the appearance, the organization, and the methods of our strange visitors. The appearance was—does this surprise you?—exactly that of today's UFO pilots. The methods were the same. There was the sudden vision of brilliant "houses" at night, houses that could fly, that contained peculiar lamps, radiant lights that needed no fuel. The creatures could paralyze their witnesses and translate them through time. They hunted animals and took away people.

*   *   *

The Salvation Myth

I find myself on a panel with Dr. Andrija Puharich, Arthur Young, mathematician Charles Muses (Young and Muses are the two authors of an excellent book called *Consciousness and Reality*), and an Army scientist, Tom Bearden. Puharich describes his latest experiences with Uri Geller. Puharich explains to the audience that he gets messages on his tape recorder, coming from a mysterious cosmic source. But the tape vanishes regularly. There is nothing he can do to prevent it, and he is totally committed to the idea that he and Uri are now guided by a very high source of wisdom and that the only course for mankind is to place its destiny in "their" hands.

The floor is given another speaker. Humanity, he says, stands on the brink of catastrophe, at the edge of a chasm. How are we to reach the safe side? A flying saucer hovers above the chasm, our only hope: "Do you want a lift?" asks the UFO, helpfully.

This topic is a familiar one in the "New Age" movement. The 1987 celebration of the so-called "Harmonic Convergence" used similar themes.

Salvation from heaven. Shouldn't we know something more about the helpful stranger before we jump on board? Shouldn't we make sure that the chasm is real, and that we cannot bridge it with our own resources? Cannot we reach the other side—our future—by our own means?

When we are asked to suspend all our rational thoughts, to forget our "obsolete" critical faculties, to throw control overboard, then the time has come to take all the data and go away with it to a quiet place to think. My fear is that the problem will not be seriously studied by scientists until it has begun to generate a high degree of public awareness, and then the approach will be an entirely classical one: millions of dollars to consultants and research institutes, thousands of questionnaires, field investigators with glass bottles, sociologists filling out correlation matrices, medical personnel adjusting electrodes over the frontal lobes of ranchers. This would only be *another wrinkle in the learning curve, another step in the conditioning.*

There is a strange urge in my mind: I would like to stop behaving as if I am a rat pressing levers—even if I have to give up the cheese and go hungry for a while. I would like to step outside the conditioning maze and see what makes it tick. I wonder what I would find. Perhaps a terrible superhuman monstrosity the very contemplation of which would make a person insane? Perhaps a solemn gathering of sages? Or the maddening simplicity of unattended clockwork?